The Malady of Islam

The Malady
of Islam

Abdelwahab Meddeb

Translated from the French by
PIERRE JORIS AND ANN REID

BASIC
BOOKS

A Member of the Perseus Books Group
New York

Originally published as *La Maladie de l'Islam*
Copyright © Editions de Seuil, 2002
Translation © 2003 by Pierre Joris and Ann Reid

Published by Basic Books,
A Member of the Perseus Books Group

Basic Books are available at special discounts for bulk purchases in the United States by corporations, institutions, and other organizations. For more information, please contact the Special Markets Department at the Perseus Books Group, 11 Cambridge Center, Cambridge MA 02142, or call (617) 252-5298, (800) 255-1514 or email j.mccrary@perseusbooks.com.

Designed by Lisa Kreinbrink

Library of Congress Cataloging-in-Publication Data

Meddeb, Abdelwahab.
　[Maladie de l'islam. English]
　The malady of Islam / Abdelwahab Meddeb ; translated from the French by Pierre Joris and Ann Reid.
　　　p.　cm.
　ISBN 0-465-04435-2 (alk. paper)
　1. Islamic fundamentalism.　2. Islam—Controversial literature.　I. Title

BP166.14.F85M4413 2003
320.5'5'0917671—dc21

2003007424

03　04　05　/　10　9　8　7　6　5　4　3　2　1

Contents

The Malady of Islam

Part I

Islam: Inconsolable in Its Destitution

1

THE SPECTACULAR ATTACK OF SEPTEMBER 11, which struck the heart of the United States, is a crime. A crime committed by Islamists. It constitutes the extreme point of a series of terrorist acts that have followed an exponential curve whose beginning I trace back to 1979, the year that saw the triumph of Khomeini in Iran and the invasion of Afghanistan by Soviet troops. These two events had considerable effects that reinforced the fundamentalist movements and helped the dissemination of their ideology. In order to understand the form this ideology takes, we have to go far back in time. We have to recognize exactly where the letter—the Qur'an and tradition—is predisposed to a fundamentalist reading. We have to rediscover the exegetical and theological tradition in order to unravel the way this letter enables and encourages those who retain from its meaning only what summons them to war. We have to discover where the tradition resists, where we must allow a new interpretation that did not express itself where such a tradition grew.

It is important to know if we can read this literal text according to the conditions offered by the mental landscape of our times. We must also denounce the legerdemain that has perverted the heroic aspect of Islam, by generalizing the concept of the enemy in peacetime. The sectarians at the origin of this operation have universalized and generalized the concepts of anathema, excommunication and jihad, holy war, whereas the tradition has often been careful when touching upon these questions. It is imperative that we follow the course of such a genesis, which has ended up producing monsters who have forgotten the reasons of existence and which has transformed a tradition based on the principle of life and the cult of pleasure into a lugubrious race toward death.

On the very day that the two New York towers collapsed in a gigantic cloud of unbreathable dust, at the very moment when thousands of innocent people (whose ethnic, religious, and national diversity is a sign of the city's cosmopolitanism) died with the world looking on, at that very instant television showed scenes of rejoicing coming from Palestine and Lebanon. In light of what followed, these images—pornographic at a human level, and politically disastrous—revealed their marginal truth, and the local authorities managed to control the street and to restore it to some decency. But from such images, there arises a feeling and an emotion shared by many subjects belonging to the Islamic masses, and I try to understand through what trials or education an individual must have passed to be capable of rejoicing in such a crime.

There are internal and external reasons for this misery. In this book it is my responsibility to insist principally on the internal reasons, without, however, excluding or neglecting the external ones. It is part of the writer's role to point out the drift of his or her own people and to help open their eyes to what blinds them. I insist, as the saying goes, on starting by sweeping in front of my own door. This book, a translation from the original French version, will be read by numerous English-speaking readers concerned in one way or another by the drama of their own Islamic origins. I address myself to all readers, but

I have a special concern for those readers who, like me, have constellated themselves symbolically within the faith of Islam.

To each entity its sickness. This affliction can become so contagious that it turns into a plague ravaging minds and souls. Voltaire thus analyzed the sickness of intolerance that had kept up its ravages until the Calas affair. In response to the death sentence imposed on Jean Calas on March 9, 1762, by the tribunal of Toulouse, the philosopher of the Enlightenment wrote his *Traité sur la tolérance* (Treatise on toleration). Begun in October 1762, in the middle of the campaign to rehabilitate Calas, the book was published in Geneva in April 1763. In this book, Voltaire recapitulates the horrors engendered by Catholic fanaticism against the Protestants after August 24, 1572, Saint Bartholomew's day, when the reformed Christians were massacred in Paris and in the provinces. One of the reasons for the spread of fanaticism is the survival of superstition among the people, and the best way to heal this mortal illness is to subject the greatest possible number to the use of reason. The word "sickness" appears in Voltaire's book when the author accuses the "convulsionary" Jansenists of cultivating superstition among the people, which predisposes them to fanaticism. I hasten to quote this passage even if the reader recognizes in it the biting irony of the master from Ferney, the effect of which may seem inappropriate to the gravity of my subject:

> If there still are a few convulsive fanatics in remote corners of the outlying districts, it's only the basest part of the population which is attacked by this parasitic disease. Each day reason penetrates further into France, into the shops of merchants as well as the mansions of lords. We must cultivate the fruits of this reason, especially since it is impossible to check its advance.[1]

Thomas Mann had to deal with the German sickness, which led him to write *Doctor Faustus* (published in 1947), an amplification and radicalization of *Death in Venice* (1919). In it the author denounces the excess of the Promethean spirit, which brought so much harm to German thought and art and, as a consequence, to the German people themselves. Mann intended to show "the flight from the difficulties of the cultural crisis into the pact with the devil, the craving of a proud mind, threatened by sterility, for an unblocking of inhibitions at any cost, and the parallel between pernicious euphoria ending in collapse with the nationalist frenzy of Fascism."[2]

Thomas Mann was thinking about Nietzsche. In the same work, two pages later, he confirms the suggestion: It is indeed the author of *The Birth of Tragedy* who is the unnamed model of the personage of the musician he invented. Even if the German sickness did not spare Nietzsche, one of his concepts of moral psychology nonetheless sheds some light on an internal state that favors the eruption of the sickness in Islam. It is this internal state that I propose to analyze. If fanaticism was the sickness in Catholicism, if Nazism was the sickness in Germany, then surely fundamentalism is the sickness in Islam.

This is my thesis. That said, I do not, however, intend to claim that there is a good and an evil Islam, that one has to honor the one and denounce the other. Nor do I insinuate that fundamentalism is a deformation of Islam. In Islam, there is no institution that legitimates absolute doctrinal magisterium, but traditionally access to the letter was protected: One needed to obey specific conditions to make it speak or to speak in its name. However, unrestrained access to the letter was not prohibited and is not a peculiarity of our times. History has often had to record the disasters such access provokes. Only today, thanks to the effects of demography and democratization, the semiliterate have proliferated and the candidates who claim the authority to touch the letter have become much more numerous. Their sheer number reinforces their ferocity.

The Qur'anic letter, if submitted to a literal reading, can resonate in the space delimited by the fundamentalist project: It can respond to one who wants to make it talk within the narrowness of those confines; for it to escape, it needs to be invested with the desire of the interpreter. Rather than distinguishing a good Islam from a bad Islam, it would be better for Islam to open itself to debate and discussion, to rediscover the plurality of opinions, to set up a space for disagreement and difference, to accept that a neighbor has the freedom to think differently. Better for Islam if intellectual debate rediscovers its rights and adapts itself to the conditions polyphony offers. May the deviations multiply and unanimism cease; may the stable substance of the One disseminate itself in a shower of ungraspable atoms.

As far as external factors are concerned, we may concede that they are not the cause of the disease that gnaws at the body of Islam. But they are certainly the catalyst. Because of them, the disease intensifies. If, by a miracle, they were to disappear, I do not know if the sickness in Islam would disappear too, but it would not find a climate favorable for the flourishing and propagation of its germs. What are these external causes? They are, to list them, the nonrecognition of Islam by the West as representing an internal alterity; the way in which Islam is kept in its status of the excluded; the manner in which the West denies its own principles as soon as its interests demand it; and, finally, the Western habit (and in our days, particularly the American habit) of exercising its hegemony in total impunity, following the politics of the double standard.

Without wanting to justify crime, many here in the Old World still thought that the attacks on New York and Washington were an answer to an American policy based on partisan power. This opinion seems to shock the Americans themselves, as Robert Malley, former member of President Clinton's National Security Council, reminds us:

> In the Arab countries, in Europe and by a handful of American intellectuals, it was insinuated that American policy was the prime culprit: sanctions and strikes against Iraq, a pro-Israeli stance, the backing of repressive regimes, that is what is understood as explaining the terrorists' choice of target. The United States as victim of its own policies? This was, understandably—and beyond the logical flaw of the argument—difficult to accept.[3]

   With all due deference to American common sense, I have to begin by confirming that the three reasons specified as hypotheses are exactly those that feed the sickness in Islam and that help in its dissemination. I would also like to know what Malley considers the "logical flaw" of the argument. And who would find these hypotheses "difficult to accept," except the very conceivers and ministers of those policies? Malley's reservations are nothing more than unsupported affirmations. I admit that the argument does not suffice to explain the attacks that brought down the Twin Towers and a large wing of the Pentagon, but it may constitute an a posteriori legitimation. The opinion was expressed not just by Muslims or Arabs, but also by the French and other Europeans. It cannot be reckoned as a basic anti-Americanism (even if such a feeling may be part of it).

   If a country, a people, a state wants to remain the leader of the world, it has to be impartial in its manner of governing. The choice clearly lies between an imperialistic policy founded on war and an imperial policy whose main concern is to keep the peace. Now, an imperial policy commends its promoter as the arbiter of conflicts flaring up in the world, and by no means to be both judge and litigant. Take, for example, the successful sequences that buttress one of the last historical manifestations of such an imperial policy: the Ottoman empire under great sovereigns like Mehmet Fatih (1451–1481) and Suleiman Kanuni (1520–1566). These leaders saw themselves as continuators of the imperial structure developed along the rim of the Mediterranean since its creation by Alexander, its strengthening by the Romans, its continuation under the Byzantines and its attempted renovation during the Holy Roman empire. It's with that mind-set that the Ottomans successfully managed the mosaic of conflicts among minorities and nationalities that have always existed in the Near East. Beyond the emotions felt at the moment, there were many who realized that the events of September 11 could constitute a response to a failure of American policies, which have seemed imperialistic rather than imperial in matters concerning Islam in some of its areas or that touch upon one or another of its sensitive symbols.

Who are those who died while spreading death in New York, Washington and Pennsylvania? Beyond their contamination by the sickness in Islam, they are the sons of their times, the pure products of the Americanization of the world: the same ones who turned the digital into child's play and television into personal memory, without having troubled to transmute the essential archaism of their minds and their souls.[4] Thus we see the technical and "aesthetic" success of the event. The terrorists used the technical means masterfully, and they accurately thought through the relays of the event's diffusion as image. In fact, one wonders if the twenty-minute delay between the targeting of the towers were not an invitation to the cameras to film "live" the banking turn that the second plane made before hitting its target at the point foreseen for impact. We witnessed the optimum use of today's means, inviting this quasi-instantaneity between the event and its transmission across all continents. That is one of the effects of the universalization of technique and of the cathodic unification of humankind in the age of the Americanization of the world.

What I insist on, though, is that we witnessed technique rather than science. Since the seventeenth century the Islamic world is no longer a creator of science; since the middle of the nineteenth century it has tried, without success, to reconnect with the scientific spirit that once upon a time radiated from its cities. But during the postcolonial era (begun in the 1960s and corresponding to the first manifestation of the Americanization of the world arising in the aftermath of the war), Islam, along some of its fringes, was able to master technique. The implication is more a mastering of the machine's functioning than its invention, or even its production. With technique, one is downstream from the scientific process, the initiation of which demands great mastery upstream.

Who are these terrorists but the children of the Americanization of the world (as I have said and as I will repeat)? Children who suffer from the open wound the Muslim subject feels from having been turned from a ruler into someone ruled. Children who refuse the state of submission in which they believe themselves to be, and who dream of restoring the hegemony of the entity to which they belong; of making Friday the universally adopted weekly holiday (rather than Sunday); of substituting the year of the hegira for the year of the Common Era (whose Christian origin they keep stressing). This is not a caricature. I draw my conclusions from what I have read of the ineptitudes they publish. But let us first see what specific historical process produced these people. If indeed they are the result of the considerations that follow, it is important to specify at the outset that no rationale inherited from the past can justify their crime. Furthermore, the process of explanation transcends the specific case of these monstrous figures whose vector is nihilism. The process I am trying to throw light on is meant to identify the anthropological conditions in which these terrorists were born, though these conditions did not by themselves condemn them to be the monsters they became.

2

THE ISLAMIC WORLD HAS BEEN unceasingly inconsolable in its destitu-
tion. It knew one very high point of civilization, accompanied by the
boldness of hegemony. If we go back to the notion of world capital, as
proposed by Fernand Braudel, it is reasonable to suggest that before
its displacement toward Europe, this concept was concretized in the
Abbasid Baghdad of the ninth and tenth centuries, in the Fatimid
Cairo of the eleventh and the Mameluke Cairo of the thirteenth and
fourteenth centuries. After that, the world capital crossed over to the
north shore of the Mediterranean with the Genoa-Venice duo, before
it exiled itself, departing ever further from the Islamic world, by setting up first in Amsterdam in the seventeenth century, then in London
in the nineteenth and in New York City in the twentieth century.
Hereafter, we will probably see a migration toward the Pacific coast in
the dense interactions between Asia and North America. Since the fifteenth century, the world capital has thus moved geographically ever
further away from the Islamic space.

For Islam, entropy has been at work since the fourteenth century, but it was only toward the end of the eighteenth (with Bonaparte's expedition to Egypt) that the Muslims themselves began to become conscious that they were no longer at the same level as the West. It was this lateness, this lag, that allowed a number of countries belonging to the Islamic territories to be colonized because they found themselves in the situation of the colonizable. The Muslim individual, who claimed superiority to or at least equality with the Western individual, cannot grasp the process that has led the Muslim to such weakness when faced with the centuries-old counterpart, enemy or adversary, or at times partner and even ally, depending on the circumstances. In reaction to this state of affairs, ressentiment against the Westerners arose among Arabs and Muslims. (I am taking up the very useful concept of ressentiment as developed in Nietzsche's *On the Genealogy of Morals*.[1]) Nietzsche himself thought that the Muslim (or more precisely, the Arab) was someone who belonged to a people who, throughout the ages, had acted more in conformity with aristocratic morality, the morality of affirmation— someone who illuminates, someone who gives without trying to receive.[2] The situation of the person of ressentiment, on the other hand, is to be in the position of the one who receives but who does not have the means to give; the person of ressentiment cannot affirm. Thus the Muslim is no longer the individual of the "yes" that illuminates the world and creates a naturally hegemonic being. From sovereign being, the Muslim has slowly become the person of the "no," the one who refuses, who is no longer active but only reactive, the one who accumulates hatred and waits only for the hour of revenge. This sentiment, initially unknown to the Islamic subject, will imperceptibly grow and take over the person's center. I believe that the fundamentalist actions whose agent is the Muslim subject can be explained by the growth of the subject's ressentiment, a condition that had historically been unknown to the Muslim since his first appearance on the stage of history as an individual.

This new feeling did not install itself mechanically after the defeat of colonial confrontation: Much time passed before the germ of ressentiment started to grow. Consider Emir Abd el-Kader (1808–1883). This Islamic ruler lost nothing of his aristocratic dignity despite the defeat of 1847, his incarceration in France and his expatriation to the Orient in 1852. He never knew ressentiment. This man of the sword and the pen dedicated himself in his Damascene exile to the teaching of the esoteric sciences, deepening the centuries-old furrow of his master Ibn 'Arabi (1165–1240), whose works he interpreted and published. During the troubles of 1860, he applied the Akhbarian doctrine that preaches the equality of beliefs.[3] Absent from Damascus when Muslims (carried away by the herd instinct that characterizes masses) attacked the Christians of the city, but hearing that vile events had shaken the city, he hurried back and saved many lives. Gathering the Christians in groups, he led them to safety in the citadel.

A Christian survivor, Mikhayil Mishaqa, bore witness to this action. Hundreds of fugitives (European consuls and Syrian Christians) fled toward Abd el-Kader's quarters on the banks of the river Barada, and the excited crowd wanted to attack them. So the emir "had his horse saddled."[4] In one of his *mawaqif* (spiritual stations), the same emir recalled how during one of his Damascus sessions, he was questioned by a member of the audience who was worried about the effects of the defeat on the Muslims. The Muslims had started to imitate the Christians (i.e., the Westerners) in the way they dressed, ate and lived. In short, one is faced with an early questioning of the acculturation being experienced by the Islamic countries at the beginning of the Westernization of the world.[5]

We cannot find the smallest trace of ressentiment in the emir's response. After a traditional theological argument (if the Muslim faced defeat, it must have been because he was tepid and negligent in the service his God asked him to perform), he presented another argument of psychological common sense (it is human nature that, through fascination, the vanquished imitate the victor and will even go as far as to learn the victor's language). He then made an accurate sociological observation (first adopted by the elite, the process of imitation then propagates like poison throughout the whole social body).

Finally, the emir remembered the theory of divine names as constructed by his medieval master, Ibn 'Arabi, the names that govern all human activities and preside over all events that occur. Thus he invented the divine name of *Khadhil* (the deserting god who abandons you) to explain the defeat of the Muslim in the face of the European (which was nothing else than the emir's own defeat).

Even if such a name can be traced to a verbal form in Holy Writ (the Qur'an says: "If Allah assists you, then there is none that can overcome you, and if He forsakes you, *yakddhulu-kum*—who is there then that can assist you after Him?"), it is clear that the emir's invention is of astonishing audacity.[6] His boldness is the sign of a freedom that can at least be assimilated to what traditional theology calls a *bid'a*, a reprehensible innovation. All through his development, the emir was inspired by the following verse: "God abandons the Muslims without aiding the infidels. The defeat of the believer is due to God's abandonment; but the unbeliever's victory does not result from His help." This vision of divine effect, negative for oneself without being positive for the enemy, preserves the horizon of faith during the ordeal.

Thus aristocratic man believes himself to have enough sovereignty to take the liberty to invent the actualization of tradition, and it is his familiarity with the hermeneutical method of *ta'wîl* that authorizes and legitimizes his action. This familiarity predisposes him to emulate his audacious predecessors. Such doctrinal boldness cannot be in the reach of the half-educated, who today are legion in Islamic societies, which during the period of decolonization have experienced democratization without ever tasting democracy. It is in such a context that the mutation took place: From being aristocratic, the Muslim subject gradually became the person of ressentiment, a frustrated, dissatisfied individual who believes himself to be better than the conditions imposed on him. Like every half-educated person, he turns out to be (in his accumulated refusals and hatreds) a candidate for revenge, predisposed to insurrection and all it demands in terms of dissimulation and sacrifice.

But the real origin of this development, which lies at the point where psychology and ethics intersect, is the end of creativity, the end of the contributions that made Islamic civilization. Aware of their sterility, the Islamic people have grown inconsolable in their bereavement. Now, this state of affairs does not date from the colonial era; the imperial role that the majority of Islamic countries experienced is not the cause of their decline but the consequence of it: For the past several centuries, Muslims have not been creative in the scientific domain, nor have they been masters of technical development. It took them more than a century to master technology, something that happened in the postcolonial phase. As I have already said, the Americanization of the world is what permitted this acquisition. It belongs to the domain of consumption and functioning, and not to that of production and invention. It is useful primarily for the expansion of markets. However, apart from some individuals of Islamic origin working in Western research institutions, Muslim individuals, inside the horizon of their own symbolic and linguistic territoriality, remain excluded from the scientific spirit. They are not involved in the conception of the airplane, its invention or even its production, but they can pilot the flying machine very well, and go as far as to steer it to destruction.

3

THE MAJOR EVENTS IN ISLAM HAPPENED VERY early on. But their mutation was interrupted too soon. The very beginning of the ninth century saw the birth of a rationalist movement animated by those whom
we call the Mu'tazilites. These thinkers tried to disrupt two then-
dominant ideas: They criticized the Islamic dogma that states that the
Qur'an (like God) is uncreated and has come down from heaven as it
is in itself and in eternity. Their answer to this dogma is that, indeed,
the Qur'an is of divine origin, but that the concretization of the Holy
Writ in an earthly language can only be created by God at the moment
of its revelation. These sectarians think that those who claim that the
Qur'an is uncreated are installing an Islamic equivalent of the Christian sense of incarnation: The Qur'anic letter would thus be the incarnation of God. The literalists could thus easily be mistaken as
Christians who identify Christ with God because he is His Word.
These Mu'tazilites removed God from the world; they gave him back
to his unknowability, they neutralized him in a transcendence that lib-

erated humankind from predestination and made humans alone responsible for their actions.

This theological movement became the official state ideology. The caliph himself, al-Ma'mun (786–833), the son of Harun al-Rashid, wanted to impose it on all his subjects.[1] The caliphate in fact set up a sort of inquisition (the *Mihna,* inaugurated in 833) that attacked with great violence the contemporary literalist school in the person of its most eloquent representative, Ibn Hanbal (780–circa 855). It is important to remember this moment in history. The genealogy of fundamentalism must include this ninth-century personage, who was subjected to the worst tortures because in the name of his literalism he refused to accept the theses of the Mu'tazilites. His resistance found resonance and support among people anxious for the return of Qur'anic orthodoxy.

The great limitation of the Mu'tazilites' rationalist movement was that it failed to evolve into an enlightenment, above all because it sought to impose its point of view through the most radical violence, using the means at the disposal of an Eastern despot. (To extend his power over the theological domain as a whole al-Ma'mun gave himself the title of imam and imposed his interpretation on the constituted bodies of the ulemas, scholars in theology.) Orthodoxy was reestablished at the center of power as soon as Mutawakkil, the third successor of al-Ma'mun, took over (847). Now the Mu'tazilites were made to suffer in their turn—first by their complete marginalization and then by their slow but certain extinction—the same hardships they had made their adversaries suffer, who not only survived them but prospered.

During this period (as precocious in its conflicts as in its complexity and promise), the caliph al-Ma'mun played an important role in acclimatizing the Greek heritage in the Arab language. This caliph, so tradition tells us, dreamed about Aristotle, who asked him to have his books translated into Arabic. It is as if every process that leads to an enlightenment were triggered by a love for the Greeks and the restoration of their ways of thinking and feeling. While on a campaign against the Byzantines, al-Ma'mun came across the Neoplatonic community of the Sabæns in the Harran. A bold *fatwa* likened them formally to the enigmatic *Sabi'un*, to whom the Qur'an had given the status of a people of the Book: "Surely those who believe, and those who are Jews, and the Christians, and the Sabæns ... "[2] So the Holy Book put the Sabæns on equal footing with the Muslims, the Jews and the Christians. The Sabæns provided Islam with a number of scholars and translators from the Greek.

The caliph al-Ma'mun encouraged the confrontation of ideas in the heart of the city by organizing debates between sectarians of diverse faiths and Muslim theologians of various schools of thought. Already at this early period, the literalists were stubbornly opposed to any foreign borrowing as well as to the presence, in the city, of contradictory voices, which their ears perceived as blasphemous. Yet this staging of a forum for disagreement was itself the work of a ruler. This point keeps us from affirming that the exercise of reason, in its triumph, was accompanied by freedom—which remained the great unknown, especially in its political form.

It was in this Baghdad of the first part of the ninth century that the great scientific adventure of Arabic literature began, an adventure that lasted into the sixteenth century. It was at this time that the school of astronomy of Baghdad was created, founded both on speculative calculations and on observation. It was also in this city that algebra was invented by al-Khwarizmi, who dedicated his treatise to al-Ma'mun.

Besides this scientific movement, there was born a poetic revolution reminiscent of the nineteenth-century poetic revolution in France. If the reader can transcend context and history, he or she can hear how the words of these Arab poets resonate with those of Baudelaire, Verlaine, Rimbaud and even Mallarmé. In the body of work created by these Arab poets, one can distinguish poetic processes as varied as those of the French poets just cited. As just one example, consider the recognizably Mallarméan case of the Syrian Christian poet Abu Tammam (806–845). His father ran a tavern in Damascus. By using odd syntactical devices, rare words, antitheses and abstractions, and by a cultivation of paronomasia, he inflected the occasional verse that was his chosen genre (panegyrics, threnodies, satires, description of battles) toward a hieratic and hermetic poetry that demands interpretation and that comes to its full realization only in the fullness of commentary. His is the following rather compassionate and limpid (he was able to write like that too) distich that speaks of the eternity of love in a dialectic of absence and presence:

> *What is it consoles me in your absence*
> *if not the memory of you which doesn't fade*

> *Of all the guests you are the closest and*
> *even if you are far sadness brings you close*[3]

To show a likeness with Baudelaire, the emergence of a critical and scandalous individual making use of transgression as the engine of the poem, I will evoke Abu Nuwas (762–circa 813), one of the most radical figures of this poetic revolution. An Arab-Persian poet writing very provocatively in Arabic, he sang the praises of wine (forbidden in Islam) and homosexual love; he was an existentialist who brought his own experiences to bear on his poems. The critics of his era saw him as the main figure of the school of the Moderns (the *Muhdathun*). In a polemical way, he turned his back on the poetry of Arab origins rooted in the desert and in nomadism. He considered that way of living a throwback to the poverty that marked the region and to the difficult life such penury engenders; to the original desert he contrasted the conquest of the metropolis and the pleasures it provides, even down to the tragedy of profligate spending and excess that make for the enjoyment of the provocative and reckless dandy as well as for the dissipation he undergoes, diverted from religious practice by what presents itself to his senses. Moreover, he helped impose a quasi-arithmetic formal unity and rigor onto a rhapsodic, discontinuous, unbridled poetic tradition. We still read this poetry from the high Middle Ages as if it had been written yesterday, as if the ink had not

yet had time to dry. Just imagine those spectacular moments of creation happening in that ninth-century Baghdad workshop! As you
can see, the attempt to reform took place very early on, but it was
aborted.

The following two poetic extracts illustrate the mischievous joy of
this lively transgressor, whose verbal lushness could certainly be
likened to the 'abath, that scandalous vanity that discredits any art
form in the eyes of our narrow-minded contemporary fundamentalists:

Serve me and serve Joseph
this tasty wine
that makes one thrill

Push trouble out of your life
keep only its peace

Fill my glass to the brim
I don't want cups
that are only half full

Put down the gourd
and beside it the Book

Drink three glasses
and recite a verse

Good has mingled with bad
and if God forgives

He will win in whom the one
has wiped out the other, basta!

Or, from another one:

To one who asks me if I want to go to Mecca
I answer yes—when the pleasures
of Baghdad will have been exhausted
For how could I make the pilgrimage
as long as I remain immersed
in a brothel or tavern?[4]

4

IF WE LOOK SIMULTANEOUSLY AT SCIENCE, the state of technology and the state of the arts, we can say that Islamic civilization kept pace with what was happening in Europe until the baroque and classical periods. There can indeed be an equivalence between what happened in Islam in the eleventh, twelfth or thirteenth centuries and what was created in Europe up to the seventeenth century. Islam came very close to the Cartesian, Keplerian, Copernican and Galilean threshold.[1] From the seventeenth century onward, and through the revolutions in thought symbolized by the names just mentioned, there evolved a movement that would lead to the Enlightenment of the eighteenth century. The Enlightenment would separate Europe from the other great civilizations, from the Islamic as well as the Chinese and the Indian civilizations. It is the eighteenth century that caused the separation of the West, with the fascinating accumulation of ideas concretized by the events of 1789. According to Hegel, rarely had a historical rupture been thought through as deeply before it actually occurred. With the French Revolution, the idea preceded the fact: The former made the latter ineluctable.[2]

And yet, at the end of the seventeenth and the beginning of the eighteenth centuries, both in regard to the material life of the societies an ! to the morality that framed them, the Islamic polis was considered equal by those Europeans who were confronted by it. Two examples illustrate this sense of equality. In his anthology of Eastern maxims, Antoine Galland (1646–1714) tried to enrich the European moral conscience by drawing on teachings of Arab, Turkish and Persian origin.[3] And in her letters, Lady Mary Montagu, the wife of the English ambassador to the Sublime Porte (1717–1718), at times judged the Ottoman situation as more positive than the European one, especially concerning religious tolerance. She expressed these thoughts after her conversations with the religious scholar Effendi Ahmad Bey, in whose house she had lived for three weeks in Belgrade. She noted that the most widely shared opinion, if one sought out the secret of the effendis, came down to a sort of deism corresponding most probably to the spirit of Akbarism (the relativist theory of Ibn 'Arabi) that pervaded the Ottoman elites.[4]

And this eighteenth century, founded essentially on the broadening of the concept of freedom, the individual and the rights of men, also experienced the explosion of the consubstantial link between the political and the religious. The problematic that flowered, crystallized and proposed the solutions that eighteenth-century Europe would experience (and on which the future would be built) was located by the historians as originating in an Arabo-Occidental text, the famous *Decisive Treatise* by Averroës (1126–1198).[5] In this book, the Cordovan philosopher systematizes the thought inaugurated by the first hellenizing philosopher from Baghdad, al-Kindi (796–873). Averroës takes up and deepens al-Kindi's reflection on the relation between religion and philosophy, theology and technique. He perceives philosophy as the logical technique that underlies his method. In Arabic, Averroës calls this *ela,* the instrument, and the *organon,* the instrument of thought as inherited from Aristotle, the aim of which is to think the inexhaustible articulation of language on the world. The first step in this long process carried this problematic to the European Averroists—Christians primarily, but also Jews.[6] In this philosophical adventure, which canonized the separation of the fields, the ideas circulated from Greek to Arabic, then to Latin, to Hebrew, and to the modern European languages. That's where the beginning of the problematic lies, and its evolution will pass through the Averroists, the European ones, notably. In Islam we truly have the same perspective as the Western one, but the process stopped in Arabic, whereas it continued in the European languages.

It would be erroneous to believe that the energy of thought and of creation died out in Islam with the lack of Averroist lineage. Henry Corbin has reminded us in his books how fertile the Avicenian influence was in Arabic as well as in Persian, especially via the Persian Platonists.[7] The latter were marked by the Plotinian inheritance (long extracts of the *Enneads* were known in Arabic from the beginning of the tenth century on, via the *Theology* wrongfully attributed to Aristotle). Add to this the meditation of Avicenna (980–1037), who spiritualizes the Aristotelian legacy; of Shurawardi (1155–1191), who integrates the Zoroastrian heritage; and of Ibn 'Arabi (1165–1240), who adds to his interpretive audacities the ardor of interior experience. This movement of thinking and being produced the great minds of the seventeenth century—such as Molla Sadra Shirazi (d. 1640)—and even beyond, with the Shaykhis school (around the city of Kerman), which continued to produce great masters until the nineteenth century. One changes horizons with this spiritualist and rather Shiite movement, though it does, however, intersect with the speculative thinkers of Sunnite Akhbarian Sufism (the latter produced great texts until the seventeenth century, such as those of the Syrian Abd al-Ghani an-Nabulusi (d. 1731), and even in the nineteenth century, such as those of the already mentioned Algerian expatriate, the emir Abd el-Kader). This perspective will end up privileging "the ontological infinite over cosmological finitude."[8]

What interests these thinkers passionately is the continent of the soul, and if politics enters this thought, it will be a politics that will put the soul in command. Those who inhabit with their ardor the very rich continent of the soul live, in fact and in thought, the separation from the mundane area of politics. It is much more a poetic and metaphysical retreat than a desertion in the face of the responsibility awakened by the fate of the polis. Through this retreat it is a spiritual tradition that gains in depth and unites with the spirit of aristocratic morality, one that represents the essence of Islamic civilization.

Just the same, scientific activity did not cease. Scholars conducted ongoing astronomical research and observations in Central Asia, in continuation of the international school of Maragha (1259–1316). There was also Samarkand (whose observatory was founded in 1420 and remained active until at least 1500) and Istanbul (which was given its observatory by the scholar Taqiy ad-Din in 1575).[9] Moreover, the arts continued to flourish, in architecture as well as in painting, in the various Islamic states: the Timurid state in Central Asia (fifteenth century), the Safevid state in Persia (fifteenth to seventeenth century), the Moghul state in north India (seventeenth and eighteenth century) and the Ottoman state on the three continents over which the empire spread (fourteenth to nineteenth century).

5

IT IS ESSENTIAL TO DETACH OURSELVES from the stereotypical notion that Islamic civilization lost its fertility at the end of the twelfth century, in synchronicity with the end of Averroism and the theological reaction this philosophic oeuvre gave rise to. At most we could say that from the fifteenth century onward, a kind of entropy took hold of minds and set them on a slow yet inexorable curve toward decline. And yet, what was built and invented in the princely Timurid environment (in the region of Samarkand, Bokhara, Tashkent and Herat) is in no way inferior to the contemporary brilliance of the quattrocento in the Florence of the Medicis and in the Burgundy of the Limbourgs. These same Timurids were abundantly quoted by Antoine Galland in his *Remarkable Sayings,* through which he sought to become the Plutarch of the Muslims. On many occasions, Galland evoked the Timurid sovereign Shah Rokh, a descendant of Tamerlane, as the figure of the smart if not enlightened monarch to present as an edifying example for the European kings.[1]

These days, in the face of the political woes of the Islamic polis and the irresistible propagation of fundamentalism, it is fashionable among certain intellectuals who claim modernity to neglect this intense creativity over so many years. They neutralize this contribution to civilization by limiting it to the princely environment and to mystics, a conjunction they see as paralyzing necessary political reforms. Armed thus with the proof of political failure, these intellectual critics preach a return to Averroës to patch together a civil viability. They relativize Western borrowings, because a self-identity without this relativization would be wounding and even ignominious, in their eyes.[2] Such intellectuals trot out yet again the dialectic of the particular and the universal to heal themselves of the sickness of identity in a world objectively Westernized, and in which everyone ought to serenely appropriate the insights of the Western Enlightenment.

It is by such appropriations that the truth of the Enlightenment will shine fully: If every non-Westerner uses its light, then this truth will finally be rid of the smoke screen that veils things when the truth is twisted by the descendants of those who first offered it to humankind. The denial of the principle by the historical actions of the Westerners does not suffice to disqualify the idea erected as a principle.

This failing was noticed very early on, as long ago as 1834, in the first Algerian text written in French, *The Mirror*, by Hamdane Khodja. This is a confused book whose value for us lies only in a remark in the preface, which formulates what will be the irrefutable argument of every anticolonial stance. At the very moment when, in the name of the liberty of the people, the French aided in the struggles of Belgium, Greece and Poland in Europe, France—creator of that concept of liberty—was enslaving another people in Africa:

> I see Greece succored and established on a firm base after having been liberated from the Ottoman Empire. I see the Belgian people separated from Holland because of some difference in their political and religious principles. I see all free peoples display concern for the Poles and the reestablishment of their nationality, and I also see the

British government immortalizing its glory by the emancipation of the Negroes, and the British parliament sacrificing half a billion pounds to realize this emancipation, and then as I return to cast my gaze on the country of Algiers, I see its unhappy inhabitants placed under the yoke of despotism, extermination and all the evils of war, and all these horrors are committed in the name of free France.[3]

This says it all. In this statement, we find one of the very first denunciations of that Western perversity that causes the European to act against the idea (that he himself set forth as a principle) when the preservation of his hegemony demands it.

Will we find ourselves forced to agree with the critique that Carl Schmitt formulated in 1926, concerning colonial empires? The German philosopher of law decries the illusion of democratic universality, which leads to the opposition between the law of the state and the rights of the people, and thinks that homogeneity and equality exist only inside sameness, which annuls the universal. Democracy was then limited to the West, which found itself incapable of creating universal equality. In a colonial situation, democracy turns out to be founded only on the concept of internal homogeneity and equality.

Colonies, protectorates, mandates, interventionist charters, and other analogous forms create a relationship of dependency, which means that today a democracy can dominate a foreign population without making it into citizens and can make it dependent on democratic states while simultaneously keeping it apart from that state. This is the political and governmental meaning of the eloquent formula "The colonized populations are politically excluded and juridically included."[4]

According to Schmitt, the idea of universal—and thus absolute—equality annuls itself; it is an empty concept that turns on itself: "Up until now there has not existed any democracy that didn't recognize the concept of the foreigner and that would have tried to implement the equality of all men."[5]

And Schmitt ends up defining colonies with this lapidary formula: "Dependency in relation to the rights of the people, otherness in relation to state law."[6]

Close to a century later this definition extends Hamdane Khodja's remark. Every Algerian who read it when it was written could recognize himself in it.

Now that we live in the postcolonial era, are we able to say that these perversions and illusions have ceased to exist? Or are they hiding behind other masks and disguises? If these failings continue to manifest themselves, we can state without risk of error that their persistence feeds the resentment of the person who experiences its effects. Such is the case with the Islamic subject.

6

THE RETURN TO AVERROËS MAY, however, not be without pedagogical value in guiding the Islamic subject through the confusion that disorients him and opens him up to harkening to the disastrous fundamentalist illusion. Certainly it doesn't seem meaningless to go back to a twelfth-century thinker who, in your own language, has analyzed and resolved problems encountered in his time and that continue to beset your contemporaries. Such concerns, for example, are the relation to the other and the inequality of women.

The relation to the other, to the stranger, is set forth admirably at the beginning of Averroës's *Decisive Treatise*.[1] And the reasoning of the medieval Cordovan philosopher can indeed provide today's anxious identity seekers with an answer. In truth, it is common sense itself that takes hold of the question through that technical aspect that deals with the legitimacy of borrowing.

In order to use his reason to gain knowledge of God and of the whole of the creation God has endowed with being, Averroës recommended the use of inference as a method that extracts the unknown from the known. This method can be assimilated to the syllogism with its premises and species; it plays the role of the instrument for theoretical thought, a role comparable to that of the tool in practical activities. Concerning recourse to the logical instrument (the rational syllogism), Averroës noted that the first generations of Muslims (who constitute the basis of the tradition) did not know this instrument. He brushed aside the suspicion of *bid'a,* the "reprehensible innovation" discussed previously in relation to the Emir Abd el-Kader and which the conservatives invoke to obstruct new avenues opened by borrowing and adaptation of foreign inventions. Averroës believed that it is foolish to waste time reinventing for oneself what has already been invented by others. The accumulation of knowledge is universal. Anybody can draw on it, whatever his ethnic, language or religious background. By calling for the utilization of the method of the Ancients (the ancient Greeks, that is), Averroës overwhelmed the dogma of the Jahiliyya, that era of ignorance abolished by the age of grace introduced by Islam. Not only did he believe that new nations have to take advantage of the memory stores of previous peoples, he further set up a welcoming formula for his borrowings: We should rejoice and thank the ancient thinkers for everything they invented that conforms to the truth, while warning the public of the excusable errors of the ancients. Until this assertion, the word that designated the ancient Greeks was the Arab word *qudâma,* or Ancients, that is, the "Ancients from before the apparition of the nation articulated by the Islamic law."[2]

In a second move, Averroës ended up by creating a rather beautiful ambivalence when, invoking "those who came before us among the ancient peoples," he used the term *umam as-sâlifa.*[3] This expression makes use of an attributive adjective based on the consonantal root *s.l.f.,* the very root of the word that designates "the pious ancient ones" of Medina. Those *salafs* are constantly spoken of through the history of Islam by all who call for a return to origins (without forgetting to count among these the nineteenth-century fundamentalists and their chief figure, Sheikh Mohammed 'Abduh (1849–1905), as well as contemporary fundamentalists).[4] It is as if the Arab Aristotelian from Spain were subconsciously expressing a desire to confuse the Greeks, heathen foreigners, with the model figures that run through the Islamic myth.

Concerning the question of women, this other form of alterity based on sexual difference, Averroës analyzes it in his paraphrase of Plato's *Republic*. The original Arabic version of the book is lost and has come down to us in a 1321 Hebrew translation by Samuel ben Yehuda, a Jew from Marseilles, in the citadel of Beaucaire.[5] We also have a 1491 Latin translation based on the Hebrew version and prepared by one of Pico della Mirandola's Jewish students. In this way Florentine Neoplatonism of the late quattrocento was in its turn able to enjoy the Arab philosopher's commentary.

Without Aristotle's *Politics* available to him, Averroës decided to read Plato's utopia in an active manner (summary, commentary, actualization). And he found himself in agreement with the Athenian philosopher concerning the natural equality between men and women. This is why either sex can take part in great things: Women can be philosophers, military and political leaders. But this equality does not hide the difference that separates the sexes: If men can be more diligent at their tasks, women can be more skillful in the practice of certain arts. This is the case for musical interpretation. Thus it is said that melodies achieve perfection if men preside over their composition and women over their execution. It is clear that since they share the same nature, men and women can exercise the same professions in the city. But since women are physically weaker, they should be responsible for less arduous tasks. They are even capable of mastering the art of war, as has been noted in the barbaric countries that stretch out beyond the frontiers of the empire. To illustrate these assertions, Averroës took up once more the animal image used at the beginning of the text concerning the class of the guardians: Although weaker, female guard dogs are as ferocious as their male counterparts when it comes to fighting the hyenas that attack the herds.[6]

After the approving summary came the actualization, concretized in the course of the commentary. Averroës attributed to certain women— the intelligent and well disposed—the possibility of attaining political leadership and authority. He must have been thinking about Islam specifically when he noted that certain laws prohibit women from exercising supreme power (what he called the great *imamat*) because of the conviction that such women could represent only rare cases.

Otherwise, the women of these cities (the demonstrative pronoun pointed to the Andalusian cities Averroës knew) remained excluded from participation in great things because they dedicated themselves to the care of their husbands, to childbearing, to breast-feeding and to the children's education, tasks that occupied them completely. In this way the women resemble plants. And as their upkeep is a heavy burden for the men, they also become one of the causes of the poverty of these cities, because they do not participate in necessary activities— they only augment production a little through rudimentary tasks like spinning and weaving. This is Averroës's calm witness, naturally favoring the equality of women and implicitly preaching their emancipation. By his recourse to the economic argument, he anticipated contemporary feminist theories that link the liberation of women to their participation in production, rescuing them from financial dependency, which leads to all the other kinds of dependency. This defense of women is written in Arabic by a Muslim man of the twelfth century; it can still serve as a plea to put an end to the inequality and the confinement that is so often women's lot in many Islamic countries, today, at the beginning of the twenty-first century.

7

WE HAVE TO ACKNOWLEDGE THE FLOURISHING of Islamic fundamental-ism and the global dimension it assumed. The event we witnessed on September 11, 2001, was made possible only by the mutation of the Western model: It has gone from European to American.

It is clear now that the European model in which I grew up, the one that arose from the French Enlightenment and formed me through a Franco-Arabic education, no longer holds any attraction. I felt the shock of that when the question of the veil, so highly symbolic in Europe, came up. During my childhood in the 1950s, in that citadel of Islam that is the Medina of Tunis, I witnessed the unveiling of women in the name of Westernization and modernity. This involved the wives, daughters and sisters of the scholars of the Law who taught at the thousand-year-old theological University of the Zitouna (one of the three most important in Islam, after the Kairaouine in Fez and al-Azhar in Cairo).

This unveiling of the women in the conservative milieu in which I was brought up was not just the result of Habib Bourguiba's emancipatory action in Tunisia. Even in the more conservative Moroccan context, King Mohammed V had unveiled his own daughters. It was in the air at that time, and not only because of the Maghreb's close connection with France. Throughout the Arab world, the unveiling of women was a process that had begun at the end of the nineteenth century, following Qasim Amin's (1865–1908) pamphlet on the subjugation of women, and the veil as sign of that servitude.[1] Inspired by the liberal interpretation of the Qur'an proposed by the Sheikh Mohammed 'Abduh (1849–1905), Qasim Amin had written his *Tahrir al-Mar'a* ("The liberation of woman").[2] His ideas had mobilized the women themselves to create the Egyptian Feminist Union, in 1925. Its president, Hoda Sha'rawi, rejected the veil officially in 1926.[3] Qasim Amin's pamphlet does not propose a complete liberation of women. In relation to the veil, for example, his proposal is for a practical veil that complies with Qur'anic recommendations without hindering the women's movements or limiting their participation in civic activities. Most importantly, he insists that the oppression of women does not come from Islam itself but from usage and customs. This appreciation is in accord with the anthropologist Germaine Tillion, who, after conducting fieldwork in the Islamic terrain of the Aures Mountains, placed women's condition of servitude inside a wider structure. Concerning women and the veil, she linked "the cloistering of women in the whole Mediterranean basin to *the evolution, the interminable degradation of tribal society.*" She also suggested "reasons why this humiliating position was so often, and wrongly, attributed to Islam."[4]

The movement that summoned women to end their cloistering has to be inscribed in a cultural context of Westernization, which, during the last quarter of the nineteenth century, even marked the thought and action of the theologians. This is the case, for example, with Sheikh Mohammed 'Abduh, the master of Salafism, which invoked simultaneously modernization and a return to the *salaf,* those ancient pious ones of early Islam.[5] It is a kind of fundamentalism, however, to be distinguished from the *integrism* that is dominant today.[6] The sheikh was simultaneously against European hegemony and local despotism; he tried to adapt the contributions of Western civilization as closely as possible to the basic tenets of Islam. He read the *Treatise on Ethics* by the hellenizing philosopher Miskawayh (932–1030) and meditated on the rise and fall of states and other civilizations by confronting the cyclical and crepuscular thought of Ibn Khaldun (1332–1406) with that of the conservative historian François Guizot (1787–1874).[7]

Like his master, Afghani (1839–1897), Mohammed 'Abduh's thinking revolved around the decadence of his civilization. To remedy the decadence, he took up the theses that Afghani had developed in his controversy with Ernest Renan: Islam is not incompatible with the scientific spirit; all that is needed is to rediscover the material conditions of greatness that would allow the city of Islam to reconnect with scientific invention.[8] Therefore, Mohammed 'Abduh admits the necessity of change. But the condition for such a change depends on respect for the principles of Islam. His open-mindedness leads him to interweave his ideas with notions borrowed from Auguste Comte's positivism. 'Abduh strained his ingenuity to find at the core of Islam the elements of a rational religion that would create or permit access to modernity. He called for the creation of an elite whose discourse was to be the interpretation of Islam in that direction.[9]

I call these known facts to mind to give an overview of the climate of European Westernization that Arab thought underwent from the end of the nineteenth century to the 1950s. It is in this atmosphere that the feminist movement of the period between the two world wars flowered. This period also saw the creation in Cairo of a modern university marked by the philological positivism that Taha Husayn (1900–1972), an Azharian educated at the Sorbonne, wanted to apply to the Arab poetry of the pre-Islamic period. A few seeds were sown, despite the storm this book created.[10] The conservative scholars knew that if they let historicity take hold of the corpus of pre-Islamic literature, they would no longer be able to keep doubt from closing in on the Qur'anic text. But as early as 1937, Taha Husayn, using his characteristically biting critical irony, wrote an essay (*The Future of Culture in Egypt*) in which he excoriated the local mandarins who confused creative adventure with administrative compunction.[11] He chided the local celebrities for their reductive and small-minded vision of Egyptian identity by reminding them of the Mediterranean and Hellenic scope of the ground on which they walk. In this book, Taha Husayn called upon his people to Europeanize themselves in all their manners of thinking and being, with the sole proviso of preserving their religion.

This process of Europeanization manifests itself in another work in Arabic: *Al-Islam wa uçul al-Hukm* (Islam and the foundation of power), written by another Azharian, Sheikh Ali 'Abd ar-Raziq (1888–1966), who continued his education in Oxford.[12] He attacked the myth of the Caliphate and showed its merely relative effectiveness in history, as well as its obsolete character. He wrote his book in the wake of the definitive abolition of the Caliphate under all its forms (by Kemal Atatürk in 1924.) The disappearance of this venerable institution was not considered a loss by 'Abd ar-Raziq, who recommended that Muslims rethink their political structures by taking into account historical evolution and the contributions of other nations. Evoking Hobbes and Locke (without being directly influenced by them), our enlightened sheikh went so far as to question the elaboration of political principles in Islam.[13] Evidently such opinions gave rise to lively polemics. And it is not untimely to recall that in the TV clip aired by the Qatar-based channel Al-Jazeera on October 7 2001, Osama bin Laden implicitly brought up the abolition of the Caliphate when he claimed that it had been eighty years since the misery, the dispossession, the state of being orphaned, had befallen the Islamic subject—a condition against which Muslims now had to rise.

8

THROUGH THE IMPLICATION OF THAT televised message of October 7, 2001, we can see how very much things have changed in the land of Islam. We have moved from the deconstruction of myths to their restoration. And we have gone from the unveiling of women to their re-veiling. In short, we have changed eras. The world in its Westernization has gone from the European to the American mode. This formulation, as I repeat it here, will become clearer in the following pages.

I must confess that I felt something like shock with the re-veiling of women in one of the strongholds of freedom and Western culture, Paris, France. I had thought that with unveiling, we were engaged in an irreversible process, in which the subjects of the territories of Islam would also participate. Later, after spending more time in the Arab Orient, I discovered to my great astonishment the cohabitation of American-style consumerism with a vision of a simplified, traditionalist thought, very schematic and far removed from tradition and its complexity. (The country in which I grew up, Tunisia, is more marked by the French model, and I myself received a bilingual education in accord with the reforms introduced by the state under Bourguiba.) I learned that the Muslim participating in the consumer society proposed by the global market does not need to reform his soul first. The individual can very well adopt the American way of life while hanging on to his archaism.

The best example of this paradox is embodied by Saudi Arabia. This country, though authentically pro-Western in its alliances and profoundly Americanized in its urban landscape, simultaneously extols a kind of Islam that is not even traditional but has gone through a series of reducing diets from which it emerges anemic and debilitated. This is an Islam that founds its belief on the negation of the civilization that engendered it. This form of Islam is constantly at war with everything that's great in its history, at war with all that's beautiful. The Islam of Saudi Arabia came about not by the application of the letter of the law but rather through the transgression or at least the skirting of that letter, in some attempt to depart from it without necessarily attacking it.

If indeed some authority chose to subject its community at any price to a univocal letter of the law, that authority would need to prohibit reading the Sufis and theosophical thinkers who, like Ibn 'Arabi, dared to think audaciously. Such an authority would be forced to destroy the beautiful texts that led to Muslims' adolescent awakening. To shred the *Divan* of that most famous ninth-century poet discussed in Chapter 3, the Baghdad libertine Abu Nuwas. To hunt down the freethinkers of Islam in the depths of the ninth or tenth century.[1] To feed the flames of an auto-da-fé with the scattered pages of their works: those of Ibn al-Muqaffa (middle of the eighth century), who for his ethical quest preferred the ancient ones (the Manicheans) to his contemporaries (the Muslims); or those of the most famous impious character of Islam, Ibn Rawandi (ninth century), who put to flight a number of Islamic myths: the inimitability of the Qur'an, the impeccability of the Prophet and the mechanism of the Revelation. Such an authority would think it urgent to throw a veil over the figures evoked by Ibn Hazm (994–1063), who managed to adopt a disillusioned religious stance by applying the principles of the Greek skeptics who claimed that all proofs are equally valid (the *isotheneia ton logon*).[2] It would insist on tearing up the books of al-Ma'arri (973–1058), the poet who revoked all religions in such a lapidary formula that it was easy for me to retain it in my student memory. The blind man from Ma'arra is a skeptical spirit who introduced me to the virtues of doubt, in this verse, for example:

> Each generation of men follows another and turns the old lies into the new religion. Which generation was given the right path?[3]

By the same token, it would be necessary to burn the *Thousand and One Nights,* which struck my childish ears so deeply and made me familiar with the evil that inhabits this world. Through a journey of words, this book confirmed the Islamic imprint that shapes me as a speaking subject, capable of symbolizing and imagining in order to respond to the violence of the real.

It is important to understand that the emergence of this scanty and impoverished Islam acts first of all against Islam itself as a culture and civilization. What remains astonishing within this fundamentalism is the cohabitation of archaic regression and active participation in technique and technology. I have cited the case of Saudi Arabia because these people are now at the core of an immense aporia: While being part of the Western alliance, while wanting to be part of the *pax americana,* they have fueled the real or virtual civil war that is threatening the whole of the Muslim world. It is they who have financed, who have backed, who have restored this idea of a return to the pure letter, to the application of the letter of Islamic law, and who are trying to put the Qur'anic letter at the very foundation of the law down to the use of corporal punishments obedient to scriptural imperatives.

Part II

A Genealogy of Fundamentalism

9

To throw light on the genesis of Saudi Arabia and the formation of its ideology, one must go far back in the course of history. Before looking at the eighteenth century, one has to go as far back as the ninth. In evoking such a sequence of events in Chapter 3, I briefly discussed Ibn Hanbal, one of the protagonists who took part in the events in Baghdad during the first quarter of the ninth century.

As discussed earlier, Ibn Hanbal created one of the four law schools of Sunni Islam. His doctrine insists more than any other on a return to the purity of the letter and on the imitation of the *salaf,* the "ancients of Medina," which amounts to trying to apply to every person and to each century the idealized model of the Prophet's city. What is omitted is that from its very beginning (only a few years after the Prophet's death), Medina, which in the seventh century experienced the birth of the Prophet's politics, was historically scarred by a bloody civil war. Three of the first four caliphs (whom myth called the well-guided caliphs) were assassinated. A great part of the history of Islam took place in the violence of civil war, and at regular intervals it has been rocked by factional disputes concerning legitimacy. Ibn Hanbal glossed over the issues and enmities that had divided the early community by promoting the adversaries and enemies of those first days of discord to the hierarchy of the Ancients; he tried to reconcile the greatest number in order to win a large consensus favorable to rallying the community to the one and incontestable truth of the Qur'an and the tradition (the *sunna*). So as not to trouble the horizon of such a truth, he advised against recourse to personal opinion (*al-ra'y*) as recommended by other schools of law. He therefore recommended that the reading of the Qur'an be literal and avoid any allegorical exegesis.

Between the time of Ibn Hanbal (the early ninth century) and the eighteenth century, which saw the birth of Saudi ideology through the intermediary of Mohamed Ibn 'Abd al-Wahhab (1703–1792), there was the intermediary link constituted by Ibn Taymiyya (1263–1328). This Syrian theologian, a radical disciple of Ibn Hanbal, lived through an uneasy period for Islam (this kind of radicalism, by the way, comes to the fore only when the entity to which one belongs is under major threat). Ibn Taymiyya lived during the time of the Mongol invasions, the sacking of Baghdad and the end of the Caliphate, with the perils posed by the Crusades barely overcome. It was an extremely dangerous, even apocalyptic situation for Islam, which felt threatened in its very being. Gifted with exceptional intelligence and energy, Ibn Taymiyya spent his life lying in wait for any protrusion that might mar the smooth surface of the letter, and he set himself the task of polishing that letter by ridding it of the variety of meanings that decorated its profile. He indiscriminately hunted down the effects of philosophy on theological discourse and its contaminations by Greek thought; he fustigated any number of esoteric sects, decreeing them heretical by virtue of the privilege they accorded to hermeneutics; he denounced the theory and the experience of the uniqueness of Being as preached and lived by the Sufis, whom he considered far more dangerous than the Christians for a belief based on absolute monotheism. Whereas among the Christians, God became human on one single occasion (through the Incarnation), with the Sufis, the human disposition toward the reception of the divine is open and universal. In everyday life, this constitutes an attack on the idea of the One God. Ibn Taymiyya also denounced pilgrimages and visits to the tombs of saints. He condemned every manner of intercession, which he identified with the detestable survival of paganism and idolatry that deserved nothing but eradication.[1]

Taymiyya also wrote a short book, a sort of manifesto, which, since its composition at the beginning of the fourteenth century, constitutes the breviary that delights the eyes and the hearts of every suitor of the pure letter. This book is titled *Politics in the Name of Divine Law for Establishing Good Order Among the Affairs of the Shepherd and the Flock*.[2] Its many small, popular one-hundred-page editions bear witness to this text's wide diffusion. The book sets out the charter that links the prince and his subjects in their submission to the *Sharia*, Islamic law. The radicalism emanating from such a book totally fulfills the expectations of the fundamentalists. This text alone is worth an exhaustive analysis to help us delineate the symptoms of what I call the sickness in Islam. I will, however, cite only a few characteristic passages, sufficient for the purposes of the book at hand.

To begin with, the author makes corporal punishment, as set out by the Qur'an, the very criterion of the law. These punishments, very few in number, involve stoning for adultery, flagellation for false accusation of adultery, flagellation of the wine drinker, the chopping off of the hand of the thief, and the chopping off of the hands and feet or crucifixion for highway banditry (depending on whether homicide is involved). These rudiments of a penal code are called *hudud,* the plural of *hadd,* which in the common vocabulary means "interval, obstacle, extremity, end, point or edge, limit, border." The *hudud* constitute God's claim, the inalienable share of justice that belongs to God and that cannot be called into question or paid for in any other way. Ibn Taymiyya adduces an anecdote concerning the Prophet, who was once asked by a plaintiff who wanted to withdraw his accusation against a thief in order to spare the latter the amputation of his hand. The

Prophet grows angry, arguing that nobody, not even he, can intervene in what he has called "God's share." The Prophet separated God and humans by an unbridgeable border, made tangible through the prescriptions that distribute bodily punishments according to the offense. The Prophet then told the plaintiff to think twice before accusing someone, because once the machinery of law has been put into motion, it is impossible to go back. The *hudud* are that share of the law that is nonnegotiable, and with which neither rank nor fortune can interfere.

This vision, which places the share of the law in the untouchable region of transcendence, seems to echo Kant's perception of penal law. In the section devoted to the right to punish and pardon, contained in the "Doctrine of law," the first part of the *Metaphysics of Morals*, he writes: "Penal law is a categorical imperative, and woe onto him who would slip into the serpentine rings of eudemonism in order to discover something which, by the advantage it promises him, would deliver him from punishment or diminish the latter."[3]

In Kant's mind, law is thus outside the world, beyond any empirical consideration or human feeling. Here too, one is inside a logic of purity that rids the law of any utilitarianism, that relieves it of any compromise: "For justice ceases to be justice as soon as it puts a price on itself."[4] The passage in Kant leads to a defense of capital punishment and a refutation of the theses developed by one of his early critics, the Marquis di Beccaria, in his *Dei delitti e delle pene* (On crimes and punishments) (1764).[5]

But is it necessary to insist that a world separates Kant and Ibn Taymiyya? For the German philosopher, the purity and absoluteness of law aim at considering man as an end and not as a means. In his company, and in the context of the Enlightenment that is his, we remain inside the horizon of freedom. With the Syrian scholar, we do not leave the theocentrism that submits man to the order of the divine. For the one, the purity and absoluteness of law are attained by recourse to divine transcendence; for the other, law is its own foundation. In the 1920s, this law became transcendence itself, if one follows the theories of the Kantian jurist Hans Kelsen.[6]

Concerning the application of corporal punishment, many other schools of law show themselves much more adaptable. Out-of-court settlement is permitted by certain jurists for false accusations of adultery as well as for theft, for these are offenses that violate a human right. Active repentance is also taken into account in relation to theft and banditry. And recourse to *shubba,* the "resemblance" of the committed act to a lawful act, can merit the accused a presumption of innocence. The jurist has set up many ruses to soften the approach of the *hudud.* Further, the establishment of proof is made very difficult. Finally, it is considered more praiseworthy to pass over in silence faults involving corporal punishment rather than adducing proofs.[7] In fact, there is a wide range of "liberal" procedures that Ibn Taymiyya does not mention.

10

In his *Siyasa*, Taymiyya makes jihad, holy war, one of his main themes. He gives it the same importance as prayer and seems to set it above the other four canonical prescriptions (the confession of faith, fasting, charity to the poor and the pilgrimage). To indicate its high status, he associates it with the image that is meant to represent religion: a column with the base representing submission to God, the shaft representing prayer and the capital representing jihad.[1] Thus he makes the fight against the infidel one of the two functions of the prince, who must devote his energies to the service of religion by insuring on one hand the triumph of virtue inside the polis (through the rigor of corporal punishments), and on the other hand by waging holy war beyond the borders.

At the end of his manifesto, Ibn Taymiyya concludes that by putting all the means of the empire (the financial and military capacities) in the service of religion, Islam will complete its religious edifice; it works toward the conquest of the benefits of the earthly world and confirms those of the hereafter. He thinks of this as Islam's greatest possible political and religious victory. Through this accomplishment, such a community avoids a double peril: The first peril is the separation between the political and the religious—political power that does not take religion into account. The second danger is religion that is only preoccupied with itself, divesting itself of power and grandeur to reduce itself to humility and compassion. This double peril is what happened to the two other religions, which grew impotent, unable to perfect the religious edifice. They took two erroneous paths: one that asserts religion without putting political, financial and military power at its disposal, and one that does possess the power, money and military might but without any plan to put these in the service of the establishment or the strengthening of religion. The first path is the one of those "who will incur divine anger"; the second is the one of those who "went astray."[2] The Jews took the first, and the Christians took the second of these paths.

We realize how much the consubstantiality of the political and the religious (which so many believe belongs to the essence of Islam) is just the elaboration of one theologian transformed into a warrior of his faith (I'll return to this question later in the book). This consubstantiality is presented as an ideal (or utopia) and as a galvanizing slogan in the framework of an ideology that is now being reactivated by contemporary fundamentalists.

And I cannot pass over in silence how wrong Ibn Taymiyya turns out to be when we compare his words with the facts of his era and the historical memory that formed it. Thus when it comes to the Jews denied political and military power, many of the poems written by the Spanish Jew Yehuda Halevi (circa 1075–circa 1141) bear witness to that privation, stressing the pathos of the situation:

> *The son of the slave robes me with terror*
> *and throws his dart with a high hand . . .*
> *I have been stripped of the light of love*
> *And a proud foot presses on me like a yoke.*

I suffer from the cruelty of his customs
In exile, in prison, in sadness, revolted
Without leader or minister of state.
The enemy approaches and the rock steps aside.[3]

A similar dispossession—sign of exile—was represented in Christianity. Witness the allegory of the synagogue shown under the south portal of Strasbourg cathedral (mid-thirteenth century.) The synagogue is represented as a beautiful lady with bandaged eyes (to signify that her gaze remained darkened to the new light emitted by the New Testament's grace) and carrying a broken lance (to recall her exclusion from active statecraft and from the use of arms). But what about Christianity? On the same Gothic portal, facing the synagogue, haughtily steps the allegory of the Church as a noble lady proudly exhibiting the attributes of power (crown and intact lance) together with the ecclesiastical symbols. Ibn Taymiyya couldn't help remembering the Crusades, a chapter barely closed when he was born and which were nothing but the adaptation of jihad in Christianity. Either the Syrian theologian was well appraised of the latest conflicts between the pope and the emperor concerning the sharing of temporal and spiritual power, or he simply dismissed the Gospel passages that separate the realm of God from that of Caesar.

It is in the long run that Ibn Taymiyya's words turn out faulty. Taking into account historical evolution, every reasonable person will conclude that the theologian's judgment is only contingent, even if it did take the long passage of the centuries to prove him wrong. Humanity's greatest political achievement took place in Europe, originating from a Christian genealogy, even if it was formed precisely on the separation from religion, through the effects of an intellectual negation that neutralized the inherited belief. With the return of Israel to statehood (Yehuda Halevi's desire was realized more than eight centuries after its poetic expression), the Jews' reappropriation of the military has known its times of glory as well as its hours of decay. Today, it is the condition of Muslims that seems politically and militarily un-happy and marked by loss and defeat.

But history has more than one trick up its sleeve. It yet again discredits Ibn Taymiyya while simultaneously derailing a stereotype dear to common sense. If I have to weigh the contributions of each on the scales of history, I would say without fear of error that the most precious legacy that may be ascribed to Islam consists in the profusion and intensity of its body of spiritual texts. This legacy owes as much thanks to the ardor and intensity of its poetic and lyrical sayings as to the exalted tenor of its speculations. The success of Islam was achieved in the Sufi corpus—which was denounced by Ibn Taymiyya—whereas the defeat of Islam occurred in the political sphere, exactly where the theologian had placed the privileged space of his faith. In contrast, according to a current credo, only in Christianity (since it is far from the political) can the mystical experience come to its full realization, as Christianity is supposedly the religion of love and not of law. And yet spiritual success recognizes itself as Islamic, whereas political success recognizes itself as Christian. In truth the lesson of these observations is that the matter of history cannot be satisfied with an essentialist vision, either of the men or of the ideas that create such a vision.

To come back to Ibn Taymiyya, in his day, he represented only one opinion among many. Though his radicalism pleased the crowd, it worried his colleagues in theology and law, and he was a source of dissension within the polis. Accordingly, he endured trials and long years of imprisonment (which he devoted to writing). His literalism, his anthropomorphic, "corporist" dogmatism, is derided by the traveler from Tangiers, Ibn Battuta (1304–circa 1369), who claimed to have met him:

In Damascus there lived among the great Hanbalite jurists one Taqi as-Din Ibn Taymiyya, a man held in great esteem and who could discourse on the various religious sciences, though he was slightly deranged.[4] The people of Damascus highly venerated this man who exhorted them from his pulpit. On one occasion he proffered words that the jurists contested, and the latter referred his case to al-Malik an-Nasir, who ordered him to be taken to Cairo. . . . Al-Malik an-Nasir commanded that he be thrown in jail. Our man remained imprisoned for several years, and in jail he wrote an exegesis of the Qur'an he entitled *al-Bahr al-muhit* ("The ocean"), which ran to forty volumes. . . . Ibn Taymiyya's mother went to complain to the sovereign, and that is when al-Malik an-Nasir ordered him released from prison. But Ibn Taymiyya continued to behave the same way. I was in Damascus at that time, and one Friday I witnessed one of his exhortations from the mosque's high chair. Among other things he said: "God descends toward the sky of the world here below as I now descend," and he took one step down from the high chair. A malekite jurist called Ibn as-Zahra confronted him and contested what he had said. The crowd rose up and beat the jurist with fists and sandals so hard that his turban fell off, revealing a silken skullcap.[5] The people criticized that piece of headdress. . . . (Ibn Taymiyya was then taken to the Hanbalites' judge, or *kadi*) . . . who had him imprisoned and flogged. . . . The condemned man died in jail.[6]

Such testimony shows the theologian as excited agitator, rousing the crowds, scandalizing his Sunni peers, even those who belonged to his—the Hanbalite—legal school. His attitude and provocation exasperated the goodwill of the political authority. He represented an ideological voice that embarrassed the state power without being unanimously backed by the scholars. On the other hand, he apparently had the vox populi behind him, the voice of the people who seemed to put up with simplifications and preferred the effortless adhesion to the apparent sense of the letter. It is that voice—bellicose, theatrical—that was the voice listened to centuries later by the firebrands of fundamentalism. And above all, by the founder of Wahhabism.

11

MOHAMED IBN 'ABD AL-WAHHAB (1703–1792) is at the origin of Wahhabism, the ideological strain named after him. In the very interior of the Arabian peninsula, he preached a cross between the theory of Ibn Hanbal and that of Ibn Taymiyya. In his native Nejd, he established ties with the tribe of the Saud which strove to take over power by conquering the deserts of Arabia. Thus was launched—at the very heart of the eighteenth century and contemporaneous with the European Enlightenment—the puritanical movement that brought forth today's Saudi Arabia two centuries later.

Through the contemporaneity of these two phenomena belonging to very separate mental spaces, a new era opens for the world. Since that time, the differential between coexisting human cultural modes has increased rapidly: We find in the same century different cultures that illustrate the multiple states that humanity has known, from the immemorial pre-Neolithic to the child engendered by the latest technological revolution. The Marquis de Sade's reaction to the events in

Arabia can be placed in the framework of this phenomenon, which thereafter was even more exacerbated, until at the beginning of the twenty-first century, it manifests itself in the cohabitation on this single planet of that immemorial being and of the cosmonaut setting off to conquer space. Here is how a postreligious man at the end of the eighteenth century judges, in his new wisdom, his fellow man who is regressing toward the all-religious:

> And once again wars of religions are ready to devastate Europe. Boheman, leader and agent of a new sect of "purified" Christianity, has just been arrested in Sweden, and the most disastrous plans were found among his papers. The sect to which he belonged is said to want nothing less than to render itself master of all the potentates of Europe and their subjects.[1] In Arabia new sectarians are emerging and want to purify the religion of Mahomet. In China even worse troubles, still and always motivated by religion, are tearing apart the inside of that vast empire. As always it is gods that are the cause of all ills.[2]

The words are by the divine marquis, who had understood the danger of that sect at the very moment of its emergence. Note Sade's discernment in associating this peril of purification not just with Islam: He makes it into a universal problem that poses its threat as soon as a zealot tries to create a revolutionary and insurrectional movement in the name of the letter, whatever the specific religion may be. To demand that human affairs be conducted in the name of God can only engender fanatics and their attendant disasters.

If we examine Ibn 'Abd al-Wahhab as a doctrinaire writer (by reading, for example, his most famous book, *Kitab at-Tawhid*, "The book of the unicity of God"), we discover a scribe without an ounce of originality. We don't even dare give him the status of thinker. The book I have just mentioned is stuffed with citations, revealing its author as a copyist more than a creator. His numerous other briefer works confirm that his short breath doesn't bestow the dignity of a genre on the short form. The pages he has covered with writing confirm his obedience to strict Hanbalite thinking. He seems to be even more rigid than the founding master. Ibn Hanbal, as it turns out, reveled himself as rather tolerant on the question of excommunication; Ibn Taymiyya himself acknowledged that the Baghdadi scholar was extremely exigent in relation to cultural obligations (the *'ibadat*) but rather liberal when it came to matters of custom (the *'adat*).

In the wake of this remark, one can see how the cult of the saints could be tolerated by Ibn Hanbal, even if in his day the brotherhoods had not yet been constituted. On that question, as on many others, we witness an increase in the scale of intensity between the three links: We go from the relative tolerance of the master from Baghdad (ninth century) via the radical critique (though it remains theoretical) of the theologian from Damascus (fourteenth century) to the violent actions and the destructions of century-old mausoleums by the Arabian disciple (eighteenth century). In fact, not one saint's tomb is left in all of Arabia today, except for the Prophet's in Medina.[3] To safeguard his faith, the Wahhabite does not hesitate to destroy the vestiges of civilization with the sole aim of preventing the redoubtable confrontation of the myth he propagates with actual historical documents.

An entire world separates the two early masters from Ibn 'Abd al-Wahhab, though he claims to follow their teachings. It is important to recall that Ibn Hanbal also had a Sufi lineage that included some great masters. Certain concepts he introduced are not incompatible with inner experience—for example, the concepts of *tafwidh* (to trust to God in what concerns the ultimate mystery) and of *taslim* (conscious surrender to the word of God and his prophet in one's acts as well as in one's words). Such dispositions can favor the fideism of an Ansari (1006–1089), the great spiritual master from Herat, whom I remember with deep emotion at this very moment when bombs are raining on what remains of his beautiful city.[4] This master combined Hanbalite rigor with the incandescence of inner experience as manifested in the fireworks of his Qur'anic meditations.[5] One fragment of Qur'anic verse captured his gaze and converted him to Sufism: "Those who believe are the most ardent in their love for God."[6]

Here is the result of his meditations, one of his "Cries from the Heart": "My God! I have water in my head and fire in my heart; inside I feel pleasure, outside I feel desire. I have foundered in an ocean without shores; there is a pain in my soul for which there is no remedy. My gaze fell on something that no language can describe."[7]

Ibn Taymiyya shows exceptional constructive abilities when he turns away from invectives and anathema. His *Refutation of the Logicians,* a work full of subtleties, offers perspectives that allow his thought to throw light on certain zones defined by modern logic.[8] We need to point out some of the nuances that make for the complexity of both Ibn Hanbal and Ibn Taymiyya's work, if only to distinguish their work from that of their rough disciple from the Nejd, Ibn 'Abd al-Wahhab, whose work, given its poverty, could well have been consigned to oblivion.

The mediocrity and doctrinal illegitimacy of 'Abd al-Wahhab have often been denounced, at times by unknown or very ordinary sheikhs who thought themselves more competent than he in matters of traditional sciences and gave themselves permission to condemn him. This is the case of Dawud al-Baghdadi, who demolished the doctrine of Ibn 'Abd al-Wahhab in a booklet containing two refutations of Wahhabism. (These treatises were completed in 1293 A.H./1875 C.E., and they were published in Istanbul in 1305 A.H./1887 C.E.)[9] Al-Baghdadi recalled a *fatwa* that had been argued in 1195 A.H./1780 C.E. by a contemporary of Ibn 'Abd al-Wahhab, the Shafiite sheikh Mohamed Ibn Sulayman al-Madani. The latter had received a query submitted to him accusing Ibn 'Abd al-Wahhab of having opened the road to ignorance and of having authorized uncultivated men to extinguish divine light. How could such a personage pretend to the interpretation of the dogma (*al-Ijtihad*) when he did not fulfill the conditions that scholarly tradition demanded of anyone exercising this art? Didn't he need to submit himself to the scholars instead of continuing to attribute the imamate (prophethood) to himself and to exhort the community to follow in the path he was laying out? Why did he call anyone who contradicted him impious and demand his death?[10]

Suppose, Baghdadi said, that the conditions of *Ijtihad* were gathered in one person who would, by his own wits, elaborate a doctrine. Did that mean that he had to impose it on everyone, when the doctrinal domain is vast and the roads through it many, as established by the hermeneutic tradition and corroborated by the scholars?[11] The critic asked for elucidation on Ibn 'Abd al-Wahhab's prohibitions of visits to the tombs of the saints, vows, intercessions, offerings, sacrifice, the invocation of the Prophet or one of his companions in moments of distress, and petitions addressed to anyone other than God. The unknown querier who formulated this juridical consultation is also asking himself by what right the man from Nejd accuses the believer who follows such practices of being a renegade. The Shafiite scholar applies himself to the task of deconstructing one after the other all the prohibitions invented by Ibn 'Abd al-Wahhab. His very technical answers rely on some of the greatest names in Islamic theology, chosen among the most orthodox and exoteric Sunnites.[12] He ends up by revealing the author of those prohibitions as an illegitimate pretender to science, an ignorant sectarian, whose prescriptions wreck the complex edifice of law built up over the centuries.[13]

12

THE MOVEMENT THAT TRIED TO take power in the lifetime of Ibn 'Abd al-Wahhab came to nothing. The troops of Egypt's viceroy, Mohammed 'Ali (1769–1848), managed to chase the Wahhabites from the Hejaz after a violent campaign. (Jacques Berque has wondered how the Egyptian generals were able to take their canons all the way to Dar'iya, the cradle of Wahhabism, where in the 1970s he had glimpsed the citadel of the Sauds still in ruins.[1]) A new attempt in the middle of the nineteenth century did not succeed any better. But the ideological seeds had been sown, and at the very beginning of the twentieth century, the conditions were ripe for reviving the movement. The tribe of Ibn Saud, forever linked to this puritanical ideology, reactivated the process; thirty years later, it had imposed its hegemony on the greater part of the Arab peninsula, pacifying all the tribes, and created—in 1932—the Saudi state, with Wahhabite ideology enshrined as official doctrine and buttressed by a zealous militia watching over its scrupulous application.

Without the wealth created by the exploitation of oil resources, the Saudi state and the ideology that underlies it would have remained marginal phenomena. Its domain would have been limited to an inhospitable terrain on which a minor sect would have survived, before either dying out or surviving in rough austerity, in accordance with the dire scarcity of desert living. But thanks to the power acquired through the petro-dollar, the Saudis were able to spread their simplistic ideology and prey on the civilization that the nations of Islam have created over more than a thousand very full years of history. Through the technological means of sound and image (which are the means of the Americanization of the world), they wounded Islam profoundly by abolishing or suspending its various creative dimensions.

Havoc has been wrought among local cultures that harbor the cult of the saints and its expression as festive theater, the live witness in this century of an ancient and totally Dionysian energy redeployed in the contours of Islamic faith. The ceremony of the trance has managed to survive into the heart of the twentieth century: I was its amazed witness during my childhood, and I found it again in the 1980s, at the *moussem* animated by the Issawa of Meknes to celebrate the Prophet's birthday. But censure is at work. Under the insidious influence of Wahhabism, political authority has decided to attenuate the intensity of ancient practice, to smooth out its rough edges, to control its creative urge.

Will such an excessive expenditure of energy slowly wither away? What can we do to help preserve the ceremonial of the trance maintained for so long by the Issawa of Meknes? E. R. Dodds has unearthed surviving aspects in the Issawa that throw light on ancient Maenadism or give an overview of the energy that leads to the loss of self, the exact sort that led Agave to fail to recognize her son Pentheus, to dismember him and to feed on his live flesh, as Euripides shows in *The Bacchae*.[2]

We might object: "How can you mount a defense of those barbarous scenes, clearly the products of irrationality, when you have presented yourself so far as a partisan of reason?" My answer to such a charge is this: For a long time now, I have made the separation of domains into an art of living, so as not be the victim of the reduction that the logic of reason imposes. In relation to politics, I use prudence, moderation, common sense; I declare myself a down-to-earth realist and submit to the teachings of Aristotle, Voltaire and Kant. In short, I see myself as Apollonian in that area. But in poetry, in art, in the adventure of inner experience, I become a man of excess, of unboundedness. I become celestial; I navigate in the wake of Plato, Rousseau, Nietzsche, Georges Bataille.[3] And I discover myself as Dionysian. In this paradoxical logic, love of the Enlightenment does not make me occult the darker face of man.

The aesthetic span immanent to the works and days has withdrawn from the daily life of the cities. The subtleties of the traditional doctrines have often exiled themselves and taken refuge in native hearts and minds that have opted for withdrawal. Or these doctrines continue among Europeans who had converted to Islam (in the wake of René Guénon) by the means of Sufism and the ardor of its teachers. Modern times have permitted the Islamic subject to prosper by joining the global marketplace while remaining steeped in tradition at home. Are we not living the time of the Americanization of the world? Are we not undergoing some of the effects of the communitarianism and multiculturalism that are shaping the American cities? This is a question I am pondering—and which remains unanswered.

Should we see in the American-Arab alliance only geostrategic considerations and a pure conjunction of interests? The very title of an early chapter of Tocqueville's *Democracy in America* announced the archeological, genealogical method.[4] The return to an understanding of the past illuminates the present of the nations and their future.[5] To understand "the great social enigma the United States presents to the world in our time," Tocqueville returned to the founding legislations, rereading the code of laws promulgated by the colony of Connecticut in 1650. Focusing their attention on the penal laws, the legislators strange to say, . . . borrow their provisions from the text of Holy Writ: "Whosoever shall worship any other God than the Lord," says the preamble of the Code, "shall surely be put to death." This is followed by ten or twelve enactments of the same kind, copied verbatim from the books of Exodus, Leviticus, and Deuteronomy. Blasphemy, sorcery, adultery, and rape were punished with death; an outrage offered by a son to his parents was to be expiated by the same penalty.[6]

When I read such a text, I have the feeling that Wahhabite Saudi Arabia and Puritan America were held over the same baptismal fonts. At their origin, both states share a legal base rooted in religious reference; by recourse to Holy Writ, they apply rough and archaic corporeal punishments in order to preserve the virtue of the social body. But it would be dishonest to stop with this astounding report, which seems to attribute surprising elective affinities to these two states. Shortly after the preceding comments, Tocqueville adds:

> In strict connection with this penal legislation, which bears such striking marks of a narrow, sectarian spirit and of those religious passions which had been warmed by persecution and were still fermenting among the people, a body of political laws is to be found which, though written two hundred years ago, is still in advance of the liberties of our age.[7]

It is these political dispositions that impose a radical difference, one that moves us away from the perceived identity. But it is possible that this dialectic of the same and the different creates a misapprehension. In truth, and with a little help from the sin of naïveté, the religious reference in the Saudi political setup should not shock the American protagonist. Even if, as Tocqueville also writes, "in America religion is the road to knowledge, and the observance of the divine laws leads man to civil freedom."[8]

This is one more paradox that can only help fuel misunderstandings. Though religion has led to freedom and knowledge in America, religion filtered through the Wahhabite schematics can only uphold subjection and ignorance. Unconscious of his servitude and blindness, the Wahhabite sectarian walks hand in hand with the American; the two partners are equipped with foundational references that, superficially, resemble each other: Such appearances can sustain the illusion of a natural alliance. On the stage of the global marketplace, the American takes the Wahhabite as an apprentice and initiates him into techniques that help him breathe in the rhythm of America, wherever in the world he may find himself. Through this association, the Wahhabite enriches himself materially and invests in the propagation of his faith. By acquiring wealth, he honors his spiritual genealogy. Didn't Ibn Hanbal declare that to become rich is a divine duty? Didn't Ibn Taymiyya insist that to put one's wealth in the service of religion constitutes an imperative it would be reprehensible to avoid?

The Saudi-American idyll will be troubled only by the birth of that strange figure, the "Wahhabite's Wahhabite." This character will denounce the Wahhabite who has not been faithful to the doctrine and who has let himself be seduced by the other side of being American, the side that blemishes the puritanical vision of Islam. Bin Laden and the numerous Saudis who took part in the attacks of September 11 perfectly illustrate the figure I call the Wahhabite's Wahhabite. The staging of such a doubling hollows out the person, opening up an aporia that confronts it with a more radical double. I adopt it here by analogy with an episode invented by the Sufi Qushayri (986–1072) when he comments on the temptation of Adam in the Garden:

> After having succumbed to the suggestions of the Demon, Adam, furious that his purity had thus been soiled, says to him: "You damned one, you have tempted me and I have acted on your instigations." To which the Demon answers: "Certainly, Adam, I was the demon who inspired you; but can you say who is my demon?"[9]

13

As I HAVE ALREADY MENTIONED IN this book, Islam knew great things very early on, but the process it initiated was interrupted. The reader has the right to demand the reasons for this interruption. Several hypotheses have been advanced to explain the drying up of the creative wellsprings. There was first of all the progressive loss of international commerce. Islam had established its greatness at the very moment when Europe had fallen into lethargy (from the eighth to the eleventh century). One of the effects of the Crusades—which lasted two centuries, from 1099 to 1270—was the reestablished dynamism of the Italian city-states (Genoa, Pisa, Venice) which broke the Islamic monopoly on Mediterranean commerce.[1]

The mathematician and science historian Ahmed Djebbar asked a fundamental question about Islam's interrupted development: "Why was this brilliant civilization . . . unable to create at its core the conditions that should have prepared the advent of modern science, with its corollaries, that is to say, the scientific and technological revolution, followed by the industrial revolution?"[2] Instead of an answer, Djebbar proposed a synthesis of what has been said about this question by researchers (notably, C. Cahen and M. Lombard). To begin with, there were the internal crises that befell Islam after the Christian and Mongol offensives (twelfth and thirteenth centuries). Then there was the weakening of the social relationships in artisanal production. Finally there was the fact that monopolies over certain resources—iron, wood and gold, for example—changed hands, which precipitated the transfer of money from Islam to Europe. In such ways Islam lost control of international commerce, a control over which it never regained mastery. The new shipowners opened up new horizons (through the discovery of America) and changed the trade routes (by way of new maritime maps that open access to Asia and Oceania by circumventing the territories of Islam).

Régis Morelon, a historian of Arab astronomy, in a discussion with me evoked the quantitative thesis developed by the Reverend Alvès de Sa, a knowledgeable Brazilian priest who spent much time in the Dominican Institute for Arab Studies in Cairo. Alvès de Sa estimates that the great civilizations crumble after about five centuries. This periodization is applicable to Islam, whose classic phase can be said to have lasted from 750 to 1250. After this time, the culture's expressions could have continued its classic phase for another five hundred years, except that Islam was not in possession of the means that would have reconciled it with the rupture of the Enlightenment and the technological and industrial revolution.

These explanations (and others as well) seem plausible, yet some part of the enigma remains. Is there in history some intervention that lies beyond human will? Could this be the part of providence? Or of the Spirit, enigmatic in the ways in which it moves among the people and visits nations and languages? Or is it possible to adapt to history the metaphor of the unconscious, to determine there those virtualities that escape reason and go beyond the panoply of causes that explain the rise and decline of civilizations? As far as Islam is concerned, the lightning expansion of its beginnings remains marked with its own enigmatic aspect just as much as its ineluctable decline.

What remains to be explained, or at least mentioned, is the series of defeats the Islamic world experienced when it tried to respond to the dawn of the twentieth century. At that moment Islam grew aware that a revolution whose outcome it could not know was in the process of transforming the surface of the earth and the manner in which humans inhabit this earth. It is important to examine these failures, because from their smoldering ruins grows the ressentiment that excites and motivates the fundamentalist mind-set.

Let's start with the failure of the modernization attempted in the nineteenth century. In this regard the Egyptian situation remains exemplary, a failure warranting further examination, because it carries in it the failure of the Europeanization that had grazed Arab thinking, the context of which I sketched earlier when I discussed women's liberation. How are we to explain the failure of the modernization undertaken by Mohammed Ali during a reign of more than forty years (1805–1848)? We cannot avoid the feeling that there was nothing lacking in his politics: the constitution of a centralized state; the creation of monopolies of production; a modern army; a broadening of the national territory to the dimensions of empire (through expanding its frontier in the direction of Syria and Palestine, Arabia, and the upper Nile); the development of technicians and translators; the sending of students to Europe; the creation of pedagogical structures, medical institutions, and factories and plants for the processing of raw materials; the introduction of industrial crops (cotton, sugar cane); the invention of an architectural style; a politics of great public works aimed at modernizing the infrastructure; the building of roads, canals and dams. This project of modernization lacked nothing except perhaps the method that would have connected the hierarchy of priorities and the necessary rigor in its execution.

During friendly exchanges with Roshdi Rashed, founder and editor of the formidable *History of Arab Sciences,* I learned from this epistemologist and historian of mathematics that the principal reason for the Egyptian failure lay in the obstacles that the Europeans placed in the path of Mohammed Ali. In a time of European expansion, it was necessary to prevent by all means possible the emergence, so close to the old continent, of a new regional power that could become a rival on an already aggressive market protected by force of arms.

When I questioned the same friend about the later case of the Japanese success initiated in 1868 by the Meiji era, he affirmed that the Japanese modernization happened without the Europeans being aware of it, or rather happened beyond their sphere of influence. The Land of the Rising Sun thus benefited from its remoteness.[3] What's more, although Japan was determined to modernize and Westernize, it also kept intact its traditional structures of authority, as much in the circulation of decisions through the social hierarchy as in the know-how of its artisans and manual workers, who had maintained the spirit of high precision that kept watch over their art. Japan's industrialization was triggered by the initiative of the great old families with the cooperation of scrupulous trade associations.

In Egypt, however, these two conditions were absent. Mohammed Ali was a foreigner who had undone a social body that lacked historical roots (he had, for example, acquired the monopoly of agricultural lands). More importantly, the arts and crafts were in a state of decay: The ethic internalized by the manual worker was no longer focused on concern for well-wrought professional work. At the end of the eighteenth century, the editors of *The Description of Egypt* already took note of the deterioration of artisanship and the rudimentary state of technology. They were impressed by the gap that separated contemporary copper work from an object such as a door of the Mameluke period, fashioned from the same material. In the manual arts, the loss was incommensurable: What a difference between the perfect beauty of the works inherited from the fourteenth century and the neglected condition in both material and form of the objects exchanged toward the end of the eighteenth! From one period to the next, the Egyptian hand-made object had already passed from an age of precision to one of slipshod work. It was a situation not conducive to the imitation of the products of engineering proposed by the industrial age, which demands high precision within a process that needs complex coordination between distinct, complementary tasks.

The only positive achievement that the reign of Mohammed Ali and his successors managed to leave to posterity are some of the political, economic and social rudiments that eventually permitted Egypt to constitute itself as a nation-state. Yet, having brought the people neither democratic freedom nor well-being, that development in its turn experienced a failure that added to the previous failures. We will come back to this.

Let us look at a writer, Sheikh Rifa'a Rafe' Tahtawi (1801–1873), who is representative of his era.[4] An Azharian who lived in Paris for five years, he was acting as the imam of the students sent there by Mohammed Ali. Upon returning to Cairo, he headed the bureau of translation; he himself translated some twenty volumes from French. He clearly showed liberalism in his handling of juridical and political authorities, though they remained Islamic. He supported a sovereign who honored justice in the exercise of absolute power; he felt true empathy for the "protected minorities" (the Jewish and Christian *dhimmis*). He legitimized borrowings from foreign juridical systems and recommended their integration into the body of the *Sharia* (Islamic law) if general welfare demands it. This frame of mind was invaluable for the evolution of law.

The sheikh, however, remained premodern in his approach to European culture. He did not succeed in avoiding confusion and clearly prioritizing his documents, unable to distinguish between those works that were foundational and those that were adventitious. He was unable to discriminate between the different levels of texts: he put a priority on school manuals not realizing that these were—like encyclopedias—an ersatz for science. In short, he gave the impression of being in a hurry and of believing that a compendium was enough to master this or that art or technique. It is clear that he could not imagine the hard labor demanded by the incessant give-and-take between fundamental research and applied science.[5]

With this remark I want to make explicit a symptom of the failure of Europeanization, even in its later phases, with authors already discussed, such as 'Abd ar-Raziq (in whom we noted a superficial knowledge of Hobbes and Locke through the use of school textbooks).[6] Even if one invokes Taha Husayn, the most prestigious of "Occidentalists," one may judge that to the very end of his career (in the 1970s), he remained, as historian of literature, the pupil if not the disciple of Gustave Lanson, and as chronicler and critic, at best an imitator of Sainte-Beuve. He revealed himself as a follower of older models and not as initiator clearing a path in solitude. He never became an innovator who participates in the adventure of his contemporaries and works for the conquest of new terrain that would be hospitable to thought and word.

14

IN A TEXT PUBLISHED A FEW MONTHS before her death, Simone Weil warned with great lucidity that "an Americanization of Europe would certainly prepare an Americanization of the whole earth."[1] She also foresaw the role America would play in the advent of the postcolonial era, and with trepidation had the foreboding that Europe would not grasp the opportunity to stop the march toward such an event, one that would metamorphose the fate of the world:

> America, having no colonies, and thus no colonial prejudices, and naïvely applying her democratic criteria to everything that doesn't concern herself, looks without sympathy upon the colonial system. No doubt it is at the point of seriously shaking up a Europe grown dull in its routines. Now, by taking the side of the populations subjected by us, it gives us, without understanding it, the best help for resisting in the future its own influence. It doesn't understand this; but it would be disastrous if we didn't understand it either.[2]

The Europeans didn't understand it, and the Americanization of the world slowly began to replace its Europeanization. Colonialism came to an end, but with a lack of awareness: with the refusal to see that decolonization constituted one of the ineluctable effects of the postwar era. Simone Weil's lucidity bears witness to this. The attempt then was to put off the inevitable. This postponement lasted for fifteen years (1945–1960), during which time the blindness of the politicians cost us much suffering and several hundred thousand dead. The case of Algeria eloquently illustrates this fatal European irresponsibility. But that is another issue, to be adjudicated elsewhere, outside the scope of this book.

For the purposes of this discussion, the point is simply that the world has gone from Europeanization to Americanization. Traditional colonialism slowly made way for alliances between sovereign countries, though these were often enough reduced to implicit protectorates in which the protecting power shared a large part of the riches with the native population it protected. In Saudi Arabia or in the United Arab Emirates, the visitor is impressed by the material comfort that has taken over the cities, whose profile bears witness to a more global Americanization, going far beyond the luxury items that clog up the people's daily lives. Yet the legislation of these countries keeps the strict appearance of archaic religious law, even if, concerning business legislation—a token of local participation in the global market—the local contracting party espouses more than it is ready to admit the shape of international law. Such accommodations are made secretly; there is no interference as long as the appearances are kept up.

There is a sort of adaptation to the global scale of the double meaning that characterizes American identity on its own territory: an identity of one's home that differs from the identity of the polis, the city; an allegiance to one's community that parallels allegiance to the state. It is this ambivalence that characterizes the American citizen. Very often a particular identity is based as much on the religious community as on the ethnic one, though it is the religious one that is recognized by the state. A range of beliefs, which in France would be considered illegal sects, have the right to register legally as official religions; every faith can acquire a judicial status protected by the authority of the state.

But it is not such proliferation that is important in our demonstration. It is rather the common feeling toward which, it seems, all these faiths converge, and that is best illustrated by the one religion native to America, that of the Mormons. Harold Bloom calls this psychological predisposition in which many faiths come together "American religion" and sees it as the attribute of an emerging post-Christian nation.[3] It is perhaps in such a bringing together that the plurality of secondary identities finds its unity. What constitutes the American being is on the one hand the duality of belonging, on the other the folding of all religious faiths into a single feeling. Maybe this structure is transposable everywhere and thus enables the Wahhabite to be an excellent and authentic participant in the Americanization of the world.

Archaic in his faith, brilliant technologist in the marketplace, this divided being can be found in America itself, as much in the psychological predisposition just described as through the support of faiths from other continents and other times. That's what I saw in Brooklyn, in the small Ashkenazi synagogues of Borough Park, toward the end of a September evening when I had found myself alongside Polish Hassidim who were celebrating the end of the feast of Tabernacles. It was Simchath Torah, when the believers take up again the first words of the Torah at the very instant when they have pronounced the last ones, so that the end of the last liturgical year and the beginning of the new one touch. The atmosphere was archaic. I had the feeling that I was witnessing an ancient rite that had migrated across the Atlantic in the very form it had taken on in eighteenth-century Poland. I went from *stiebl* to *stiebl* only to discover men celebrating the Torah as an object of adoration, on great scrolls that the bearded, black-clad celebrants wrapped with satiny shawls I imagined to be pure silk. They cajoled the scrolls thus covered, as one would cajole a child or a lover.

The hat-wearing men danced alone, the women did not have the right either to dance or come within the interior of the temple. The next day, these same men would gather again in Manhattan to deploy their skills in jobs that covered the breadth of the information chain, from the conception of software to the sale of hardware.

15

THE MODERNIZATION THAT GRIPPED other Islamic countries during an earlier phase (that of the nation-state) was conducted on the European model. This was the case, for example, for Kemal Atatürk's enterprise in Turkey (starting in 1922) or for the venture triggered by Habib Bourguiba in Tunisia a generation later (in 1957). Bourguiba had had dealings with the juridical spirit of the French Third Republic and was determined to found a state and a society that were both secular. But the principles he had learned from his university education were accompanied by reflexes emanating from local atavism. The democratic principles of his Western genealogy were annulled by an actual use of power resembling that of an Eastern despot. The flourishing of this tyrannical atavism was explained as a necessary circumstance in Tunisia's situation. To adapt Tunisian society to the change that would remedy its ills, Bourguiba needed to institute an authoritarian state capable of sustaining the pedagogical vocation that he had bestowed upon himself.

In the relationship between religion and sovereignty, it was not easy to move from the *Sharia* laws to a legal system devoid of theologico-political influence. Even in the most advanced constitutions, such as the Tunisian, the legislature stipulates that Islam is the religion of the state. The citizen is accordingly not free to choose his belief (or lack thereof), which must conform with the prince's. Such an arrangement brings us much closer to the situation analyzed by Hobbes than to the spirit of French law expressed in the Constitution of the Fifth Republic. We are indeed not very far from Hobbes, when he writes:

> Subjects can transferre their Right of judging the manner of Gods worship on him or them who have the Sovereign power. . . . [In all Christian Churches, that is to say, in all Christian Cities] the interpretation of sacred Scripture depends on, and derives from the authority of that man, or Council, which has the Soveraign power of the City. . . . [And thus in Christian cities] the judgment both of spirituall and temporall matters belongs unto the civill authority.[1]

This theory was lucidly reformulated by Diderot in an article he wrote on Hobbism for the *Encyclopédie*. His article is in tune with the spirit of several contemporary Arab constitutions. Despite all their other differences, these agree in subjecting the governance of religion to political authority: "It was up to the sovereign to prescribe to the peoples what was to be believed of God and of things Divine."[2]

Some residues of the theologico-political order have not been completely removed in these experiments of judicial modernization. This state of affairs manifests itself at the minimum through the central position accorded the executive power, which takes the form of a leader as a pregnant incarnation of the state. It is as if in the mind of the modern—and even modernist—legislator, there persisted unconsciously the idea that the one who represents sovereignty casts the shadow of God on the earth, an idea that was articulated by a number of medieval Islamic pens despite the theological controversy it created.

The liquidation of the theological by the political turns out to be at least as difficult, if not impossible, as Carl Schmitt shows it to be, in his response to Peterson when discussing the much more profoundly secular Western tradition.[3]

Whatever state was created in the era of the nation-state, whatever the principles on which the legislator based himself, these states unconsciously did nothing except modernize the tradition of the emirate and give it a new form.[4] The institution of the emirate was theorized by Mawadi (d. 1031); it is polymorphous and changes form according to circumstances. The form that seems to fit best with the modern version has the emir take power by force (*imarat al-istila'*).[5] Mawardi regarded seizure of power as legitimate if recourse to it prevents rebellion or secession in the prince's territories. On this basis, the cult of the leader can find fertile soil in which to flower. Carl Schmitt's theory now easily explains the preeminence of the leader: The exceptional condition that legitimizes it becomes the norm. The one who makes the decisions in an exceptional situation holds the power to suspend the law temporarily, or at least in such a situation the executive trumps the legislative.

Incidentally, provision for this can also be found in the constitution of the French Fifth Republic, and Charles De Gaulle invoked it during the exceptional situation created by certain events during the Algerian war.[6] This double explanation accounts for the universal presence of an incarnated state in the Islamic countries. Such a state reanimates the theologico-political imprint that marks dictatorships; the imprint fades away to the point of becoming nearly invisible in the republican and democratic state.

In the countries under consideration, political power is nearly always wielded by the armed forces. Now, the role of the military in the political field does not come from the model of the caudillo as realized in Spain or in Latin America. This phenomenon has a genealogy all its own, to be traced back to the figure of the emir. Here too it is a matter of a tradition of Islamic history; since before the suspension of the caliphate, starting at the beginning of its decline (i.e., from the tenth century onward), the military militias, becoming conscious of their power, took over the state apparatus and decided to govern at their own pleasure. The emirates formed as soon as the caliphates started their decline.

16

WITHOUT GOING FURTHER THAN GLANCING at the chronicle that is the history of Islam, one realizes that each of its pages denies any dogma that affirms the consubstantiality of the religious and the political. Many Western Islamologists share that belief with the fundamentalists; it is an idea that also haunts the media. But I dare to maintain that this judgment (which takes itself to be dogma) is only an allegation. Political power has very often been exercised by military men who clothed themselves in the attributes of the emir and who then had to negotiate the kind of relationship they were to have with the constituted body that speaks in the name of religion, the *ulemas*. These scholars in theology represented the juridical-theological authority.

When historians have an essentialist vision of human affairs, they invoke the Prophet of Islam, who was a warrior-prophet, a founder of a political society. Historians repeat that in the very genesis of Islam, at its very foundations, any rational being will detect the consubstantiality of the political and the religious. This latter of course did exist, and was prolonged with the creation of the caliphate, assumed by the successor, the delegate of the Prophet. This caliphate is apparently characteristically Islamic: A sovereign succeeds the Prophet in the fullness of his functions, as leader of the community. The concept has another use, revealed in the Qur'an: Man is established in his sojourn on this earth as "caliph [of God] on earth."[1] Theocentrism is thus bound to anthropocentrism. With such double binds, to which can be added noninternalization of the Galilean discovery, the Islamic subject feels ill at ease in making his way toward his destiny while bearing the same narcissistic wounds already suffered by Western man: the decrepitude of the geocentric, the theocentric, the anthropocentric.

Let us return to the figure of the caliph. No scriptural arrangement (either in the Qur'an or in the Sunna) can turn it into a religious obligation. Sheikh 'Abd ar-Raziq recalled this in his treatise already cited: "The caliphate was not only neglected by the Qur'an, which never so much as evoked it, but also by the Sunna which does not mention it at all."[2]

However, the second Qur'anic mention of the term concerns a prophet-king. God addresses David as follows: "We have made you a caliph on earth."[3] This reference may thus at best lend legitimacy to a theory of sovereignty around a theologico-political vision. The result would be an overdetermination of the person of the sovereign: He is the vicar of God on earth as all men are, but he is God's shadow as prince. This quality, which we encounter in both the Orthodox and the Catholic traditions, makes it impossible to imagine an Islamic specificity for the caliphate, the latter legitimizing the political function by prophetic delegation. The inference triggered by the Davidic attribute concerns only the theological intervention sanctifying the political function. It is not the other way around, in which the caliph would gain his legitimacy because he is a successor of the Prophet, and as such would be entrusted with temporal power as one who from the onset is vested with the sacred function.

History concretized the ideal figure of the caliph only for a brief period. The possibility of regulating the question of legitimacy by sharing the power between caliph and imam likely arose very early on, starting with the first Arab empire in Damascus, that of the Umayyads (640–750). The civil war triggered by the struggle to determine legitimacy caused a trauma, which curiously enough did not interrupt or even slow down the irresistible rush of the first conquests. The conflict came to a head between the "people of the house" (the descendants of the Prophet) and the mercantile aristocracy of Mecca (whose chiefs had fought Islam at the beginning of the prophetic predication and who had heard in the first revealed verses only a mystic's ravings). The assumption of power by the Meccan clan of the Umayyads can be understood as a usurpation. With reconciliation in view, the caliphate could have split in two; the festering question of legitimacy could have been resolved by a separation between the spiritual function (assigned to the imam, a descendant of the Prophet) and the temporal function (assumed by one or the other of the clans that made up the Meccan tribe of the Quoraysh).[4]

The notion of this separation must have passed through the minds of the time. I find these premises in a poem improvised by the official poet Farazdak (d. 728). Literary tradition does indeed recall that Prince Hisham (who was to be the tenth Umayyad caliph, from 724 to 743) was in Mecca at the time his father, Abd al-Malek, reigned in Damascus (he was the fifth caliph of the same dynasty, from 685 to 705). While Hisham was performing the ritual circumambulations of the veiled cube, he tried to approach the Black Stone in order to touch it, but was unable to draw close to it, because of the dense crowd.[5] He was brought a seat on which he sat to gaze on all these people jostling each other. He was accompanied by Syrian notables. While he sat there, the Imam Zayn al-'Abidin, the son of Husayn, son of Ali, approached and started his circumambulations.[6] When he found himself at the level of the Black Stone, the crowd drew back and let him through so that he could touch the stone. At this, one of the Syrian notables asked Hisham, "Who is that one whom the people venerate with such fear?" To which Hisham answered, "I do not know him," out of fear that the people from Syria would in their turn start to worship him. Farazdak, who was present, spoke up: "I do know him." And then started to declaim:

The flagstones recognize this one's footfall
The temple recognizes him as does the sacred enclave
This one is born from the greatest of created beings
He is the pious the pure the lord of holiness
He is the Grand-son of Fatima if you don't know who he is,
Know that his ancestor is the last of the prophets
It is not by saying who he is that you would diminish
The fame of the one you pretend not to know
The Arabs recognize him and so do the foreigners
God has honored him always and has glorified him
Thus has it been ever since the Prophet's pen first inscribed the sheet
He who thanks God does so by thinking of this master first of all
From his house religion has been given the nations
The prophet's grace has bowed towards his ancestor
And the grace of his nations has conquered the other countries
He belongs to a tribe that by an act of faith one has to love
Hating them plunges you into the very heart of impiety
Their proximity confers refuge and asylum
They are the masters for all pious people
And if you are asked who are the best on the inhabited earth
You'll answer it is they and nobody can supplant them.[7]

Far from being the enemy of the Umayyads, the poet who improvised these verses was their official thurifer. But, faced with Hisham's denial, he could not repress this cry from the heart, bearing witness to the charisma of the "people of the house." The scene that this poem represents makes everyone aware of the division of the two functions: The reader of the poem recognizes that the crowd of pilgrims (representing the people of Islam) receives the son of the caliph, and a future caliph himself, with indifference, while greeting with veneration the imam, whose grandfather was assassinated in Koufa (in 660) and the father massacred in Karbala (October 10, 680), a tragedy of which he was one of the survivors.

This story alone proves that in the mind of the people, there was a clear difference between temporal power and spiritual charisma. This anecdote was probably not unique; its repetition might have established a fact that the law could then have registered and formalized. But the truth of the fact was neither theorized nor taken into account by the jurists.

17

IN 750 THE ABBASIDS UNSEATED THE Umayyads by trying to charge the function of the caliph with sacred character through the spiritual legitimacy conferred by belonging to the "people of the house." This lineage had been forged by a descent that the new pretenders to power claimed emanated from the loins of Abbas, the Prophet's uncle, whence their name. After less than two centuries of glory, the caliphate had been emptied of its substance by the middle of the tenth century, the era that saw the institution's decline and the extension of the caliphal function to three figures. Besides the caliph of Baghdad, two others declared themselves caliphs, namely, the Fatimid Mahdi of Cairo and, after him, the Umayyad emir of Cordoba. The caliphal function, eroded by this competition, had become symbolic with time; it had nearly breathed its last at the moment of the Mongol invasion, the fire of Baghdad and the assassination of the last caliph to reside in the Mesopotamian capital (1258).

Baybars (1223–1277), the fifth Mameluke sultan of Egypt (of Turkish descent), was said to have saved Islam by kicking out the Crusaders and by stopping the Mongol invasion.[1] The sultan had a stroke of genius: He took in a descendant of the Abbasid family after the destruction of Baghdad (1258), set this Abbasid up in Cairo, and returned the title of caliph to him. This gesture helped Baybars integrate the holy cities of the Hijaz (Mecca and Medina) into the domains he ruled, and from Cairo he could now hold out the bright prospect of an Islamic empire. Until 1517, the caliph played for the Mamelukes the role of the pontiff who gave religious legitimacy to their secular and military power, in turn controlled in its theological-juridical function by a third institution, the one comprising the corps of *ulemas*.

This era of exceptional greatness—modern-day Cairo bears witness to the splendor and architectural monumentalism of the Mamelukes—was founded on a power structure in which the sacred, the politico-military and the theologico-judicial functions were truly separate.[2] The whole structure was placed under the authority of the prince, who, as the bearer of sovereignty, enjoyed the glow of sanctity, which fell on him doubly. Any human who attained the supreme function bore the mark of divine selection; on the other hand, the prince who watched over the application of justice represented the shadow of God on earth.

The last radiance of Islamic civilization over Arab lands took place under the Mameluke dynasty, with the domination of the separation of the temporal from the spiritual on one hand and the redistribution of the sacred over the secular on the other. This was the epoch when Cairo had become the last world-capital that Islam was to know. Ibn Khaldun (1332–1406), who arrived there at the very end of the year 1382, could not hide how dazzled he was.[3] Faced with Cairo, the great historian became truly enthusiastic. Up until then, Khaldun was rather reserved in his reactions, sober in his expression, but when describing the universal capital, he is on the verge of lyrical exuberance:

Cairo: metropolis of the world, garden of the universe, place of as-
sembly of the nations, human anthill, high place of Islam, seat of
power. Palaces without number rise everywhere, and everywhere
flower *madrasas* and *khanaqat* where scholars shine like brilliant
stars. The city spreads out along the shores of the Nile—the river
of Paradise, the receptacle of the waters of heaven, whose floods
quench the thirst of men, and give them riches in abundance. I
have walked through its streets: a press of crowds, and markets
overflowing with all kinds of goods. How often have I heard the
praises of this capital, which has attained the truest degree of civilization and prosperity? Concerning her I have gathered a wide variety of impressions, some from my masters, some from friends
and others from pilgrims or merchants. Here, to start with, is the
impression of my friend al-Maqari—the grand Qadi of Fez and the
greatest scholar of the Maghreb—which he shared with me upon
his return from the pilgrimage in the year 740 (1339): He who has
not seen Cairo will never be able to judge the power and the glory
of Islam.[4]

The caliphal function was again revived in 1517 for the benefit of
the Ottoman sultan, but in an exclusively symbolic manner, precisely
to signify that the religious function supplements the figure of the sultan, whose primary function is imperial. Philip Mansel reminds us of
this when he refutes Fernand Braudel's description of the Ottoman
state as a counter-Europe. The concept of empire, which enlightened
the politics of the sultans, was the very concept that had been active in
Western history:

From 1453 Mehmed II, like his successors, also saw himself as heir
to the Roman Empire and the only true emperor in Europe. . . . The
Turkish metaphor for worldly dominion was the Red Apple. Before
1453 the Red Apple was believed to be the globe held in the right
hand of a giant statue of the Emperor Justinian in front of Haghia
Sophia. After the statue's destruction in 1453, the apple moved

West and came to symbolize the Ottomans' next goal: the city of Rome. . . .

The Ottomans were also inspired by a desire to equal the glory of Alexander the Great. . . . One of the favourite epithets, both of the sultans and their city, soon became *alem penah*, "refuge of the world." It appeared appropriate to create a multinational capital for an empire which, it was later calculated, contained seventy-two and a half nationalities. [Gypsies were considered half a nationality.][5]

The subjects of this empire were aware that the political structure allowed them to live a double identity. This imperial attribute constitutes an astonishing foretaste of today's situation in the United States and whose effects I have previously discussed.

The caliphal dignity came as an addition to the sultan's imperial identification: a happy supplement that adds glory to majesty. Its adoption enriches the symbolic field of the empire, strengthened as much by the Western reminiscence as by the Eastern inheritance. The imperial idea thus gave itself a wider universality. Although after 1517 the caliphal function further sanctified the position of the sultan, the Prophet's remains that arrived the same year from Cairo and Mecca constituted the visible elements of that sanctification. These relics included

The Prophet's cloak, seal and swords, one of his teeth, and the hairs from his beard. His banner, of black wool, arrived from Damascus in 1593. These relics were not exposed in a mosque for public reverence but, like the Holy Shroud of Turin, remained secluded in the ruler's palace, as a private dynastic treasure. . . . The special Pavilion of the Holy Mantle, faced with marble panels taken from Cairo, was built for them in the third court of the imperial palace near the Sultan's bedroom.[6]

As mentioned, the caliphate was to remain one of the Ottoman sultans' attributes until the abolition of the sultanate by the Turkish republic in 1924. Let us note, however, how this concept is exceeded everywhere when one approaches it in its actual historical manifestation, and not as a myth used as a symbolizing tool by those who are haunted by a culture of the proper, of the specific, the very ones who preach an imaginary purity. That utopia is the one that Osama bin Laden and his minions cry over, agreeing in chorus that for them the beginning of Islam's misery lies in the abolition of the caliphate. But we have just seen how, among the Ottomans, this caliphate constituted nothing but one more authority interested in further justifying the sanctification of the universal and already holy figure of the emperor.

18

IF WE TURN BACK TO THE THIRTEENTH century, it would be useful to examine the standpoint of a foreigner, the Emperor Frederick II (1194–1250), who was in contact with the Islamic power structure. He had negotiated in Arabic with his Muslim interlocutors, after having spent time in the Holy Land during the peaceful Sixth Crusade he had initiated in 1229. Before leaving the shores of Italy, the emperor was still engaged in the process that he had set in motion at the very beginning of his reign: to restore and reinforce the imperial structure. Because of this, the conflict with the papacy remained open, the positions of the two parties were irreconcilable, whether the adversary was Innocent III or Gregory IX. Furthermore, Frederick was in Palestine on his own authority, without having consulted the papacy. How could he have done so, given that he had been excommunicated? The problem that confronted the emperor was the same one that confronted the Muslim princes: What are the relations between temporal power and spiritual power, and what place should be accorded to religion and sacred symbols in the power structure as well as to the persons that incarnate it?[1]

It was al-Kamil (d. 1238), the Ayyubid sultan of Egypt, son of the famous Saladin, who encouraged Frederick II to come to the East, because of a foreboding that his brother Al-Ashraf, who reigned in Damascus, was plotting against him.[2] Frederick himself sought to take advantage of this intra-Islamic dissension. When Frederick landed on the coast, al-Kamil was encamped in Nabluz with a formidable army. Once Frederick had disembarked, the sultan sent the emir Fakhr ed-Din as an envoy to him. The two became friends and spent much time discussing philosophy and the art of rule. As mentioned, Frederick was a highly cultured man, educated in the Arab tradition; he shared the same concepts and references as his interlocutor. The discussions must have been fruitful, and the emir no doubt would have reported them to his monarch al-Kamil, himself a scholar and poet who loved to exchange ideas with the scholars of his city.

> The Orient had different connotations for these two great men. Unstinted admiration of the Arab mind was the weightiest factor with the Hohenstaufen Emperor. For Frederick II lived in a day when the East was the source of all European knowledge and science, as Italy and Roman culture were to the barbarian North, as of old the art and philosophy of Hellas were to Italy. The spirit of the medieval Church was imprisoned in formula and dogma, the fetters could be loosened only by oriental Hellenistic knowledge, chiefly knowledge of the laws of Nature. Frederick was more determined than any contemporary to unlock these stores of knowledge, and was destined to be, in virtue of his mental receptiveness and his Sicilian birth, the great intermediary and reconciler of East and West.[3]

After many mishaps and much temporizing, Frederick II, much appreciated by the Muslim negotiators, signed an advantageous treaty on February 18, 1229. It stipulated that the emperor extended his sovereignty over Jerusalem, except for the sacred enclaves that surrounded the Dome of the Rock and faced the al-Aqsa mosque. Bethlehem was also ceded, with the proviso that Islamic believers would have access to it in order to offer their prayers. This retrocession provoked the anger of the Muslims. Many recalled that Saladin had told Richard the Lion-Hearted how this city was as sacred to the Muslims as it was to the Christians, "and even more so, for that is where one night the Prophet ascended to Heaven, and where the angels assemble."

So Frederick did not even maintain the pretense of a war for the faith: His Crusade was purely an affair of state, a matter concerning the empire, not the church, and this could not have been made clearer than by the existence of his Muslim retinue. It was perfectly natural for Frederick, from a political point of view, to pose as an Oriental here in Syria.[4]

In his conversations with Fakhr ed-Din, Frederick brought up many questions regarding the state. They discussed the figure of the caliph and the ineffectiveness of his political clout—Frederick had negotiated with political and military leaders and had obtained the kingship of Jerusalem. If the caliph had added his voice to those of the protesters, his dissent had no effect. Frederick was fascinated by the Muslims' neutralization of their "pope." The emperor himself was forced to deal with the competition of his own pope, who had set himself up as *versus imperator*. Furthermore, Muslim sultans did not have to submit to excommunication, as he had to. He also learned that the caliph was descended from the Prophet through his uncle Abbas and that the power had remained in the family:

> "That is excellent," said Frederick, "far superior to the arrangement of those fools, the Christians. They choose as their spiritual head any fellow they will, without the smallest relationship to the Messiah, and they make him the Messiah's representative. That pope there has no title to such a position, whereas your Khalif is the descendant of Muhammad's uncle."[5]

It was as if Frederick had realized that Islam had truly managed to resolve the problem of the relationship between the two powers, the temporal and the spiritual. By concluding that the role of the caliph, descendant of the Prophet, was limited to the spiritual function, he is in agreement with what we have learned from the encounter in Mecca of the Imam Zayn al-'Abidin and the Umayyad Prince Hisham. It is as if the potentiality we discern in this tale from the beginning of the eighth century had become the reality of the thirteenth century. Before his own eyes, Frederick saw the realization of his idea: the subjugation of the spiritual to the temporal order. And the way in which thirty years later Baybars exploited the figure of the caliph for the sanctification of his own temporal glory was a consequence of that same reality.

Frederick, the excommunicated emperor, ultimately staged his self-coronation at the Church of the Holy Sepulcher, placing on his own head the holy crown of Jerusalem. This event had as its actor an excommunicated prince and as its stage the most sacred site in Christendom. But there was no intermediation by the Church, no bishop, no coronation Mass. The ceremony took place on Sunday, March 18, 1229, and on that day, Frederick restored the principle of a kingship that connects directly with God without mediation by the Church.

Frederick II brought Western "monarchy" back from the East. The Hohenstaufen descendant wavered between the model of the old Christian empire (in which the emperor incarnates the dual glory of majesty and holiness) and the new format introduced by a secular monarchy. Through this ambivalence, the emperor cut the domain of the immaterial in two: He left matters of the soul to the Church and assigned matters of the mind to the State. The ecclesiastical hierarchy of grace was given as its counterpart the secular and intellectual hierarchy of law. On this point, he must have profited from his conversations with Fakhr ed-Din. Indeed, he did try to adapt the theologico-judicial institution of the *ulemas* to his own culture and founded the University of Naples to attract juridical scholars, "twins" of the *ulemas*.[6]

Frederick's authorities were not exclusively Eastern. He also cited such figures as Justinian, the emperor of the legal code, and Augustus, the emperor of peace. Nevertheless, Frederick's viewpoint and resultant actions show an astonishing likeness to Islamic structures of power founded on a tripartite division of three concepts: nature, mind and soul. Through the first, sovereignty is invested in the monarch. Under the authority of the state, the second gives intellectual power to the *ulemas,* or the juridical scholars. The last is conceded to the caliph-imam (or to the pope). The emperor's power structure was very close to what Baybars will accomplish around 1260 in Cairo.

But Frederick's imperial experience gains its autonomy and Christian specificity in the tension between two legitimate cults of divinity: the law and the mystery of the sacraments. Such a philosophy of the State and of Justice expresses all the violence that bloodied the relationship between the Church and the State, both in direct contact with God. Dante elegantly pondered that tension in his *De Monarchia* and all his other works. According to the Florentine poet, although the contemplative life can be saved by the Church, the active life can realize itself concretely only under the reign of the law and of a sanctified State.[7]

Part III

Fundamentalism
Against the West

19

ISLAM NEVER HAD A DANTE WHO summoned the intellectual audacity to make his writing address political events as they appeared in the reality of history. I dream of this genius that Islam did not create: He would have constituted the opposite of Ibn Taymiyya. An exact contemporary of Dante, Ibn Taymiyya wrote his *Siyâsa* in the same period that Dante devoted to his *Monarchia*.

Until today, the world of Islam also lacked a figure like Frederick II, who did not allow himself to be guided only by the light of the dominant culture of his time. Wasn't it he who introduced political forms and ways of thinking borrowed from a foreign land because he deemed them more conformable to nature? Wasn't it he who knew how to adapt them to the conditions of his state? How splendid it would have been if such a figure had arisen in the twentieth century to introduce democracy into the lands of Islam and spread it through the whole of its civilization, as Frederick II did at the end of the Middle Ages, when he brought secular monarchy (even if it was by divine right) to the West. Kemal Atatürk and Bourguiba, the most "Western" political leaders of Islamic stock, did not manage to rid themselves of the despotic tradition they had inherited. In its persistence, this despotic tradition clouded the process of borrowing from the Europeans; Western ideas were skewed or, in any case, not made attractive. On the contrary, the vain expectation of civil liberties and material comfort was a source of disappointment. These experiences in their turn increased the political and cultural deficit. This incomplete borrowing of a Western model constituted an additional failure, to add to the series of failures enumerated throughout the preceding developments.

Such failures leave the way open for questioning. It is easy for xenophobic detractors to belittle the foreign model without letting themselves see the perversion it undergoes in application. By calling for a return to their own tradition, the semiliterate agitators forget that the cause of the failure of democracy is the despotic atavism at the foundation of the tradition they invoke. But they turn away from this difficulty by idealizing a return to Medina, to origins.

We have seen how the utopia of Medina was often revived. Using an example from modern times, recall that the Medina vision was at the origin of Wahhabism, and that it constituted the credo of fundamentalists, the *salafis* of the nineteenth century. It was also at the center of the system cobbled together by the fundamentalists from 1920 to 1930, with the emergence of the movement of the Muslim Brotherhood. Despite all their differences, these tendencies have a common viewpoint in their unanimous reference to Ibn Taymiyya, even if their adherence to that Hanbalite doctor varies in intensity.

But an important attribute does distinguish them: their relationship to the West. The West was not an issue during the appearance of Wahhabism; that movement was born in the eighteenth century, before the success of the West, before the conquest of the world by bourgeois imperialism. Furthermore, the cradle of Wahhabism did not undergo colonial aggression, but only the wounds of internal violence, the military violence inflicted on it by the viceroy of Egypt and by the Ottomans. As a doctrine, Wahhabism expressed its polemical violence and its prescriptive coercion wholly within the conceptual field of Islam. Its exclusivity manifested itself through an extremely rigorous theoretical position against the protected people of the Book, the Jews and Christians. But the feeling of hostility directed at Christians was not accompanied by political conditions that could have converted it into anti-Westernism. Further, the benevolence of the English during the formation of the Wahhabite state, followed by the early arrival of Americans for oil, quickly sealed the alliance with the West. This alliance of the Saudis with England and the United States was strengthened when Arab nationalism solidified its opposition to Europe and above all to the United States (during the 1950s up to the defeat of June 1967). In this hostile context, the Americans, always taking support from the Saudis, encouraged Pan-Islamism against Pan-Arabism. These same Americans will remember those times when in the 1980s they helped organize Islamic resistance in Afghanistan. They did not know that they were feeding the viper that would turn against them to plant its fangs and spit its venom into the heart of the symbols that embody their financial and military power.

Let's return to the fundamentalists of the nineteenth century, especially the masters of that school of thinking, Jamâl ad-Dîn Afghâni and his disciple 'Abduh. In politics, they were opposed to European hegemony (as manifested through colonial domination). But when it came to matters of the mind, they were completely fascinated by Western culture: By invoking the political categories inherited from the Age of Enlightenment (parliamentarianism, freedom of expression), they led the fight against local despotism. Their aim for civilization was to rediscover greatness by reconciling Western ideas with fidelity to tradition. In their theology, they sought to find in the Qur'an even the elements of rational religion of the kind theorized by, for instance, the positivist Auguste Comte.

In reality, the birth of anti-Westernism did not occur until 1920–1930. One indication in two different periods of time signals the shift from fascination with to revulsion toward Europe. The disciple and spiritual heir of Mohammed 'Abduh, the Syrian Rashid Ridha (1865–1935), changed his opinion at the end of his life about the Wahhabites, whom he had treated as heretics in an essay of his youth. He had the courage to retract his statement by singing their praises even before their victory in Arabia (in 1932).[1] After seeing them as followers of a deviant doctrine, Rashid Ridha thought that the disciples of Ibn 'Abd al-Wahhab represented tradition itself (the *sunna*).

This recantation reveals Ridha's evolution toward a greater conservatism, which distances him from the breakthroughs of his master 'Abduh, especially concerning borrowing from the West. There was on his part a new insistence that the Islamic subject had to fight the moral influence of the West and oppose it with an ethics reconstructed from his own origins. This breach was later enlarged by Hassan al-Banna' (1906–1949), the founder of the Muslim Brotherhood, who had belonged, in his youth, to the inner circle gathered around Rashid Ridha. Al-Banna' even tried to keep publishing the master's journal (*al-Manâr*) after his death. Rashid Ridha would certainly have approved of the political program of the brotherhood (in harmony with the evolution of his doctrine), but it is clear that he would have distanced himself from the violent and illegal methods toward which this same brotherhood evolved when it used secrecy and political assassination.[2]

To make the new moral order a reality, the program conceived by al-Banna' called on excluding any form of Westernism in teaching. He demanded that primary schools be attached to mosques. He rejected the adoption of European institutions in the field of politics, forbidding political parties and wanting civil servants to have religious training. At the end of World War II, he even went so far as to assert that the Western city was failing, that he saw in it the convulsions of death, that, in the wheel of history, the end of Western hegemony had arrived. The triumph of Islam would follow:

Here is the West, then: after having sown injustice, servitude and tyranny, it is bewildered, and writhes in its contradictions; all that is necessary is for a powerful Eastern hand to reach out, in the shadow of the standard of God on which will float the pennant of the Koran, a standard held up by the army of the faith, powerful and solid; and the world under the banner of Islam will again find calm and peace.[3]

This text, written in 1946, might have been interpreted as a stance taken to confront the moral bankruptcy Europe experienced after the Nazi disaster. But such an interpretation proves hollow when history teaches us that the Muslim Brotherhood had established ties with the forces of the Axis. We should see in this quotation only an example of an anti-Western diatribe amounting at worst to delirium, at best to a pious wish, proceeding from a magical and millenarian attitude that does not reckon with the balance of power. The intervention of a supernatural power, an apocalyptic upheaval, would have been necessary for al-Banna's wish to come true. What the predictor ignored is that the West is not magmatic; it is divided.[4] It had just been traversed by hostile armies, the shock of which had left millions of dead behind it. Faced with absolute barbarism of a kind never before seen, which had seized one of its most advanced peoples, and confronted by those who were the agents of the disaster, other energies had arisen that had resisted these agents and had triumphed over them.

I would have dismissed such proposals because of their vanity, their inanity, their logical and conceptual poverty, if they did not constitute a formidable vector for the diffusion of hatred, which, since September 11, has proven itself capable of carrying crime to its summit. In al-Banna's text, we can see the master plan of anti-Westernism, which is expressed through a simplistic discourse, hurling out his convictions as obvious facts. We have seen how poorly the discourse of eighteenth-century Ibn 'Abd al-Wahhab compared with that of medieval masters, and now, with this 1946 text, we are faced with an even poorer discourse. Mediocrity deepens; it is bottomless. The leveling down seems to be the sign of the poverty in which we recognize one of the symptoms of the sickness of Islam. With such a quotation, readers find themselves faced with a pathetic sample of rudimentary speeches welcomed by the greedy ears of the semiliterate consumed by resentment.

20

OTHER, LESS FRUSTRATED MINDS, belonging to that same sphere of influence described in Chapter 19, developed the logical subtleties of demonstration, at the cost of manipulations and conceptual attacks. Such was the case of the Pakistani Abû al-A'lâ Mawdûdi (1903–1979) and, to a lesser extent, his Egyptian disciple, Sayyid Qutb (1929–1966). These two voices have a considerable echo in the present fundamentalist milieu, for whom terrorism is one of the weapons. A considerable difference, however, distinguishes these two names: Mawdûdi remained pacifist and did not call for war, even if what he wrote led to it, whereas Sayyid Qutb was a follower of the reactivation of jihad and of recourse to violence to accomplish his aims.

Mawdûdi constructed a coherent political system, which follows wholly from a manipulation. "*Hukm* is God's alone," says the Qur'an.[1] The noun *hukm* (the translation of which I'll leave open for a moment) derives from the verbal root *h.k.m.*, which means "to exercise power as governing, to pronounce a sentence, to judge between two parties, to be knowledgeable (in medicine, in philosophy), to be wise, prudent, of a considered judgment." Thus, *hukm* signifies power, empire, authority, judgment, order, commandment, wisdom, knowledge, science, strength, rigor, law, rule. Most translators of the Qur'an, in French as well as in English, translate *hukm* as "judgment" or "power"; others seek the sense of "commandment" or "decision."[2] Exegetic tradition does not linger over this phrase, which is situated in a verse whose context is an address to idolaters:

> Those whom you adore outside of Him are nothing but names that you and your fathers have given them. God has granted them no authority. *Hukm* is God's alone. He has commanded that you adore none but Him. Such is the right religion, but most people do not know.[3]

Commentators never forget to remind us that this verse is devoted to the powerlessness of the companion deities (*paredras*) that idolaters raise up next to God. The idols worshipped by pagans are considered as names that do not refer to any reality. In sum it is a matter of an antinominalist critique. And in such a context (which associates a theological question with its linguistic and aesthetic consequences), the word *hukm* is likened to other words that have to do with divine order (*amr*) or with the responsibility its application implies (*taklîf*).[4] But here we see that Mawdûdi is the only one to associate *hukm* with sovereignty: "Sovereignty belongs to none but Allah."[5] By this interpretative move, Mawdûdi, by attributing sovereignty to God, makes the entire political field change into the divine.[6] Starting from this scriptural justification, he wages war against all political systems.

Legitimacy resides only in God. This legitimacy cannot come from a democratically elected majority. Nor can it come from a national tradition of public consent, a unanimous agreement in a convention, the hegemony of a class or a party, or even an aristocracy. It cannot come from a lay republic, a secular monarch or one by divine right, or even from a dictatorship marked by arbitrary power (the political form that best corresponds to Mawdûdi's interpretation).[7] Legitimacy can be based only in God, in the transcendent instance that exceeds the ambitions of men and the greed of factions. And the human rights that are at the foundation of society acquire their effectiveness only if they are submitted to the law of God. Starting with *hukm*, Sayyid Qutb, the Egyptian disciple of Mawdûdi, forged a neologism constructed on the morphology of abstract ideas, so that the word is consonant with the dignity of the concept: *Hakamiyya*, "sovereignty," becomes one of the divine attributes.

Thus religion has to be put back in the center. Islam itself, under the influence of Western secularization, had marginalized the religious principle and had a tendency to privatize religious practice by assimilating it with individual piety. So to restore the religious absolute in human society, Mawdûdi constructed a dyad that was the driving force behind this restoration: Worldly order will know its perfection by reconstituting the indissoluble link between *rububiyya*, the lordship of God, and *'ubudiyya*, the servitude of man dedicated to God alone, and no one else. Sovereignty (or lordship) belongs to God alone. And, brought back to servitude, man will retain the complex notion of "subject" only as subjection, constraint, submission, subjugation.

> The law of God is for the world and the universe the only framework in which man can live: so he must submit to it. . . . Man wants to conform to the divine plan. God is thus the only legitimate authority and the only source of the Law; He is Legislator. Man owes obeisance only to Him. And since he is created free and responsible, he is responsible towards God. If man wants to be realistic, he must choose submission to the only authority that exercises a real sovereignty: God. Political leaders, monarchs, saints, angels or spirits, rabbis or priests can never exercise a legitimate authority through themselves.[8]

Thus the total empery of religion over society and the humans that compose it is conceived. Democracy, secularization, the nation-state, all the contributions of the modern West turn out to be absolutely illegitimate. Such is the program. Should we add that Mawdûdi insisted that this revolution take place through peaceful means, through persuasion, through respectful dialogue with the believers of the two other revealed religions? The point is superfluous when we measure the violence with which those who claim to follow this ideology act. Furthermore, in the dialogue that Mawdûdi prays for, he grants no place for beliefs not based on monotheist foundations. He does not even recognize the statues of the Buddhist representatives that inhabit his immediate environment, although, for a Pakistani, those who worship the Buddha would have to comprise an internal otherness within his cultural sphere.

Moreover, can a place be found for the Other in such a total system? Can one find the truth of the world and be confronted with the heterogeneity and diversity that color its rough relief when one limits a religion to such an exclusive and self-sufficient way of life? Can one still keep the fibers of emotion and feeling alive so that one can love and respond to the beauties handed down by the many peoples of Islam through the variety of their historic contribution? How can one benefit from the past and the present if one comes to the conclusion that the only Islam that conforms to the sovereignty of God is that of Medina and the first four caliphs? In this insane, absolute theocentrism, never before in the tradition of Islam so radically developed, the world is transformed into a cemetery. If Mawdûdi reproached the West with the death of God, we can accuse him of having inaugurated the death of humanity. His outrageous system invents an unreal totalitarianism, which excites disciples and incites them to spread death and destruction over all continents. That is the kind of negation of life, the nihilism to which theoretical reasoning leads when it is not subject to the control of practical reasoning. And the judgment I pass on such a work is in the same vein as the criticisms made of Mawdûdi (eight years after his death) by his closest disciple, Mariam Jameelah, an American Jew he had converted.[9]

This radical and terrifying vision establishes a tabula rasa and transforms the world into a postnuclear place in which we find desolate landscapes wherever we look, on pages blackened by Sayyid

Qutb. Everything is at fault in the history of humanity as well as in its present; all thought, all representation is so insufficient that it merits annihilation. Everything must disappear, except the word of God as it is reported in his Qur'an. Through the word incarnate as a book, the world will know "the liberation of man," and even more "his true birth." After having submitted himself to the subjugation that the sovereignty of God requires, after having placed himself in the service of His Lordship, man will be freed from all the other servitudes of the century, that of the machine as well as whatever man seeks to exercise over man. This is the summary of the conclusion of one of the books by Sayyid Qutb, whose work is read by thousands of fascinated people, dreaming of that promised liberation that would transform man into one of the living dead, on a scorched land.[10]

In the conjunction between this theory and Wahhabism the most fatal fundamentalism was formed; the members of this sect are spread out over all the corners and recesses of the planet. This conjunction had two major sequences. I have already said that fundamentalism prospers on the rubble of experiments that fail. I must add, on the pages of the repertory that registers failures, the collapse of Arab nationalism in its Nasserian version, a consequence of the June 1967 debacle. That is when Arabia's doors opened to the semiliterate Azharians, who emigrated en masse in search of material gain. It is in these comings and goings from one side of the Red Sea to the other that the first operational tie between fundamentalism and Wahhabism was woven. But it was not until the early 1980s that the second conjunction was realized. This ideological coalescence was even more formidable, since it took place on the ground of the war in Afghanistan, and in Pakistan, the very country where Mawdûdi propagated his ideology among his own people, and in their language. From this double conjunction, the Afghanistan of the Talibans was born, and al Qa'ida of the Wahhabite Osama bin Laden and his lieutenant, the Egyptian fundamentalist Ayman al-Zawahri, were created.

21

WE'LL BEGIN WITH THE FIRST CONJUNCTION and its effects on Egypt. In the beginning of the 1970s, to fight against the left, Anwar al-Sadat supported the return to legality of the fundamentalists whose political, if not physical, presence Gamal Abdel Nasser had abolished. The legalization of fundamentalists, given their numbers, created an explosive situation. At the same time, the democratization of learning corresponded to the soaring demography; the number of university diplomas increased but at the cost of third-rate education. The masses of the semiliterate inflated in their turn. Low wages forced the pseudoacademics to emigrate to Arabia. In this political and social context, Egypt was subject to an active re-Islamization that accompanied the strategy of *infitah* (advocating the opening up to the West)—the best way of liquidating the state economy, inherited from Nasserism.

Integration into the market economy was strengthened by an alliance with the United States. Regional solidarity was established, with the convergence of Egyptian and Arabic perspectives. Egypt would come close to the Wahhabite example, at the risk of deviating from its Western tradition, still evident in literary experience. Literature found itself relegated to the margins; the reading public was reduced as the television audience widened. That is the effect of the Americanization of the world. The triumph of the window of light, the new box of wonders, brings cinematographic and literary creation, which was the vector of Europeanization, toward the periphery. One had to adapt or die. Resistance, especially of a literary kind, could create the conditions of a survival at the margins, where there was no lack of experimentation. But the great majority remained riveted to televised images, as others did elsewhere in the world. In the lands of Islam, though, because of the contrast between a heterogeneous way of life and the kind that television shows, change seems more obvious; it can be seen on the surface of things. There is no need to dig deep or even to scrape the surface to unearth its evidence.

I will not linger over the emergence and entry of the fundamentalist phenomenon into society; it is described in its time by Gilles Kepel.[1] Nor will I recall the inflammatory sermons of hysterical imams, who exulted in adorning their verbal anti-Westernism with flowers of rhetoric that belong to the resources of the language they use. Such an anti-Westernism resounds in the walls of the city with a thousand mosques at the very time when the politicians place their hopes in a Western alliance, which will make Egypt (especially its army) an example of this new form of protectorate of which America is fond. The re-Islamization of society and the American alliance will go hand in hand and will constitute another paradox, which I will call the Egyptian paradox. As the society becomes Americanized (through incitement to material consumption and through the media), the quest for the specific gains in intensity.

This phenomenon will have as its emblem the sequence animated by the deception of the Islamic banks, adapting financial investment to the divine law that forbids the earning of interest, which is considered usury. I will not insist on the bankruptcies that interrupted the activities of these banks; nor will I evoke the technical details that disguise bank interest as licit earnings. The aim of such institutions was to answer to an ideological demand: They were supposed to make the Islamic quality of participation in the market visible. Such subterfuges prove illusory when any reasonable person knows that the immense Wahhabite fortunes flourished in the spheres of high finance and according to the rules of the Stock Exchange, which is not moved by any inclination to bend to the prescriptions of Islam. The Islamic banks' vocation was to symbolize the articulation between Egypt and Saudi Arabia, between Nile fundamentalism (heritage of the movement born in the 1920s, as I recalled earlier) and Arabic Wahhabism. This was a way to give a color of Islam to the money earned by the Egyptian expatriates in Arabia.

Should we connect the fundamentalist word with its deed, with the appearance of terrorism at the beginning of the 1980s, of which one spectacular victim was Anwar al-Sadat, who was at the origin of the return to this political radicalism in Cairo?[2] Recall that behind this political assassination stands the specter of Ayman al-Zawahri, the right-hand man of Osama bin Laden during the second conjunction between fundamentalism and Wahhabism, the one that inducted the Afghan scene, as prelude to the attacks of September 11, 2001. Should we also bring to mind the merciless war that the Egyptian government directed against fundamentalist terrorism, guilty of a long list of executed or excommunicated victims? This list featured politicians and people belonging to the intellectual milieu or civil society, punished for having remained faithful to what's left of the values spread by Western modernity. In this war, Hosni Mubarak, the Egyptian president, almost joined his predecessor in death during the assassination attempt made on him in Addis-Ababa in July 1995.

But I would above all like to stress the consequences of such a political process devoted to violence. Through its imprint, a society has changed its face. Even if, politically, the fundamentalists have not won, their ideology has marked the whole of the social body. Some of their precepts have been adopted by official Islam; in the war of words, the state thought it had to take away from the fundamentalists the argument denouncing the nonconformity of their society to Islamic norms. To defuse this criticism, the state decided to entrust to al-Azhar the governance of souls, provided it would minimize the reach of political Islam. After such a tacit agreement, society found itself metamorphosed. The signs of European modernity were obliterated, while Islamic signs (adapted to an Americanized urban landscape) were restored; the most obvious of these signs, and the most polemic, is the wearing of veils by women. With a few rare exceptions, even the most Westernized women conformed to this return to Islamic norm; the elegant ones created headgear to fit the circumstance, which fit tightly around their hair and kept it hidden. The memory of the feminist Hoda Sha'rawi is as effaced as the beautiful neo-Mameluke house where she used to live. The house is destroyed; the land where it sat now serves as a garage for the tourist buses visiting the pharaonic museum.

At best, we are witnessing the unfurling of a devout society, the realization on earth of a human ensemble obeying what the Savoyard St. François de Sales had thought and imagined (in a different age!) when he recommended

> accommodating the practice of devotion to the strength, business, and duties of each particular. . . . "The bee," Aristotle said, "draws its honey from flowers without disturbing them," leaving them whole and fresh as it found them; but true devotion does even better, for, not only does it not spoil any kind of vocation or business, but on the contrary it adorns and embellishes them.[3]

In such a way, through your devotion, you can contribute to founding a society subject to Islamic virtue while still keeping your profession, your economic activities. Nor does devout practice prevent you from satisfying the desire to consume or to succeed in the affairs of business the market offers.

The reeducation of such a society occurred through the intervention of televised sermons and instruction, which have had their stars, among whom Sheikh Sha'rawi stands out. The sheikh had a large audience and even an influence over the modern, enlightened minds that thought they were discovering the subtleties of traditional theology through the obscurantist theology spread by this sheikh, one more avatar in whom the semiliterate, emboldened by their very resentment, can feel triumph.

Confusion was at its height, the loss of reference points impaired judgment, and the public took the theatrics as vitality. It responded to the literalist analogies the sheikh propagated. With drops of spit accompanied with emphatic gestures, the pedagogue of the poor submitted his role to a well-received theatricality despite (or because of) his elementary expressiveness.

Using the new form of literalism he glorified, he located Qur'anic references to technological innovations, from electricity to the atom. It was as if the masses of Islam could find an additional reason in this subterfuge to authenticate their book (which is supposed to enclose the very word of God) and credit it with an omniscience anticipating the inventions that changed the way humans live on the earth. As if from such a sense they distilled an appeasement that could console them for having excluded inventions produced by those evil, strange Westerners. As if such a divine premonition expressed in their language made them free of guilt, as if it placed their ressentiment in reserve to help them enjoy the material goods of postindustrial society while keeping the illusion of having been their heralds if not their actual inventors.

This is the kind of magic thread on which depends adherence to such a religion (whose rational dimension, which frees it from myth and legend to found it in history, its incense-bearing admirers praise). This claim—shared, moreover, by the proud epigones of three monotheisms—is pushed to the height of its exuberance in fundamentalists like Sayyid Qutb.[4] But none of them knows that with such ideas thrown together in haste, they themselves are fabricators of myths.

22

AMONG THE PREACHERS AND EVEN among the "secular" editorialists, an extreme xenophobia illumines the disasters undergone by their community. Thus they invent an imaginary conspiracy attributed to the Other, in the role of the enemy. The faults of the group and the deviances of individuals are attributable to the evildoing and malevolent foreigner. Is there a better way of removing responsibility from the individual after having discharged him of guilt? The misfortune that plagues the Muslim has the West as its origin . . . and Israel, whose success is irritating: The counterpoint is in fact his own failure, which he cannot acknowledge. That is how traditional anti-Semitism is changed into modern anti-Semitism. A world separates the two ways of expressing hostility against the Jews. Traditional anti-Semitism involved the theological controversy in which the Jews themselves participated, as was the case of Yehuda Halevi, who, in Arabic, sang the praises of "the despised religion" (translators' note: Judaism) after having refuted the two rival monotheisms.[1] Such a feeling of hostility inscribed itself into a competition for legitimacy. The goal was to establish the authenticity of one's own theological ground, all the more necessary since it had to distance itself from the potential influence that the earlier exercises over the later, from the very moment you decide to found your own building on the site and with the materials of those who preceded you.

Current anti-Semitism stems from unthinking Westernization; its engagement is fed by the use and adaptation of falsehoods made up by the anti-Semites of the West. This is the case of the translation and distribution of *The Protocol of the Elders of Zion*. Another example is the use of the anti-Semitic document created in the 1920s by the American extreme right and attributed to Benjamin Franklin (1706–1790), editor of the U.S. Constitution. The document makes him express the suspicion that the migration of the Jews should arouse, for if they were to multiply on American soil, they would usurp the state and manipulate it to make it defend their own cause. This text is considered a blessing by those who, in their anti-Zionist war, don't care about protecting themselves from the drift toward anti-Semitism. Relying heedlessly on such falsehoods, they attribute the American alliance with Israel to Jewish infiltration of the most powerful state in the world. They fail to see how basic the legitimacy of Israel is in the vision of Anglo-Saxon Protestantism, marked by its messianic reading of the Old Testament. They do not know that the Zionist idea emerged in the beginning of the nineteenth century in Puritan writings, from believers who found it unbearable that the Holy Land was not in the hands of its legitimate owners. The idea of Zionism was born in a Protestant land before being formulated in a much larger way as a Jewish aspiration.[2] Let us add to this historic truth the inscription of the Holocaust into the symbolism of the state and in the civic education of the United States, a holocaust whose accelerating role in the process that led to the foundation of the Hebrew State is well known.[3]

It is important to remember this reality in an effective approach to the Palestinian question. We must avoid the mistake of the great imam of al-Azhar, Sheikh Tantâwi, who imprudently used the falsehood attributed to Benjamin Franklin and made it the epigraph of the thesis he devoted to what should be a theological subject par excellence, *The Children of Israel in Koran and Sunna*.[4] This epigraph became the syr.ptom that revealed that a traditional theological treatise had been transformed into an ideological tract, shot through with tendencies evoked by current events. The Jews of Medina (contemporaries of the Prophet Mohammed) are judged in the same way as the Jews of Israel at war with the Palestinians and the Arabs. Anti-Judaism is mixed with anti-Zionism and is changed into an anti-Semitism that is not even aware of being made from a Western import. In the generalized confusion, a theological controversy is assimilated with a political question that in its turn is mixed with a racist perversion. The wound Israel inflicts on Arab consciences remains exposed to all purulence.

No one is spared, not even the least obtuse and least fanatical minds, such as Sheikh Tantâwi, one of the reasonable voices of authority of official Islam, representative of a semimagisterium to limit the damage that uncontrolled access to the word causes. He denounced the deception of Osama bin Laden and denied him any legitimacy in attributing to himself the position of imam; he reminded the Saudi millionaire that he had neither the moral authority nor the doctrinal competence to call for holy war, which had to obey particular conditions to be proclaimed canonically unimpeachable—at a time when that notion was valid. After saying all that, I am under the obligation to reveal that even the antidote to fundamentalist poison is not safe from the sickness of Islam, one of whose symptoms is xenophobia and anti-Semitism.

Thus we propose to ourselves the theoretical and abstract foreigner as a scapegoat we overload with falsehoods. Almost unanimously, Egyptian opinion was that the Luxor attack (November 1997) was the result of a conspiracy hatched by the U.S. Central Intelligence Agency (CIA) and its Mossad hirelings. In vain I explained to my interlocutors that beyond the obvious fundamentalist implication, such a massacre of innocent tourists could be perceived as the implementation of the discourse spread in the name of official Islam by the organs controlled by the state.[5] The problem stems from the Azharian brand of Islam that the state put in charge of souls. To defuse adherence to fundamentalism, this Islam felt it was in a favorable situation to take over the discourse of Islamists without shouldering its ultimate consequences, those that preach violence and insurrection.

Can one lead a society with such a discourse toward piety and devotion without inciting it to found the Islamic State that would accord with its moral condition and would assure it, if not permanence, at least endurance and coherence? Are we still living the separation between religion and politics? That is certainly the case today in Egypt, but the distance between the values emanating from the two modes of thought is such that it risks producing schizophrenic citizens, susceptible to mending their interior division by soldering it into the unity that the fundamentalism of secrecy and violent action promises. This situation has engendered one of the leaders who directed the September 11 attacks, the one the press has talked about most of all: Mohammed 'Atta did not fall from the sky; he is the product of Egyptian reality, which produces many other similar figures.

In the commentaries revived by the latest attacks on New York, we again find at work the same way of disengaging responsibility. The attacks were attributed once more to the Mossad, on the pretext that the instant the planes hit their target, four thousand Jews were not at their posts in the Twin Towers. Supported by large segments of public opinion from the fringes of the intellectual milieu, the press for a long time gave the spotlight to Mohammed 'Atta's father, who did his utmost to explain that his son had been abducted by the Mossad so that his name would be sullied and used in an operation led by the Secret Services of Israel in order to harm Egypt and Islam. It's not hard for a father in distress to clear himself of having engendered a criminal and a monster! We should point out too that such attitudes are not unique to Egypt. While visiting Damascus during the last ten days of September 2001, I discovered that the official Syrian press was still attributing the destruction of the Manhattan towers to the Mossad.

Anti-Western xenophobia combined with anti-Semitism needs rumors to keep going strong. When I was at Abu Dhabi in May 2001, a number of my interlocutors, of various Arab nationalities (Lebanese, Syrian, Sudanese, etc.), confirmed the warning, spread by the local newspapers, to the public of the countries of the Near East not to buy the very inexpensive belts with the label *Made in Thailand*. These belts, the people told me, were actually Israeli products in disguise and carried a kind of flea that propagated an incurable disease: one more Zionist trick to weaken Arab bodies, if not eliminate them. These interlocutors, otherwise reasonable and likable, gave credit to information as fantastic as that. Those are the fantasies in which the symptoms of the sickness of Islam can be seen, the receptive compost in which the crime of September 11 could be welcomed joyfully. Didn't the press report that, in a Cairo bus, when the radio revealed the first estimates of the number of victims pulverized in New York, the passengers had spontaneously applauded and congratulated each other as if they had just received the happiest news? If such a crime brought such joy to these people, how could it be attributed to the Mossad? It is true that opinions afflicted with blindness are not accountable for their contradictions.

23

THE SECOND EFFORT AT RE-ISLAMIZATION is visible through the transformation of the social body in its relation to pleasure and enjoyment. Islamic society went from a hedonist tradition, based on love of life, to a prudish reality, full of hatred of sensuality. Prudishness has become a criterion of respectability. The urban scene teems with Tartuffes and other bigots. The city arranges its stages to take away the rights of the body, a consequence of the resentment taking root in the souls of the semiliterate, who are legion. The streets, repellent in their new construction, negligent, disrespectful of the fabulous architectural past, increase in ugliness when they are traversed by oafish bodies, cut off from care of self; aesthetics withdrew as soon as seduction in the relation of the sexes was abolished. The maintenance of beauty, and its emphasis, are in turn eliminated.

What an eclipse this is of the religion that has so fascinated foreigners by its cult of the body and the call to pleasure, which are at its foundations! Behind what screens of repression has Islam sheltered itself so as to forget that, according to its medieval wise men, one made love in the name of God, not just to beget but also for pleasure?[1] What breakdown has paralyzed the entity in which the word that designates religious marriage is the same that designates coitus (*nikâh*), which authorizes the jurist to decide that it's enough to invoke the multiple meanings that pervade the word to know that, canonically, coitus is the reason for marriage? How has the society that had devoted so much to the rights of the body been so vaporized? What mutation has caught hold of belief whose promise is carnal, of faith that venerates desire on the stage of this world as at the heart of the theater promised to the elect in the beyond? What has happened to the community, perceived by medieval Christians (whose credo establishes a nihilism of the body) as an association of debauchees (because of the carnal promise as much as because of the legal dispositions that make polygamy, cohabitation, and divorce licit)?[2] Why were ears stricken with deafness to stop hearing the language the *Thousand and One Nights* spread, those tales immersed in the satisfaction of the senses procured by earthly enjoyments—pleasures that were considered divine gifts? Their words traveled, and their European diffusion through the Gallimard translation (1702–1714) contributed to liberating the Western body and inventing the fantasy of the harem, which pervaded the century of the Enlightenment. Without speaking of Turkophilia and the fashion for oriental artifice, can one imagine the fable that reveals the truth and secret of sex in Diderot's *Les Bijoux indiscrets* (Indiscreet jewels) if Diderot and his public had not been impregnated with the *Thousand and One Nights?*

What metamorphoses the lands have undergone, lands that so fascinated travelers and writers of the nineteenth century, for the same reasons that had scandalized the European clerics of the Middle Ages! What a blanket of shame has covered the countries that saw Flaubert engulfed in pleasure! To find the scene again, what can one do but recall the ardent hours the Norman writer spent with the almah Kuchuk-Hanem on the shores of the Nile in Upper Egypt?[3] Or bring to mind Guy de Maupassant, who grew passionate about the Arab manual of medieval erotology and wanted to write a new translation of it? This manual, *The Perfumed Garden,* was written in the fifteenth century by my compatriot Sheikh Nafzawi, a theologian who exalted the body in the name of God.[4] Or we should also quote Nietzsche, contrasting the nihilism of the body (which the Christianity in which he had grown up inculcates) with the cult of pleasure and the bodily hygiene of the citizen formed by Islam: The German philosopher illustrates this difference by an anecdote that recalls the first thing the Christians did when they took back Cordova: "Here one despises the body, one rejects hygiene as sensuality (the first Christian act after the expulsion of the Moors was to close the public baths, which in the city of Cordova alone numbered two hundred and seventy)."[5]

Now, though, the tradition that reveres the body seems to be disappearing from those Islamic lands ravaged by the moral order that the semiliterate, sick with resentment, impose. Cairo and Egypt have been transformed from paradise into hell; to be convinced of this, it is enough to see the bodies of livid women, suffering from the heat, burdened by their scarves or their black veils (a color that absorbs the sun's heat, in a country where the sun is the tyrant of the day). Maltreated bodies in a megalopolis in which sixteen million people bustle about, breathing the most polluted air, between the gas from old, unregistered cars and the clouds of steam spit out by the cement factories, billowing fumes that are joined in season by the bitter, heavy smoke from the rice husks that the peasants of the region burn after gathering the harvest. Living in Cairo, you find your lungs become just as blackened as those of an inveterate smoker, though your lips have never touched a cigarette or the mouthpiece of a hookah.

And then there is the noise pollution, caused not just by the continuous mass of car horns and the rumbling of motors (of cars as well as air conditioners), but also by the vehement calls to prayer, semipolemic calls diffused by the ubiquitous and parasitic loudspeakers that would disturb the sleep of the dead. Unchecked access to technology corrupts one of the beautiful aesthetic contributions of Islam, the one that exalts the voice, one of the vectors by which the word can be celebrated. Besides the assaults that the body endures in this polluted urban atmosphere, we see in these untimely exercises of the voice one of the symptoms that aggravate the sickness of Islam. What a difference there is between that noise and the unison that the choir of muˁzzins modulates with their bare voices, sweet tones emanating from chests, from throats, from tongues, from palates, from physically present lips, sent out from the clerestory that crowns minarets! Going from one method to the other, the listener passes from the highest emotion to the most odious of aggressions.

Such an aesthetic loss stems from the way bodies are mistreated: They are no longer surrounded by the care that the cult of beauty, one of the attributes of ancient Islam, requires. For the body to blossom, it must move in an architectural space, metaphor for geometric and musical harmony, as much in relation to concord as to dissonance.

It is important, too, that the body come into physical contact with objects that in turn honor the principle of beauty. This is why Islamic civilization has been one of the great cultures of the so-called minor arts: profusion of objects produced through work in wood, leather, stone, ceramics, fabric, cotton, wool, linen, silk, so many beautiful things designed to exalt the body in its movements. What shipwreck has pushed them out of sight? To the bottom of what sea depths have they fallen? If I were a cleric and a censor, I would return the message to the sender. I would tell these semiliterate people sick with resentment, so ready to accuse and excommunicate, that with this shipwreck of the beautiful, they abolish the aesthetic dimension that accompanies the ethics of Islam, and that they dishonor the famous *hadîth,* which affirms that "God is beautiful and loves beauty."

Cairo is the largest city of Islam, one of the vastest and most populated on the planet. It has multiplied all the defects of megalopolises, but it does not possess the highest virtue of them, that of anonymity, which enlarges the adventure of freedom and rescues you from the social control the community exercises over the individual. In short, Cairo combines the defects of the metropolis and the constraints of the village. What seems to save it and make its present and its future impossible to suppress is the energy that pervades it: Everywhere it is overflowing with those who circulate in it. Also saving it is the splendor of its site, between the Moqattam, the Nile and the desert, and its venerable age, the centuries that have succeeded each other in it and that have all bequeathed wonders for eternity. I say eternity, for the monuments remain standing despite the negligence and indifference of the humans who are their unworthy inheritors. Finally, it is the epiphanic potential Cairo holds, bringing the material of poetry to the visitor who finds himself immersed in it.[6]

Today, we are witnessing a curious inversion in the politics and economics of the human body. Islam proposes a prudish city, whose inhabitants are sick with nihilism and resentment. Meanwhile, the Western body has freed itself from inherited constraints. This is an extravagant inversion of which Islamic devotees are not aware, since they are proud enough of their state to propose their virtuous society as a counterexample to the Western society, which is supposed to be one of vice. Don't they oppose their modest society to the immodest foreign society? Don't they sing the praises of discretion and dissimulation, and belittle the exhibitionism of the West? Don't they celebrate the veiled, or reclusive, feminine body by lambasting Western nudity and promiscuity? They never realize that they are being proud of the very signs of their illness. And they are not embarrassed at cultivating their difference by insisting on what distinguishes their virtuous and pious society from that of the foreigner, marked by debauchery and atheism.

In this East-West contrast, in the respective judgments that Islam and Europe make about each other, we are witnessing the inversion of the medieval stereotype. Never has misunderstanding remained so tenacious. Between amnesia (which obliterates the memory of tradition) and oversimplification (which believes that the moral person disintegrates in the freedom of the individual), humans formed by contemporary Islam are at best naive. They let themselves be pervaded by the tricks of the unthinking, at worst hypocritical, arranging the scene of their transgressive desire in hidden alcoves, or in so-called shameful countries, far from the gaze of their own people.

24

THE OBJECTIVE OF ALL FORMS of Wahhabism is to make one forget body, object, space, beauty; these obscurations mean to impose a generalized amnesia, one of the symptoms of the sickness that has afflicted the disciple of Islam. This sickness can be observed in many different areas and acts in various strata of society. Christian Jambet, one of the rare thinkers who have mastered both Western and Islamic philosophical traditions, in his Arabic and Persian versions (he is a specialist in the Neoplatonists of Persia), teaches at L'Ecole des Hautes Etudes Commerciales in Paris. Many of his students come from French-speaking lands like Morocco and Lebanon. When Jambet presents his students with thoughts from the Islamic Middle Ages, and especially when he evokes the hermeneutic tradition, very often his Muslim students, future administrators of "corporate capitalism," protest and interrupt him, asserting that such doctrines cannot belong to Islam. By acting in this way, they reveal Wahhabite influence: Forgetful of their own culture, they think they are the real guardians of the true Islam. These future executives of international finance are marked as well by that simplistic Islam, cut off from its civilization. The diffusion of such an elementary Islam comes from Saudi Arabia and from its petro-dollars, and it prospers on the accumulation of failures whose detrimental effects I have outlined.

These failures reinforce the idea that it is possible to achieve modernity by following one's own course and adapting the technical advances of the age to one's own principles. Simplified to the extreme, these principles seem adaptable to the space of modernity. Wahhabite oversimplification and the aptitude for Americanization again find themselves clearly united: The individual does not blink at the contradiction between belonging to a traditional society and the use of the material goods of modernity. No place is made in this scheme for critical thought, so the work of contradiction cannot produce the rupture necessary to insure the passage from a traditional structure to the adventure that modernity opens up.

These tendencies toward Americanization were united in Afghanistan, where the second conjunction between Wahhabism and militant fundamentalism occurred, still under the aegis of the United States, which did not seem shocked by the ideological content of the Islamist mobilization against the Soviet invasion. Their objective was to neutralize the USSR. To fight while reviving archaic religious sentiments that invoked Holy War did not seem to the Americans to embody a fatal potential for which they could be the future target. Military operations were conducted involving trusted allies, Pakistan and Saudi Arabia. The archaic soul combined with wealth to insure technical initiation into the most sophisticated weapons for the fundamentalists.

In this spirit, an international community of warriors of Islamic origin was created, formed under the control of the CIA with Saudi money. And in this context appeared Osama bin Laden, who took part in these battles, weapons in hand, before placing his personal fortune at the service of the cause and recruiting for the jihad everywhere in the lands of Islam, especially in the Arab countries. Many of the semiliterate, the potentially unemployed, and other militants, perhaps less frustrated but still children of resentment, possessed by revolutionary aims, responded to his summons. A dozen years of training and military exercise on the field of battle (1980–1990) were enough to form the international brigades of fundamentalism. Victory over the Soviets embedded in the fundamentalist milieu the idea that, through weapons and the use of terror, it was possible to reach one's goals.

After the war in Afghanistan, thousands of militants, marked by this ideology of battle, were suddenly available. Armed and experienced, some returned to their country of origin to fan the flames, stir unrest, revive dissidence. Algeria's misfortune was intensified by the influx of "Afghans," those Algerians who had gone from the maquis of the Hindu Kush or the Pamirs to the maquis of the Aurès. When they disembarked in Algiers, their compatriots were surprised and impressed by their appearance. The militants were wearing an outfit that didn't belong to local traditions: ample robes, turbans from elsewhere, full, uncut beards contrary to local custom. They had returned to their homeland with a new habitus, symbolizing an unknown violence, in a country that had not been unaware of the experience of violence and that was not peopled with angelic choirboys. Representing violence in violence, these "Afghans," in the euphoria of the victory over the Soviets, decided to create the sinister GIA (Groupe Islamique Armé), in Peshawar in 1990, to transport their "skills" into their own country. They were the first to be convinced that military violence was the only answer to the interruption of the electoral process of 1992. When in 1993 the conflict between the leaders at the core of the GIA was exacerbated (between the locals and the "Afghans"), Osama bin Laden (who supported the movement and financed its support groups in Europe) decided in favor of the Afghans.[1]

The dispersal of "Afghan" Arabs brought them to Egypt, the Sudan, Yemen, Saudi Arabia, the United Arab Emirates and Jordan. They were also attracted by the European wars that involved Islamic communities—Bosnia, then Chechnya. These wars came to an end or ran out of steam. The states targeted by political terror resisted. Some of these fundamentalists found themselves once more free, or harassed. After the asylum granted by a hospitable Sudan, they proceeded to a second fallback position in Afghanistan and its Pakistani borderland (around Peshawar). At that time, in May 1996, Osama bin Laden came to settle down in the region, non grata in Sudan (he had been living in Khartoum since May 1992). He found shelter with the Taliban, pure products of the local (Mawdûdi) fundamentalist tradition reinforced by Wahhabism (the propagation of which is officially financed by Saudi Arabia through a network of religious schools that stretches its tentacles everywhere it can reach). The Taliban movement represented the extreme point of irredentism in the linking of a basic Wahhabism with the radicalism brought by the Egyptian tradition of fundamentalism within the totalitarian system developed by Mawdûdi. This tradition will be physically present on Afghan soil in the person of Ayman al-Zawahri. Mullah Omar is nothing but the spiritual son of these hybrids.

25

IT WAS SUCH AN INDOCTRINATION that reanimated a caricature version of a Medinese utopia in the Afghanistan of the Taliban. The ridiculous regime of the Afghan mullahs was judged by Osama bin Laden to be the unique earthly realization of the ideal city of Islam, after the Medina of the first four caliphs (called in myth *al-khulafâ' ar-Râshidûn,* "the well-guided caliphs"). But what a difference there is between the Medina of history and the stupid and archaic sublimation of Kabul!

I have some sympathy for the Medina of the beginning, where rumors were whispered and the first tentative attempts at a new civilization began, starting from almost nothing. And the voices of women were mixed with those of men in that setting, a context in which the great violence of civil war did not stop the momentum of conquests. This sequence of foundation constituted just a first step in the chronicle that the city would come to know in the course of the first century after the hegira. The blessed city would live a second, illustrious time when the political center of the nascent empire moved to Damascus, when the wealth of the booty won through conquest would accumulate in its caves. This was a propitious time for the culture to flourish, especially since there was no lack of money for the expenses of luxury.

One can easily admire those primitive Muslims, who were the protagonists of the beginning, poignant in that they had a commitment to a great destiny, but were always torn between pagan impulses and the imperatives of the new law. Despite all their glory, though, my personal preference is for the second Medina. This city gave birth to a famous school of song, which welcomed a gallant poetics, supported by beautiful discourses intensifying in the truth of their difference the relationship between the sexes. This Medina did not impose on its women the status of the oppressed, but of lovers and celebrated singers, worldly women who held literary or musical salons, hosting concerts and poetic jousts, admirable for their teasing and pleasing coquetry.[1] Recalling those obscured times, what can I feel but revulsion toward the Medinese caricature the Afghanistan of the Taliban embodies?

The United States continued to negotiate with the Taliban until August 2001, promising the group a large reward for bin Laden. The nation must have been naive to think that a disciple would, for wealth, hand over his master. With the same Taliban forces, the surest Islamic allies of the United States (Pakistan, the United Arab Emirates, Saudi Arabia) continued to have privileged relationships. How could they let the Taliban apply its sinister law with impunity? It would appear that the state of people and things in Afghanistan shocked no one. I can understand such an attitude on the part of the Pakistanis, who are affected by ethnic Pashtun solidarity, anxious to develop a profound strategy, and not unaware of the Islamist ideology that watches over the least transactions in the hinterland. The same is true for Saudi Arabia. After all, the members of the Taliban are its ideological children, though poorer, more frustrated and more excessive. But in the end, they are only applying the dogma the Wahhabites had taught them; at most they add to the received doctrine the zeal of the neophyte. But why didn't the United States rank the Afghanistan of the Taliban as outcasts? Why did the suffering of the Afghan people count for nothing with the chancelleries?

Since the Gulf War (1991) one of the themes dealt with in the mirror of democratic opinion has been the right to interfere. But no one had recourse to this idea when the Taliban announced its decision to destroy the Buddhas at Bamiyan in the name of the battle against idols. Yet that was an ideal occasion to exercise such a right legitimately. An intervention to save the Buddhas would have set a legal precedent; it would have given efficacy and moral legitimacy to the idea. Perhaps it was too much to ask of our Western friends, who had destroyed Iraq by running to the aid of Kuwait. In that war, the principle of interference was invoked, but I know it was invoked only because oil interests were at stake. Without such considerable economic stakes, Iraq's aggression would have aroused only verbal protests not followed by any action.

I should make this clear: I have never defended the invasion of Kuwait by Iraq; faced with the event, I took a stance acquiescing to the theses defended by Kant in his treatise entitled *Toward Everlasting Peace*. Iraq had fomented disorder by rejecting the borders of an already established nation. "A State is like a stock with its own root; to attach it as a graft on another State amounts to suspending its existence as if of a moral person, and making it into a thing, and thus contradicts the idea of an original contract without which no right over a people is conceivable."[2]

Since it was the origin of a casus belli, Iraq deserved to be punished. But between the punishment of a state and a leader, both of which sow trouble, and the protection of such a leader combined with rage against a people, I see two irreconcilable aims. Still, the Iraqi dossier lies outside the scope of this book. I will just recall that, without oil, no coalition would have been formed to destroy Iraq. I remember especially the speeches and reflections that accompanied that sad episode. A number of intellectuals evoked great principles, the same ones that are easy to recall when your comfort is threatened and that are better to silence as soon as your interests require it. Linking the survival of a principle to one's own interest ruins the principle itself. With similar considerations, on the subject of colonialism, I have already mentioned one of the symptoms of Western sickness. I will only evoke it in passing, but I don't want the reader to read into that a method of symmetry: sickness for sickness. If such were the case, my project would be emptied of its substance; it is far from my intention to neutralize the sickness I am treating by applying the sickness of the other.

26

IF SOMEONE HAD INTERVENED TO prevent the destruction of the Buddhas, the principle would have been preserved; the right to interfere would have acquired its virtue. Precise, limited, materially not costly, such an action would have smelled neither of oil nor of gas; it would not have been aroused by greed for gold or uranium. Art alone, which belongs to those who love it and take pleasure from it, surpasses territorial borders. Such an action was within the scope of the United Nations: Weren't the statues designated a universal heritage site by UNESCO?

The giant Buddhas, sculpted out of the walls of the mountain between the third and fourth century of our era, remained significant for a still living religious practice. From my point of view, all beliefs deserve to be considered: This is a teaching I take from Sufism, notably the Akbarian tradition, elaborated in the framework of Islamic faith by Ibn 'Arabi, the Andalusian master who recommended being "*hyle* so that all beliefs can take form within you."[1] That is to say, for the

Sufi from Murcia, the Islamic disciple had the capacity to internalize all forms of beliefs and to progress with their truth without trying to reduce them or make them disappear. He was even ready to sing the praises of tenets that shock common Muslim opinion, such as the Trinity of Christianity, assimilated into Islam in a form of polytheism, and that Ibn 'Arabi celebrates in one of his poems in which he reveals a perfect complicity between logic and the mystery of the hypostasis.[2] In such an economy of inner experience, the celebration of Buddhism by a spiritual member of Islam is entirely possible. We could have put this theory into practice if we had landed in Afghanistan to save the Buddhas. Such an undertaking would have consecrated a gesture of tolerance in harmony with the Islamic tradition itself; from the depths of the Middle Ages, this gesture could give a lesson in complexity to the frustrated Wahhabite fundamentalists who rage in this beginning of the twenty-first century.

First, we should recall that the image in Islam constitutes more a question than a taboo that prohibits questioning. The problem is not raised by the Qur'an; and the *hadîth* treats it in a quasi-Platonic way, especially if one seeking to understand it consults "Bâb at-Taswîr" ("Chapter of the image") in the *Sahîh* by Muslim (born circa 820), commented on by Nawawi (1233–1277).[3] Leaving aside the anecdotes that are useful from an anthropological viewpoint, I note that it virtually poses the philosophic question in its relation to mimesis (*muhâkât*). Such *hadîth* denounces the element missing from the image in the exercise of imitation. The Prophet says that a challenge will be given to painters and sculptors: On the day of judgment, they will be asked to bring to life the creatures they had imitated, and they will not be capable of doing so. Thus, the Prophet recommends that painters imitate the inanimate (which corresponds to the iconographic plan of the mosaics that decorate the courtyard of the Omayyad mosque built in Damascus in 705 by order of the caliph Walîd I). In the theological debate that the question of images has aroused, one of the most radical *fatwas*, forbidding all representation, even of inanimate subjects, is the one pronounced by Ibn Taymiyya, the ancestor of the Wahhabites. He equates the use of the image, its production or its likeness, with an act of idolatry. On the other hand, Ibn 'Arabi legitimizes the likeness of the icon on the scene of the imagination. The practitioner of Islamic belief, he tells us, as inheritor of Judaism and Christianity, must resolve a paradox as to the status of the image. How can one reconcile the taboo of representation in the Decalogue (somewhat confirmed by the *hadîth*) and the iconophilia related to Christ? Taking support from the tradition of virtuous behavior (*Hadîth al-Ihsân*), the Murcian Sufi recommends that the practitioner of Islam adore God "as if he saw Him." This "as if" opens the curtains of the imaginary stage where the one who prays fabricates what I have called elsewhere the "mental icon."[4]

The same Ibn 'Arabi tempers the monotheist refutation of idolatry; he demystifies it. The cult of images is not considered negligible; it can manifest in belief as a lower degree of adoration. The worshipper is subject to a hierarchy in his spiritual exercises: Adoration that seeks out the image remains inferior, but it is not worthless. What characterizes beliefs, what unifies and authenticates them beyond their formal differences, is that they are all based on passion (*al-h'awâ'*). And whatever the object of adoration is (stone, tree, animal, human representation, star, angel), the practitioner is always confronted with an imagined form of the divinity. For this reason, some pagans say, "We adore them only so that they can bring us closer to God."[5] And even those who call their cult objects gods have cried out, "Has he made of the gods one single God? That is indeed an admirable thing!"[6] Pagans did not deny God, they marveled at God. They fixed on the plurality of forms, which all lead back to the divinity. The Prophet invited them to adore one single God, who can be known but not seen. The passage from one degree to the other was easy for them, since, by saying, "We adore them only so that they can bring us closer to God," they knew that their idols were only stone. The Prophet encouraged them to adore God at the top of the hierarchy, that of the impenetrable, unrepresentable God, whom sight cannot grasp, but at the same time, Ibn 'Arabi recommends that it is up to the individual to develop himself through experience, which is epiphanic, and epiphany is realized through forms. Thus, if God does not show himself in the perceptible, it is not because He is forbidden from representation; in epiphanies many images illustrate the manifestation of Him. If you no longer feel the need to grasp God in forms, it is because you have reached the summit of divine knowledge.[7]

In his impressive book on India, on the subject of the representation of the Buddha, Bîrûni (973–circa 1050) says no more than this in the chapter he devotes to "the principle of adoration of statues and the method of erecting them."[8] He sings the praises of idols by attributing them with an educational function for the masses who, in all cultures and beliefs, have easier access to the perceptible than to the intelligible. The latter is limited to scholars who constitute everywhere an elite characterized by small numbers. Thus, in numerous beliefs, initiates have decorated the figures of books and temples. Faced with the image, an ordinary person's adherence to belief is more immediate. Bîrûni takes pleasure in depicting an ordinary Muslim to whom the image of the Prophet, of Mecca and of the Ka'ba, is shown. The person's reaction would be entirely joyful; identification would lead him to imagine that he has seen the Prophet in person and that he could postpone performing a pilgrimage, since he thinks he has visited the Holy Places by having the image of them in front of his eyes. Many of the figures Bîrûni saw in India are ancient, but the wheel of the centuries has turned, the reasons for their presence were forgotten, the faithful would visit them out of custom alone if priests did not intervene to recall their function and especially their iconographic symbolism.

I would also like to evoke the way in which Buddha and Indian idolatry are described in the two great treatises devoted to religions and sects by the Muslim scholars of the Middle Ages. Ibn Hazm the Andalusian attributes to Hindus the belief in the stars that govern the universe: "Thus act the Hindus with their idols (bidada). They give them form and celebrate them by invoking the stars."[9] Shahrastani (1088–1153) devotes a fragment of his treatise to Buddhists: "'Buddha' signifies for them an individual of this world, who was not given birth to and did not take a wife, does not eat or drink, does not get old or die."[10] Buddha is called in Arabic *al-budd* (pl. *bidada,* from which comes *ashâb al-bidada,* or "the Buddhists"). The term comes from the Sanskrit *buddha,* "the Awakened One," epithet for Siddhartha Gautama, the man who founded Buddhism and who died at the age of eighty years, around 480 B.C. A note from the translators tells us that Sharastani's description, "authentically Buddhist," does not correspond to the historic Buddha: "It concerns the 'body of law' (Sanskrit: *dharmakaya*), that is to say the supra-worldly and infinite reality of the eternal Buddha." This remark is a sign that Islam kept its curiosity open to India. The potential awareness that developed was restricted by the common notion that Buddhism is idolatry, so that the word *budd* signifies in Arabic simply "idol." The fact remains that the Islamic view of Buddhism and India was enriched by other, more complex viewpoints.

> Everyone can admire the extraordinary Shiva Nataraja, "the Lord of the dance" with four arms, in the Musée Guimet in Paris. The architrave of Nepalese stupas, like the one in Bodhnath, turns three eyes of the Buddha toward each cardinal point: his "normal" eyes of omniscience and universal compassion, surmounted by the vertical eye of wisdom. Somewhat similarly, why not say that Islam regarded Hinduism with four eyes: the normal eyes of observation and science, underlined by the eye of discernment and surmounted by the eye of benevolence?[11]

The eye of judgment is the organ of the polemicist theologian; when condemning idolatry, he thinks first of India. The eye of observation brings back tales that interested travelers. It is the picturesque India as it appears in the two major works of the tenth century: *Al-Fihrist,* by Ibn Nadîm (who died at the very end of the tenth century), and *The Fields of Gold,* by Mas'ûdi (d. 956).[12] The eyewitnesses are especially taken by the exploits of ascetics. The scientific viewpoint is embodied by Bîrûni, already quoted, whose book devoted to India, finished in 1030, draws from a profound knowledge of Sanskrit and diligent conversations with the pandits he had met during his pilgrimages in the northwest of the subcontinent. Finally,

> Islam waited many centuries to open its fourth eye, the selective eye of benevolence. Selective, because this eye of syncretist Sufism functioned as a prism, breaking down the light of India into Muslim colors. A prestigious monarch, Akbar, the third Mughal emperor, who reigned from 1556 to 1605, adopted the movement of rapprochement with Hinduism. . . . In the seventeenth century, the Mughal prince Dârâ Shikôh, who wrote in Persian, translated fifty upanishads . . . and composed a treatise, *Majma' al-Bahrayn,* on the confluence of mystic Islam and Indian religion.[13]

Through the example of the Buddhas, the hole dug by these Wahhabite fundamentalists, simplistic and one-dimensional, is once more revealed, deviating from the traditions of Islam, polyphonic, questioning, problematic, plural in its answers. This is the gap between ancient Islam, intelligent and likable, and the political forms of present Islam, stupid and detestable. By this yardstick we can measure the distance that separates someone overwhelmed by ressentiment, reacting to abolish Otherness, from the sovereign subject, who dares to confront the Other in his difference, to deepen his knowledge of self and to maintain the diversity of the world. Such occultations exactly characterize Wahhabite teaching, which is intended to establish a generalized amnesia. When I see the uncrossable abyss that separates classic Islam from some of its current manifestations, I feel the sorrow that Hölderlin expresses in *Hyperion* for the irreparable loss the spiritual extinction of Greece represented: what a depressing present contrasted with ancient genius! It is difficult to feel "the atrocious alternation, in you, of joy and pain: that is because you have both everything and nothing . . . because you are a god among gods, in the admirable dreams that invade your days, and because upon waking, you find yourself again on the soil of present-day Greece."[14]

But the Greece of today is a small country with no ambitions of glory or claim to hegemony; Ancient Greece is a dead civilization, with a dead language, which Hölderlin hoped to revive and reclaim as an inheritance to retrace his own experience. Arabic, however, is still living, since Islam has the ambition of existing and mattering in the world solely by virtue of its territories and the number of its practitioners. Perhaps the creative among the native speakers of Arabic will have to learn how to die with respect to their language, and the brightest among the adherents of Islam will have to carry their origin to the cemetery of history, so that the language can become like a phoenix who could make the poets and thinkers of Islam fruitful, assuring them a return to themselves, and cause them to be reborn from the ashes of the entity to which they belonged. Perhaps then Islam could rediscover the blossoming that would aid the women and men who want to add their voices to the murmur filling the world scene.

During the destruction of the colossi of Bamiyan on March 9, 2001, the world was not taken by surprise. The members of the Taliban had announced the intention to commit their crime many days before carrying out the act. They had taken the time to organize its spectacle. Iconoclasts, mixing archaism with technology, they had no phobia about the televised image. They knew what kind of weapon it represented. Narcissists of the small screen, they took pleasure in defying the world by publicizing their misdeeds. Slaves to the news flash, subject to the rhetoric of publicity, mixing the brevity of the excerpt (the American sense of the news bite) with the special effects of video, they broadcast their attack on a venerable product of Buddhist aesthetics in a series of hard-hitting and ostentatious shots.

Aren't they, in their very archaism, unconscious children of the Americanization of the world? Can I dare to assert that, if we had exercised the right of intervention to save the Buddhas, New York would have escaped the loss of its twin towers? Don't the two sequences of destruction constitute two phases that strangely belong to one single tragedy? Aren't the images of September 11 the crescendo of those of March 9? From Asia to America, from the rocky walls of Bamiyan to the shores of the Hudson, tall forms that had spread the pride of their erection were instantaneously pulverized into a cloud of dust. Video recordings in the form of news clips bore witness to both disasters. Didn't you feel, after twice witnessing two disappearances, the same sensation of emptiness stretching out from the annihilated site to the rest of the universe? Why couldn't the politicians who govern our world foresee that the destruction of the two Buddhas in Bamiyan was only the prelude to, or the warning sign of, the implosion that made Manhattan's Twin Towers collapse and crush thousand of humans within it with steel and glass? Our decision makers are exclusively possessed of a technical reasoning, which prevents them from discerning the relationship between the symbolic and the real, the place where that part of the disappeared is measured, whether they are two age-old figures in rock or three thousand of our fellow creatures, perishable flesh and bone.

27

I WOULD LIKE TO TAKE UP AGAIN the question of the decline, and to understand the gap that separates ancient Islam from present Islam, to grasp the causes that led from splendor to wretchedness. As discussed in the previous chapter, Bîrûni contrasts the elite with the common, the few with the many, by distinguishing, in idolatry, between those who study abstract principles and those who are content with physical appearances. It is the dichotomy between *khâœa* and *'âma*, between the elite and the ordinary, that gives structure to the Islam of greatness.

These categories are at work in all realms of society and in all expressions of culture. The writers, thinkers and poets I have previously quoted invoke a hierarchy whose degrees are divided up in the light of this dichotomy. We find its effect in Averroës when he considers the meaning of the Qur'anic literature: The elite is obliged to interpret by arguments that can be understood only by analysis, whereas the mass keeps to the obvious meaning.[1] The same distinction is present in

Sufism and the spiritual experience. It is active in Ibn 'Arabi through his theory of the image mentioned earlier. Even the masters of nescience and unknowing discern between elite and common people. Another example is Bistâmi (778–849), whose inspiration is marked by the ladder of the elect, and who does not place the initiate ('*ârif*) and the commoner on the same level.[2]

Yet another example is Shams ud-Din of Tabriz (thirteenth century), the vagabond foreigner, the invulnerable wanderer whose arrival and enigmatic disappearance overwhelmed the master Jalâluddîn Rûmî (1207–1273) and branded him with the iron of passion. By converting the master from Konya, Shams became the master of the master; he belongs to the first rank that the Sufis call *khâsat al-khâsa,* elite of the elite. His mastery is based on the ability to make the invisible God visible. And this ability is not comparable to ordinary mastery. Being the master of the master, he revived the love that makes one mad, and forced Rûmî, who had become his disciple, to renounce his high status and share his retreat in his cell. After the unexplained disappearance of his initiator, Rûmî, inconsolable, composed the scorched poems that the burning of nostalgia inspires. Shams abolished the learned scholar in Rûmî to bring the poet to life. Master of the master, he "is both the most powerful of men and the weakest, in that his mastery is also infinite precariousness, sign of absence, where, as enigma, is revealed, inverted, the divine effusion."[3]

These various examples indicate that the distinction between elite and common is more technical than economic or social. The nuance is made more obvious by the example of the mystics who disrupt the structures of power-knowledge, and are subversive. That is the case with Bistâmi, or for the unknown man from Tabriz, whose incursion transformed Rûmî's life: The master of science trembled before the master of learned ignorance.

The people of the spiritual elite are recognizable even in our day. The traveler can meet them in those Islamic societies that preserve tradition, as in Morocco. I recognized one of them one evening in Tamesloht, halfway between Marrakech and the Atlas, in that small town marked by sanctity. I saw him under the arcades that lead to the kasbah of the Chorfas; he was wearing the rags of a mendicant. The atmosphere was impregnated with the sharp smell of oil from the olive presses. It was the harvest season; the forest of olive trees that surrounded the village was providing a rich crop. With a fine beard and shoulders high, the beggar who came toward me looked as if he had escaped from Caravaggio's "Death of the Virgin"; he was as humble, as robust as one of the characters that surround the dead body of the saint, in that painting I had just seen in the Louvre. Facing me, he sought out my eyes in the half-light, and as simple as he was solemn, he put together two gestures that summarized his condition, his involvement, his itinerary. With his left hand, he showed me the earth and the disgust it had inspired in him. And he raised his right hand with a gesture that gave his approval to the sky; a concentration of energy straightened his body, which seemed suddenly as if ready to ascend. By this sequence of theatrical mimes, he seemed to mean, Nothingness is here below; up above is existence. Such is the silent eloquence of the aristocratic beggar marked by nescience, belonging to the elite of the elite that unknowing enlightens, brother and emulator of Bistâm as well as the man from Tabriz, surviving into our century in lands saved from petrodollars and Wahhabism.

It is this distinction between elite and common that collapsed under the pressure of a democratization without a democracy, a populism that generalizes the doctrine without considering its quality and without readapting the hierarchical principle to establish a new republican or democratic elite. This, then, was the triumph of the common, which, when it acquires mastery of a technique, proceeds from alphabetization to specialization, without training in the tradition, which in the old days was called the humanities and in our time is considered useless. In this way of inculcating the mastery of some specialty in an amnesiac or virgin soul, I see additional evidence of the Americanization of the world. Thus the common man, even if he is a master of a technical specialty, is not transformed into an aristocratic figure, simply because he is the product of an instruction without culture. It is the

uncultivated educated ones who most damage humanity. Without hes-
itation, I prefer the highly cultured illiterate, like the Tamesloht beggar, to them.[4] In the absence of democracy, the aristocratic spirit that
once deferred the osmosis between the elite and the mass has withdrawn, ceding its place to the man eaten away by resentment, a candidate for terrorist and insurrectional fundamentalism. That is how a
great civilization, which had maintained its bearing during its long decline, lost its last safeguards. Such are the conditions that made fundamentalist propaganda attractive.

In fact the candidates rushed to the door of al Qa'ida, which since
1996 had made the Taliban's Afghanistan its base of operations. The insurrectional movement founded in 1989 by Osama bin Laden became
more radical with the crystallization, in its founder, of an unbridled
anti-Western sensibility during the Gulf War (1991), with the arrival of
foreign troops on Arab soil. Without those troops, all the regimes of the
peninsula would have been swept away, but in Wahhabite logic, such a
presence on the holy ground of Arabia was perceived as a defilement.
They had to fight those who were the cause of it, first the Westerners
(especially the Americans), then the Islamic states unfaithful to the
Medinese utopia.

Actually, this widespread line of argument does not delve into the
areas of the deepest motivation. Without offering it as an alibi, I will
say that it constitutes the rational thinking and conscious analysis of
bin Laden. But the motive that comes from the nagging wound that
festers in the humiliation of the Muslim is too poorly understood. Despite Islam's wealth, despite its numbers (1.2 billion people), the Muslim remains excluded from the decisions that satisfy the desire to
enforce a worldview. Starting with this sorrow that poisons the outcast's days, I can grasp the insane motivations of bin Laden and his
followers: It is the desire for recognition (the denial of which creates
the man of resentment) that incites them to act.

I must confess that I cannot grasp the logic that predisposes a person to inscribe humiliation in the innermost core of his being. If you

cannot bear being outcast, if you have trouble living with the lack of recognition, instead of complaining about it, wouldn't it make more sense to act, to create, to work patiently on your development to make yourself indispensable and objectively recognizable? I would like to answer again those who act from humiliation by referring to a ninth-century woman, the venerable Sufi Umm 'Alî. A woman of great wealth, she supported her husband, Ahmad Ibn Khudhrawayh, one of the spiritual masters of the Khurasân. She was notably the sublime consort of Abû Yazîd Bistâmi; and Sulami (937–1021) reports this magnificent saying of hers: "It is better to lack a thing than to have to suffer humiliation for it."[5]

This woman's saying is an excellent precept; those who feel themselves humiliated and rejected would do well to meditate on this advice. Maybe they can find another way than that of resentment, which only fixes them in a murderous hatred, so that to assuage their vengeful rage, they choose to join the insurrectional movement created by the Wahhabite billionaire who has become a man of shadow and caves.

Let's consider the word *qâ'ida* that bin Laden chose to designate his movement and the active or dormant networks that make up its web. By its density, this word acquires the value of a symbol. It has a polysemy at least equal to the English word *base*, its equivalent, which comes from the Greek word *basis* ("step, point of support" and, by metonymy, "foundation"), whose Latin derivatives extend into many languages, including French and English. Archaic meanings and the most modern usage intersect in it.

But let's return to the verbal root in which the noun takes its source, as if to honor the etymology in which the Semitic languages excel, where words that share the same root, the same *basis* the linguist would say, are distributed under one single rubric. The meanings that radiate from the combination of the three consonants *q. 'a. d.* are distributed over two ranges. The first plays on degrees of passivity: to be seated, to wait for someone, to be seated and ready to serve someone, to prepare, to ready someone for something. The second leans toward an active intensity: to be firm, to keep oneself firm, to be in ambush and be on the watch for someone, to be of equal strength, to be able to stand up to someone.

To illustrate this semantic contrast between waiting and acting, the medieval lexicographer, my compatriot Ibn Manz'ûr (thirteenth century) interprets the Arabic proverb in which the word *q. 'a. d.* appears in two opposite ways: *Idhâ qâma bika ash-sharru fa-'uq'ud.*[6] In the first sense, the proverb is translated thus: "If evil attacks you, wait and don't get upset." In the second, it is altered to the following: "If evil provokes you, be firm and confront it." Thus the imperative of *q. 'a. d.* (*'uq'ud*) provokes two contrary strategies: Faced with evil, the first recommends passive resistance, which is allied with temporizing if not with nonacting; the second exhorts the subject to hurry into warlike heroism.

The substantive term *qâ'ida,* however, designates "what a building rests on," "foundation or support," as well as "all that serves as a basis" and "base, pedestal." The same Ibn Manz'ûr quotes two Qur'anic verses to support this meaning: "Abraham, with the help of Ishmael, raised the foundations (*qawâ'id,* pl. of *qâ'ida*) of the temple."[7] "God attacked their building at its foundation."[8] The word also has an abstract meaning that means "law," "a general rule," "a fundamental principle"; it is used in geometry for the base of the triangle, and in linguistics, used in the plural, it means "grammar" (*qawâ'id al-lûgha,* the rules of the language). In metaphoric usage, it can designate the capital of the kingdom (*qâ'idat al-mulk*). And as in a number of European languages, the word, in modern Arabic, is widely associated with military establishments: base of operations, naval base, air base, missile-launching base, and so forth.

Two other senses of the word deserve to be emphasized in order to shed light on the choice of the word for an insurrectional, terrorist movement. The movement tries to create adherence, or at least sympathy, to "a popular base" (*qâ'ida sha'biyya*), and it uses in its subversive methods computer terminology (the height of technology) by using a *data base*, the "base of givens," called in Arabic *qâ'idat al-bayânât*.

We see how revealing this chosen word is. The technological and "aesthetic" success of the September 11 attacks can be the perfect illustration of it.[9]

Part IV

The Western
Exclusion of Islam

28

SACRIFICE AND SECRETIVENESS HAVE often been mentioned in explaining how the terrorists acted on September 11. We should be careful when analyzing these two characteristics and not try to shed light on them only by invoking Islamic history and culture. These terrorists are as much children of their time and of a world transformed by Americanization as they are the product of an internal evolution, unique to Islam. Nonetheless Bernard Lewis's book devoted to the Assassins confronts readers with troubling analogies that they will be tempted to project onto the actions of the terrorists belonging to al Qa'ida.[1]

The agents who, on September 11, committed suicide while killing others are even more clearly illuminated by Dostoyevskian nihilism. I imagine their personal experiences as close to those of the characters described in *The Possessed,* with perhaps less hysteria and more effectiveness in their actions. Actually, the recent attacks seem to be the product of a condensation of all the forms of revolutionary action. If the ideological content of revolutionary movements varies from system to system, it is still certain that the method that unites secrecy with suicide will end up failing, despite the terrible blows it strikes against established states.

The frequency of references to the Ismailians is more Western than Islamic. From the time of the Crusades forward, it has been the European historians and chroniclers of the end of the twelfth through the thirteenth century who contributed to the fabrication of the myth of the Assassins. Their names include Gerhard, envoy of the Emperor Frederick Barbarossa in Egypt and Syria; William, Archbishop of Tyre; the chronicler Arnold de Lübeck; the English historian Matthew Paris; the monk Yves the Breton; Joinville, the chronicler of Saint Louis; Jacques de Vitry, Bishop of Acre; and the travelers William of Rubruck, Marco Polo and, half a century later, Odoric of Pordenone. Through their reports, accounts, and chronicles the figure of the Assassin was made famous: a person completely subject to his master, ready to seize the dagger the master holds out to him and plunge it into the chest of the victim the master designates. The influence that the Master of Alamût had over his accomplices has been romanticized at every possible opportunity. Beyond the magical dimension attributed to this wonder-working master, the medieval witnesses of Europe imagined the setting of a Muslim paradise. Here, in a shadowy garden, girls and Adonises dabble, ready to welcome disciples and initiate them into the voluptuousness that awaits them in the true Garden of Delights promised as an eternal resting place to those who sacrifice themselves for the master's cause. This fantasy was assimilated with the material reasoning that explained the control over captive souls and their unswerving obedience.

In modern times, the first ideological uses of the Ismailian phenomenon were also Western. With the memory of the revolutionary terror still fresh, the beginning of the nineteenth century, haunted by political crime, revived the memory of the Assassins. The Austrian Orientalist Joseph von Hammer, in *History of the Assassins*, made these Assassins the universal model of conspirators, members of secret societies who "prostitute" religion to serve their ambition. He also likened to Assassins all those whom he perceived as spreaders of discord during the past centuries or among his contemporaries. With the n are identified the Templars, the Jesuits, the Freemasons, the Illuminati, the regicides of the Convention:

> Just as in the West revolutionary societies were engendered by Freemasonry, so, in the East, the Assassins came from Ismailism. . . . The insanity of the Illuminati, who thought that through simple preaching they could free the nations from the tutelage of princes and from the chains of religious practice, was revealed in the most terrible way in the effects of the French Revolution, as it was in Asia under the reign of Hassan.[2]

The Assassins have been evoked again to denounce the extremism of Italian or Macedonian nationalists, clandestine militants and violent terrorists who bloodied the European soil later in the nineteenth century.[3] Thus the reference to the Ismailians, offered as a key to interpret the attacks of al Qa'ida, agrees more with the terrorist act than with its Islamist origin. Through the disaster in New York, the myth of the Assassins is again used to shed light on a massacre whose motivation is political and whose success is due to the combination of dissimulation and sacrifice.

The leader of the Assassins, Hassan-i Sabbâh, in his turn became a literary myth in the West. The initiator of this was Edward Fitzgerald, who, in the preface to his translation of the quatrains of Omar Khayyâm, repeated a tale spread by Persian literary tradition. Hassan-i Sabbâh, Omar Khayyâm and Nizâm al-Mulk were the disciples of the same master. They took an oath that the first who succeeded would come to the aid of the two others. When Nizâm al-Mulk became vizier to the Seljuk sultan, his former codisciples reminded him of the pact between them. He offered them posts as governors that they both refused. Omar Khayyâm contented himself with a pension that left him with his freedom and his passion for poetry and mathematics. Hassan-i Sabbâh asked for an important position in the court, which he obtained. But soon he developed the ambition to rival Nizâm al-Mulk for the position of vizier. The latter then conspired against him and discredited him with the sultan. Hassan-i Sabbâh vowed to take revenge. In this way his seditious plan was born, which he concretized by going to Cairo, the capital of the Fatimid caliphate, to strengthen his involvement in favor of the Ismailians.

> Nizâm al-Mulk was born at the latest in 1020 and was assassinated in 1092. Omar Khayyâm was born in 1048 and died in 1131. If the date of Hassan-i Sabbâh's birth is unknown, we know that he died in 1124. Keeping these dates in mind, it is hardly likely that all three could have been students at the same time. For most modern researchers, this picturesque tale is a fable.[4]

But the myth was launched. Many writers seized it and illustrated it in works that turn out to be deceptive when they take the form of a historical novel. From this body of work, I will mention one of the last appearances of the figure who founded the fortress of Alamût in the mountains of Alburz, near the Caspian Sea. In *Cities of the Red Night*, William Burroughs imagines an America in the hands of libertine pirates, and his fiction is preceded by an "invocation," which begins by announcing that "this book is dedicated to the Ancients" and which ends the list of dedicatees with the "nameless divinities of dispersion and emptiness" and with "*Hassan I Sabbah,* master of the Assassins."[5] The evocation of this character in a libertarian literary context seems to me much more in agreement with the esoteric theory that underlies Hassan-i Sabbâh's political project.

In fact, Hassan-i Sabbâh sought to destabilize Sunnite society by creating a political terrorism to honor an eschatological call, intended to precipitate the return of the hidden imam, and to proclaim the *qiyâma,* the Resurrection, in which the law is abolished in order to give way to a systematically transgressive way of life. The epoch of the abolished Divine Law was proclaimed by Hassan-i Sabbâh's successors and was lived out in the jubilation that the lifting of prohibitions produces, in Alamût as well as in the fortresses of the Syrian mountains. The ideological horizon of the political terror invented by the Isma'lians presents no affinity whatever with the person who directs the actions of those fundamentalists and Wahhabites who people the networks of al Qa'ida, who dream only of imposing *Shariah* (Islamic) law on the world, the same *Shariah* that was abolished by the Assassins. The heroes of the medieval insurrection prove to be heralds of the anarchist movements of modern times, whereas today's terrorists wallow in a terrible regressive archaism, determined to apply the letter of the law that the Ismailians had abolished, after they had extracted its hidden meaning through recourse to interpretative science. According to the hermeneutic system of the Ismailians, the letter of the Qur'an that is revealed to the Prophet remains a dead letter if the imam does not give it life by illuminating the secret it conceals, one that is in his authority to disclose. The fundamentalist Wahhabites' approach to Qur'anic literature is the complete opposite of the esoteric Ismailians: The former are maniacs of the apparent meaning, the latter devote a cult to the hidden meaning. Within the Islamic landscape, Wahhabism and Ismailism constitute two irreconcilable positions.

This incompatibility is not just doctrinal; it also concerns the method of action. The Assassins never proceeded to blind massacres, aiming at innocent victims. Nor did they attack foreign targets, aside from the execution of the Marquis Conrad of Montferrat, king of Jerusalem (April 28, 1192), on orders of the formidable Sinân (d. 1193), the true "old man of the mountain," named by Hassan-i Sabbâh to direct the Syrian branch. (Sinân lived in the Castle of Masyaf and coordinated the activities of the surrounding fortresses.) And even this execution was not gratuitous; its aim was to revive dissension among the Franks, which in fact arose, since Richard the Lion-Hearted was suspected of having ordered the crime. Otherwise, all the victims of the Ismailians were politicians, members of the army, religious practitioners, administrators, intellectuals belonging to the

Sunnite state apparatus (from caliph to sultan, from vizier to prefect, from mufti to cadi, from governor to scholar). Here again, there is a staggering difference between the Ismailians practicing deliberate assassinations, and the contemporary terrorism, blinded by the power of the symbol and the search for shock images designed to last as long as possible on the ephemeral scene of news programmed for a society that grants its attention only to spectacular events.

The other distinction is qualitative. From the Wahhabites to the Ismailians, an interstellar distance separates the oversimplifications of fundamentalist ideology from the sophistication of theories developed by intellectuals. These intelligent minds constructed cosmologies in harmony with a cyclical vision of history, associating each era with a prophet accompanied by his own interpreter, who enriches the literature of the Revelation. Ismailian thinking evolved toward an adoption of Neoplatonism and the cult of the intellect, the imprint of which is seen through the epistles that make up the encyclopedia written by the Brothers of Purity in the tenth century. This text, which was distributed throughout all of Islam, still preserves a freshness that brings pleasure to the contemporary reader. The spiritual legacy of the Ismailians thus bears no comparison with the destitute productions of the fundamentalists and Wahhabites, of which I have given a few samples that are, to say the least, repellent in their intellectual poverty and their fanaticism.

The horizon of thought traced by the Ismailians attracted the greatest thinkers of the time, like Nâsîr ad-Dîn Tûsî (1201–1274), doctor, physicist, philosopher, mathematician and especially astronomer, founder of the famous observatory of Maragha in the province of Azerbaijan. Or like Nasiri Khusraw (1004–circa 1078), author of a book of travels that unites the topographer's exposition with the descriptive art of the novelist.[6] This book constitutes a precious historical document, which helps to reconstruct the state of eleventh-century Jerusalem or Cairo. Its author is also a poet who confesses in odes to his doubts and the perplexity that his interior debates arouse in him. Similarly, he practices *ta'wîl*, the hermeneutics that extracts the profound meaning of Islamic practices and dogmas. As a philosopher, he tries in his *Jâmi' al-Hikmatayn* to reconcile the language of the Qur'an with the logical discourse of the speculative sciences.

> If, in order to spread knowledge and establish the worship of God, we expect to wait till the tyranny of ignorance is eradicated from living beings, then these beings will leave this world still ignorant and rebellious. No, wise men are like fruit trees that stand laden with their fruit; seekers of wisdom are like famished children, agile, clever and cunning; the ignorant are like beasts of burden who drag themselves along, head to the ground, dulled, unable to look up at the tree, or even to know that there is anything in the tree. The children pick juicy, fresh, sweet, tasty fruit from the trees, and nourish themselves with it, while the beasts do not even suspect what they are doing.[7]

If the ghost of Nasiri Khusraw returned among us and were made aware of the deeds and writings of our fundamentalists, there is no doubt he would liken them to the ignorant creatures he had compared to animals, who can neither see the tree of wisdom nor discern the fruits that cover its branches.

29

TWO REMARKS IN BERNARD LEWIS'S book invite the reader to connect the Ismailian phenomenon with contemporary terrorism. The new method invented by Hassan-i Sabbâh consists in using

> a small disciplined and devoted force, capable of effectively striking a considerably superior enemy. "Terrorism," writes a modern author, "is maintained by a narrowly limited organization and is inspired by a sustained program of large-scale objectives in the name of which terror is applied."[1]

And the last paragraph of *Assassins* is an explicit summons to find an echo of the medieval terrorism of the Ismailians in our current affairs:

> The wave of messianic hope and revolutionary violence that had carried them along continued to roll, and their methods and ideals have

found a number of imitators. And the great upheavals of our time have provided those imitators with new causes for anger, new dreams of fulfillment and new instruments of combat.[2]

This summons intensifies when terrorism emanates from some Islamic site. At once people refer to the Assassins as if it were a basic part of Islamic culture, absolutely legitimate and completely obvious. It turns out to be exactly what happens when people discover that Palestinian fighters use the same term as the one that designated the Ismailian agents of political assassination: Both call themselves *fidâ'i*, a word that derives from the root *f.d.y.*, which means to buy someone back at the price of a ransom to save his life or free him. This word is used in a fixed expression, *fadaytuka* ("I am buying you back at the price of my life"), to express limitless devotion. *Fidâ'i* is thus one who is ready to sacrifice himself for the cause. From the point of view of the differentialists, that explains the sacrifice of September 11. Yet Bernard Lewis himself admits that there is no place for human sacrifice or for ritual murder in Islamic law, tradition or practice.[3]

On the other hand, it is possible to elucidate the question of martyrdom from Islamic history and theology. The martyr is one who falls on the path of God, he is *shahîd*, a "witness." The word comes from the root *sh.h.d.* which means to be present at, to attend something, to bear witness to something, to testify, to render a solemn testimony with an oath to the truth of a thing. Thence comes the meaning to utter a declaration of Muslim faith ("There is no god other than God"); and in the passive (*ushhida*), to be killed in war while fighting for religion, or to suffer martyrdom, to be wholly summoned as witness to Muslim faith. And *shahîd* changes the voice of the verb into a substantive: It means true witness, truthful in his testimony, who knows everything, who has omniscience, martyr for the Muslim faith (either killed in holy war or who had suffered martyrdom), and, by extension, who died from any death other than natural death (drowning, plague, killed in self-defense). In its first meaning, we find the same etymological meaning as that of "martyr," emanating from the Greek *martur*, a late form of *martus, marturos* "witness" (in legal terminology).[4]

When one dies for the cause of God, to what is one a witness? Perhaps to the face of God, which is the sign of being chosen and of the beatific sojourn, the guarantee of eternal residence in paradise. The words that derive from the root *sh.h.d.* are many in the Qur'anic text, and they are essentially oriented in two senses: that of legal witnessing and that of omniscience. The word *shahîd* is almost exclusively devoted to God who witnesses everything, who testifies to everything, who sees everything—in short, the omniscient God. And *shuhadâ'* are not martyrs; they are rather the legal witnesses and the witnesses of truth after God. I would say that the Qur'anic sense of the word remains generic and is distributed as witness of truth both on the legal axis and on the metaphysical axis: to testify to the truth of a deed (of adultery, for instance), to testify to the truth of God as this truth appears in revelations transmitted by his messenger, the prophets. There is only one verse that anticipates the figure of the martyr: "Above all do not believe that those who were killed on the path of God are dead; they are living next to their Lord, provided with goods."[5]

Fakhr ad-Dîn Râzî (1149–1209), taking up the exegetic tradition, recalls first that this verse concerns the martyrs (he uses the word *shuhadâ'*) of the two battles led during the time of the Prophet against the Qoraïshites, the battles of Badr (March 624) and of Uhud (November 625). He then says that the prepositional phrase "next to" (*'inda*) in the sentence, "they are living *next to* their Lord," is the same one that places the angels in their divine proximity, which gives those who die as martyrs of the jihad the bliss of angels during the celestial stay in the divine dwelling.[6] That is the scriptural basis that legitimizes the holy war and clarifies the reward awaiting the martyr. This basis has been submitted to all sorts of manipulations to construct the mythology of martyrdom. It has been used over and over in our time, notably during the wars of national liberation against colonialism. The Algerian nationalist fighter was called *mudjahid*, or one who devotes himself to the jihad, the victims of which are "living next to their Lord," enjoying a proximity, a beatitude and a joy equal to that of angels; they are touched by the blessing of angelic light.

It remains to be determined if the passage from war to guerrilla warfare and terrorism still justifies the notions of jihad and *shahîd*. That is where the brute access to literature invites all sorts of manipulations. In the spectrum of present interpretation, opinions vary. Those who advocate minimal interpretation invoke the holy war and all its mythology in cases of attack and situations of self-defense, as is the case for nationalist struggles. The Palestinian question is included in this minimal position. And the maximal position is, for instance, expressed in many books by Sayyid Qutb, who attacks those scholars who minimize the range of jihad. He calls for its intensification and its universalization to make Islamic law triumph on the scale of all humanity, for such law is considered the ultimate expression of divine truth.[7]

The terrorist fundamentalists claim to follow this interpretation in conducting their violent actions. Those who carried out the September 11 attacks must have thought they were martyrs of this universal jihad, not dead at all but living next to their Lord. Such is the conviction that devotes them to sacrifice and makes them internalize the mythology of martyrdom, in an elemental drama that requires them to purify their bodies beforehand for the celestial honeymoon that awaits them. This naive scenography takes us far from the angelic interpretation proposed by the rationalist interpreter of the twelfth century. But such is the scriptural basis on which we project the representations that best illustrate the need to compensate for the frustrations we undergo during our earthly stay.

It seems to me that this scriptural basis and its maximalist interpretation suffice to explain the choice of death by the terrorists of September 11. There is no need to have recourse to the Ismailians or to the idea of sacrifice as it appears among the Shiites. The Shiites are perceived as the downtrodden ones of Islam; they think they have undergone an injustice. The idea of martyrdom was exacerbated among them because their model was one of the imams they venerated the most, Husayn, one of the sons of 'Ali, horribly massacred in Kerbala (on October 10, 680). This massacre is considered by the Shiites as their primal scene, which they celebrate every year. Thus they have a cult of martyrdom, in the Christian sense of the word. It is a martyrdom that preserves the guilt of not having been ready to sacrifice oneself to defend the imam and prevent his massacre. In this kind of martyrdom, the notion of buying back and of redemption exists. The imam let himself be massacred; he sacrificed himself so that his blood could redeem those who believe in him. It is a matter of a ceremonial and ritual grieving intended to appease a guilty conscience. The celebration of this sacrifice has no relationship with jihad or the martyr, the *shahîd* who joins his rank in divine proximity when he loses his life while fighting on the path of God.

The idea of martyrdom, which accompanies terrorism, reappeared on the Near Eastern scene following a terrorist act that belongs to another cultural tradition: The first kamikazes of the present Near East are the three militants of the Nihon Sekigun (the Japanese Red Army) who, on May 30, 1972, carried out a suicide attack on the airport in Lod. Muammar al-Qaddafi even wondered why the Palestinians wouldn't use this method.[8]

After the September 11 attacks, the government directed by Ariel Sharon immediately likened the New York attack to the ones that Israel undergoes because of the Palestinians. And the Arab governments allied with the United States were careful to make a distinction between the terrorism of resistance and the terrorism of the jihad proclaimed against the West by al Qa'ida. They refused to equate these two types of terrorism. Those nations intervened so that the United States wouldn't add organizations like the Palestinian Hamas and the Lebanese Hezbollah, which they called organizations of resistance, to their condemned list. The press and the Arab political classes created this dogmatic distinction, reminding us of the terrorism of the French and European Resistance against Nazi occupation, as well as the recourse to such weapons by Jewish organizations during the struggle that led to the creation of Israel. In the Palestinian case, the terrorist act, in its very horror, is comparable to the weapon of a weak man whose despair is amplified by the hatred caused by impotent rage.

The question of sacrifice is thus posed through the terrorism practiced on the Near Eastern scene. A veritable mythology of martyrdom and sacrifice was constructed by the Hezbollah, drawing perhaps from the cult of martyrdom as it survives in the Shiite circles of South Lebanon. A form of ceremonial and iconography in keeping with myth was elaborated to prepare the suicide candidate for the honeymoon that awaits him in the Garden of Delights, peopled with virgins with large black eyes. In this dramaturgy, I see the last anthropomorphic, literalist reincarnation of contemporary fundamentalism, which turns out to be as elementary in its fictions as in its approach to the meaning present in the Qur'anic text.

As for me, I have already become radical in my rejection of the terrorist act, whatever its motive. I know how terrorism exercised in the name of a noble cause can be perverted by myth and re-arise in political culture:

> As to terrorism and Islamist extremism, I will be decisive: both represent the unacceptable for me, nothing can legitimize them, and I stand completely and with all my strength against them, even if I feel powerless before their intrigues; but I fight them and will continue to fight them by the means I have, that is to say through writing and speech that denounce the scandal they project on the world's screens. I take this irrevocable position simultaneously with their sacrificial and bloody acts.
>
> As to terrorism, I take on the lineage of Camus, who was one of the rare people to have the lucidity to refuse this barbarism, whatever its cause; it was, you will remember, in the 50's, during the Algerian War; and Camus was isolated in the Parisian intellectual scene; and, twenty years later, I counted myself as one of his detractors; but it is not from infidelity or from a taste for recanting that I have changed my position; it is time, the revelator, that dispenses

justice to those who have kept their lucidity in apartness and solitude. Why should we repeat the transgressions of the past when a
prior example appears openly in the light of day? I will add that the
experience of terrorism for a noble national cause got recorded in
the nation's memory as glory and not as horror. Thus it turned into
a fact of culture, and a habitual recourse. Now the Algerians learn
that this weapon has been turned against them.[9]

Islam does not practice human sacrifice. To carry out their terrorist actions, contemporary fundamentalists have redirected the idea of
sacrifice and have acclimated it to the Islamic imagination by a series
of manipulations. On the other hand, every year, the Muslim celebrates Abraham's sacrifice, based on an action of substitution in
which God redeems the son for an animal. Abraham's sacrifice is re-
counted in the Qur'an:

> When the son was of an age to accompany his father, he [the father]
> said: "O my son! I saw in a dream that I sacrificed (*adhbahuka*) you;
> what do you think of that?" He said: "O my father, do what is com-
> manded of you; you will find me, if God wishes, among the pa-
> tient."/ After they had accepted God's decision, and Abraham had
> thrown down his son, forehead on the ground,/ we cried out to him:
> "O Abraham/ you have authenticated the vision, this is how we rec-
> ompense those who do good./ That is truly an indisputable test."/
> We bought him back (*fadaynâ-hu*) with a victim destined for a major
> sacrifice (*dhabh*).[10]

Thus, in the very text of the Qur'an the link between ransom and
sacrifice can be found. And we find the same root *dh.b.h.*, implied by
the verb "to sacrifice" and by "the victim destined for sacrifice"; its
primary meaning is "to split, to tear up, to break," whence "to slice
the throat," to kill by cutting the throat of cattle, and, by the same
procedure, to sacrifice a victim or to kill a man without pity.

In the Scriptures of Islam, it is said that Abraham's sacrifice constitutes "an indisputable test." This evaluation predisposes the scene to tragic interpretation. In his commentary on Aristotle's *Poetics*, Averroës, unaware of the corpus of Greek tragedians, saw in Abraham's sacrifice the best illustration of one of the characteristics of the genre stressed by the Stagirite.[11] Tragedy must arouse fear and pity by presenting "the arising of violence within relationships."[12] And Goethe uses Abraham and Agamemnon to illustrate the catharsis associated with human sacrifice:

> In tragedy, *katharsis* is realized through a sort of human sacrifice, whether it is actually accomplished or only in the form of a surrogate, thanks to the intervention of some benevolent divinity, as in the case of Abraham or Agamemnon.[13]

I experienced this range of tragic feeling when as a child I attended the annual throat-cutting of an animal in commemoration of Abraham's act and to give thanks to God who, through his gift of the animal, had redeemed the son. That is probably a way of celebrating the historical transcendence of human sacrifice. Thus the actual celebration of this symbol makes the Muslim familiar with the death rattle that accompanies the cut throat. After this gesture, the child I was saw the steaming blood flowing out of the animal until the last drop and following its red course toward the sluice, on the paved slope of one of the paths that separated the flower beds. I could not help but think of this commemoration of Abraham's gesture when the scenes of slaughter of entire families reached us from Algeria, the work of the GIA (Groupe Islamique Armé), which had emerged from the Afghan crucible with the complicity and blessing of the members of al Qa'ida. The ceremony of bloodshed from the animal makes me think of that other form of sacrifice, due not this time to the suicide of the terrorist, but to how the fundamentalist makes himself the priest of an Islamic adaptation of the ritual crime. An additional perversion abolishes the divine ransom and reverses the substitution, by going from animal to man. Living the reality of symbolic sacrifice by sacrificing the animal with one's own hands does not save one from the madness that seizes someone when he decides to reproduce a symbolic gesture in a real action (which literally defines insanity). To live the symbolism in the reality of bloodshed perhaps predisposes someone to this swing towards madness.[14]

30

SHOULD WE THINK BACK TO THE Ismailians when we recall the secrecy so complete in the conduct of the September 11 terrorists? In fact, the examples of dissimulation and disguise as concerns the Ismailian *fidâ'is* are just as impressive as the behavior of the present terrorists. Those who executed Conrad of Montferrat were dressed as Christian monks. Those who terrorized Saladin had waited patiently for months to become the two most intimate Mamelukes of their master. Those who executed the vizier Mu'în ad-Dîn were disguised as two servants. The one who killed Nizâm al-Mulk played the role of a Sufi. And the *fidâ'i* sent to kill off Fakhr ad-Dîn Râzi, who was criticizing their doctrine in his public courts, had passed for months as an assiduous student, winning the master's confidence before attacking him when they were in a tête-à-tête. Râzi saved his life only by promising never again to criticize their actions or their doctrine.[1]

Should we recall the tradition of dissimulation that recourse to *taqiyya* implies, used in the Shiite logic of Ismailism?[2] The word *taqiyya* derives from the root *w.q.y.*, which means to watch out, to be careful, to protect, to preserve. When you are unable to practice your religion in the open or to make your faith public, it is recommended that you hide your belief to take all the necessary precautions to keep, preserve, protect your private thinking. This practice was observed in two situations: among Muslims who had the status of foreigners under the authority of another law, and among those of the Islamic minority when Sunnite power persecuted those it considered heretical, that is, various Shiite sects (including Ismailism) or the Khawarij.[3] These sect members were advised to practice *taqiyya* in periods of persecution: Concealing your conviction saves you from being pursued. This strategy of dissimulation helped the survival of a number of sects. The Shiites are the ones who formed this idea and who theorized it, saying that, when the Muslim fears the danger of the enemy, God authorizes him to deny his faith with his tongue if he remains a believer in his heart. They took this idea from a scriptural reference: "Believers should not take the infidel as friends instead of believers. Whoever does that in no way honors God, unless you protect yourself (*tattaqû*) from their misdeeds."[4]

For the Sunnites, recourse to *taqiyya* was not valued, although it is acknowledged practically in all the sects that its use is permitted, even without the requirement that it be used only to save you from danger of death. In this vein, another Qur'anic verse is invoked: "Work in the path of God and do not throw yourself with your own hands into danger and do good, God loves those who do good."[5]

This idea is considered dangerous by the Sunnites, who think it weakens the holy war and martyrdom. The Hanafites, for instance, prefer martyrs who die under torture to those who, resorting to *taqiyya*, save their lives by verbally denying their faith.

The use of *taqiyya* is sometimes recommended to Muslims when they are in a minority and threatened by intolerant authority, as was the case with the Moriscos, the last Muslims of Spain, who found themselves obliged to choose between exile and conversion. This impulse toward intolerance had been begun in 1499 by the pious but fanatical Franciscan friar Francisco Jiménez de Cisneros, who had become confessor to the king before becoming inquisitor general of Castile. He carried out the forced conversion of four thousand Muslims in Grenada, dishonoring the pact of 1492, which authorized the practice of their religion for those Muslims who wished to remain in Grenada after its surrender by their monarch Boabdil.[6] This distressful situation elicited a *fatwa* formed by an Oranese theologian from Almagro; it is dated, according to the copies, December 1503 or 1504. The rescript begins with an ardent sentiment addressed to the Moriscos of Grenada forced into conversion: "Brothers, you seize your religion like one who seizes live embers in his hand."[7] The mufti of Oran calls those Muslims who become Christian through force the *ghurabâ,* or foreigners, thinking of the beautiful *hadîth* that says, "Islam was born foreign, it will end as it began, foreign; blessed are the foreigners."[8] Then he recommends that they live the Islam of *taqiyya,* dissimulation, and he explains how to act so as to hide their doctrine and their practice, to maintain their faith in the secret of their heart while pretending to adhere to Christianity. This is

> what is called in Muslim theology "the status of constraint to say words of denial by force." This case goes back to the beginning of Islam, when Qureysh made the first Muslims undergo unbearable tortures to make them deny their religion—and that clearly resembles the case of the Muslims of Andalusia forced to embrace Christianity.[9]

A Qur'anic verse had been revealed to the Prophet on this subject, promising the worst punishments to "whoever denies God after having believed, except for one who has suffered constraint and whose heart remains peaceful in faith."[10]

This, then, is *taqiyya,* which is to be practiced in a situation of violence where the Muslim finds himself oppressed in his belief, and is led to come to terms with the contradiction between hidden faith and evident behavior. This practice is dominated by the notion of intention (*niyya*), which is central in Islam, as the *hadîth* proclaims when it says that "actions count only by their intentions." It is the intention that counts when, subjected to constraint, the Muslim is forced to declare himself a Christian. For him to preserve his faith, it is enough for him to declare his Islamic intention while practicing Christian rites.

Must we return to theological considerations to understand the way in which the September 11 terrorists prepared their murderous attack in secret for months, if not for years? Why not see in it simply the clandestine action common to secret societies motivated by insurrectional and revolutionary aims? If one insists on satisfying the cult of the specific, why not refer to the clandestine movements that existed in the Near East, with the Arabs, in the beginning of the century, struggling against the Ottomans, at a time when the emergence of Arabism was encouraged by the English to weaken the Turkish empire? Concerning these movements, T. E. Lawrence writes that the Arabs

> read the Turkish papers, putting "Arab" for "Turk" in the patriotic exhortations. Suppression charged them with unhealthy violence. Deprived of constitutional outlets they became revolutionary. The Arab societies went underground, and changed from liberal clubs into conspiracies. The Akhua, the Arab mother society, was publicly dissolved. It was replaced in Mesopotamia by the dangerous Ahad, a very secret brotherhood, limited almost entirely to Arab officers in the Turkish army, who swore to acquire the military knowledge of their masters, and to turn it against them, in the service of the Arab people, when the moment of rebellion came.
>
> It was a large society, with a sure base in the wild part of Southern Irak, where Sayid Taleb, the young John Wilkes of the Arab movement, held the power in his unprincipled fingers. To it belonged seven out of every ten Mesopotamian-born officers; and their counsel was so well kept that members of it held high command in Turkey to the last. . . .
>
> Greater than the Ahad was the Fetah, the society of freedom in Syria. The landowners, the writers, the doctors, the great public ser-

vants linked themselves in this society with a common oath, passwords, signs, a press and a central treasury, to ruin the Turkish Empire.[11]

If one insists on an explanation that takes cultural difference into account to grasp the principle of dissimulation, one might as well offer the one that contrasts the civilization of telling all with that of discretion and silence and modesty, qualities that would predispose one to keeping secrets. Although I doubt the effectiveness of such a shortcut, it is not useless to insist on this real cultural difference. Western civilization has created the telling all of autobiography, especially beginning with Rousseau's *Confessions.* I insist on this true beginning, though still aware that, in Western tradition, there was a precursor to the *Confessions,* written by my compatriot Saint Augustine, who allows the child he was to speak (which is a distinctive trait of the genre). But finally, this work discusses sin only in connection with faith; Augustine's life is divided into periods by it: before and after his conversion. Another forerunner was Montaigne, who revived Pascal's attack on "the detestable self."

What's more, there have been at least three famous autobiographies in the Islamic tradition, all of them translated into French. The one by the Syrian Usama Ibn al-Munqîdh (1095–1188) constitutes a precious firsthand account of the Crusades, revealing to us the character and truth of a person through the vivacity of his involvement in major historic events.[12] But it ignores childhood, does not make personal avowals, confesses nothing, does not internalize sin, does not play the card of guilt, the very thing necessary for the establishment of the subject. Even if faults did not exist, one would need to invent them, to create the drama that would show the subject being formed as something unique. It is the Sufis who, in Islam, perceived the importance of this, following the example of Bistâmi.[13] But it is already a feat for Ibn al-Munqîdh to have arrived at the truth of the self-portrait merely by the description of his involvement in events. This constitutes an appreciable achievement for a society based on the reserve, if not the effacement, of the self, in the strategy of social and intersubjective relationships.

There is also the autobiography of my other compatriot, Ibn Khaldun, born in Tunis, died in Cairo. In it, the author recalls neither his childhood nor his family nor his feelings. In short, in his *Voyage,* the self is eclipsed and the work very eloquently illustrates the culture of the secret, of reserve, of retreat from the ego. It is a culture that is distinguished from the one that establishes confession as its center.[14] Ibn Khaldun's book, on the other hand, leaves a precious account of the workings of institutions in which the power of authority and knowledge is exercised in the Arab Islamic societies of the fourteenth century. Additionally, the book contains some beautiful descriptions (like that of Cairo quoted earlier) and some fine stories, including one that recounts the author's meeting with Tamerlane at the gates of Damascus.[15]

Finally, the last famous autobiography was written by a monarch, the famous Babur (1494–1529), who would go on to conquer northern India and found the dynasty of the Mughals.[16] What characterizes this book is again the modesty with which the man gives us his notes on daily life, his youth, joys, regrets, ambitions, failures and triumphs. The subjective part is conveyed in the emotions that certain landscapes or certain portraits arouse, as well as in the sensations that describe the experience of the senses, as when he discovered the taste of mangoes in India, a new taste of an unknown fruit to which Babur continued to prefer the taste of melon, the fruit of his childhood and his native land.

31

IN A WORLD IN WHICH INTERFERENCE reigns, on a planet subject to globalization, one must use the dialectics that combine the particular with the universal, the specific with the general, the different with the similar, all with the requisite nuance. For centuries, borders have been drawn not just to prevent migration, but also to be crossed as much by ideas as by people. Such journeys do not constitute a singularity of our time, even if in our day the migration of people and things has intensified.

The phenomenon of the Assassins is best approached from this perspective of travel, a phenomenon that is an Eastern, Islamic fact, but which has been constructed as a myth by the Christian West since medieval times. The same West reactivated it in the seventeenth century and then again in the nineteenth, so that every form of political terror was associated with it. When it is used as an analogy to shed light on another Islamic fact, one should keep in mind the Western construction that such a reference requires. Where one imagines one has found a cultural coherence between two facts—an ancient, "archeological" fact that is supposed to decode another, contemporary fact, both of which are supposed to belong to the same historical space—one only carries out a linking of heterogeneous elements. If one feels that there is a universal analogy between terrorism and Ismailism, the specific loses its specificity. From here on, the analogy between the Assassins and Qa'ida terrorists no longer constitutes proof of a cultural coherence or continuity. That the two phenomena belong to the same scene of belief might correspond to a coincidence, where it is understood that the Ismailian reference serves as a model for any terrorism based on secrecy and sacrifice.

I see only two similarities between al Qa'ida terrorists and the sect of the Assassins. On the one hand, their leaders took refuge in impregnable mountains. Hassan-i Sabbâh based his fortress of Alamût on a mountain crest in Elburz, not far from the Caspian Sea, in a region belonging to the sphere of Central Asia. The stubbornness of the Mongols was needed to overcome it and win its surrender, almost three centuries after its foundation. The citadel had been founded in 1090 by Hassan-i Sabbâh in the region called the land of the Daylam, northeast of the city of Qazvin, a country reputed to be difficult of access. It was also, after its Islamization, a refuge for a number of sects persecuted by the orthodoxy. In fact, it was a permanent home for Shiite agitation. The castle, said to be impenetrable, was finally besieged by the Mongol Hülagü in 1256.

At the moment I write these lines, though, I wonder how much longer Osama bin Laden, his lieutenants and their guard will resist there in the mountains near Qalât, in the province of Zabul, contiguous to that of Kandahar, from which comes the tribe of Hottaks, to which Mullah Omar belongs. If they aren't crouching in the caves of Qalât, they might be somewhere else in the mountain. Eventually they might take refuge in the underground base whose tunnels were dug beneath the high reliefs of Tora Bora, that place called "black dust." It is a scene of desolate mountains and naked rocks that rise southeast of Jalalabad, more to the north of Qalât, but still in the opposite direction from where Alamût rose, on the other side of that territorial sphere called Central Asia.

The inevitable failure of the terrorist enterprise constitutes the second similarity between the two movements: Al Qa'ida is destined to fail just as the Assassins failed. The organization created by bin Laden will fail just as every similar movement throughout history has failed. It is a lesson taken from human experience. Historical accounts have recorded only failure for this kind of irredentist activism, animated by the fury of hubris. In politics longevity is won through prudence and the art of compromise. The only question that remains is how much such a failure will cost the world.

Those who have taken up the Assassins as a reference to shed light on the events of September 11 turn out to be in agreement with Huntington's theory of the "clash of civilizations."[1] The purpose of this thesis was to strengthen a shaky history, to give it a new reason for being, after the fall of the USSR and the end of the Cold War. What mattered was to respond to "the end of history" and to redefine the shape of the enemy. Among the eight civilizations considered as potential rivals of the West, Islam was chosen as the future enemy, the one that would be the first to challenge Western hegemony. Some have seen in the events of September 11 the realization of this prediction. The very first American reactions invoked the Crusades as if by reflex, to respond to what was no doubt implicitly understood as an act of jihad. But soon official discourse took a more prudent turn, leaving an at least symbolic place for Islamic allies, to organize a rejoinder to fundamentalism. The distinction between Islam and Islamism distanced us from the hypothesis that invokes the clash of civilizations.

Huntington's theory was severely criticized by the Iranian philosopher (who writes in French) Daryush Shayegan. He writes that Islam does not constitute a structured, coherent entity. Under the effect of modernity, accepted or suffered, conscious or unconscious, Islam, like the other traditional civilizations, lives in an in-between state, between the loss of what it was and the infinite expectation of what it will be. This situation is the consequence of the Westernization of the world, which is irreversible and which provokes a rupture involving the fate of all of humanity. It is a rupture that has the same qualitative importance, the same amplitude, as the rupture of Neolithic times. The final avatars of the industrial and scientific revolution transform man wherever he is and whatever the civilization is to which he belongs; such is the precondition that makes globalization objective and establishes the common cultural scene. All the other civilizations identified by Huntington as potentially anti-Western (Japanese, Chinese, Indian, Slav-Balkan, Latin American, even African) are in the same situation; with varying degrees of subtlety and means, they are all forced participants in the common scene. Hierarchical mobility and hegemonic restructuring can be developed only on this unique scene and can only be involved in a shared axiology.[2]

Edward Saïd criticized the same thesis heatedly, when a number of commentators reanimated it to analyze the events of September 11.[3] He recalled that Huntington relied for his demonstration on Bernard Lewis's 1990 article, the hostility of which is apparent in the title itself: "The Roots of Islamic Rage." Thus, a man who had chosen the Ismailian connection to give a specific genesis to Islamist terrorism is also one of the first to identify Islam as the prime enemy of the West in the scenario revived by the clash of civilizations. Saïd tries to demonstrate that Islam was a complex phenomenon, whose experience has not been a single confrontation with the West. Many times the two entities have intersected, met, enriched each other; they have been participants in the common theater of the Mediterranean. Quite simply, Saïd recalled the obvious: Islam has been inside Europe, it is within the West. And as an example he gives Dante (1265–1321), forced to recognize the centrality of Islam by placing the Prophet and the imam, Mohammed and 'Ali, in the heart of his hell.[4]

I will add that among the troublemakers of schism and discord, the presence of the founder of Qur'anic literature and his interpreter in the ninth *bolgia* of the eighth circle confirms first of all the medieval stereotype that equates Islam with a heretical sect. Second, the predicament Dante created for them reveals the poet's refusal to recognize the debt he incurred by drawing from the wealth of Islamic culture. His salvation of Saladin, Avicenna and Averroës (all three placed in limbo along with the great figures representing the thinking and politics of Greco-Roman antiquity) is not enough to discharge the Tuscan poet's debt.[5] The amplitude of that debt is perceptible through the extraordinary poetic and metaphysical proximity of the Florentine's work with that of his Murcian predecessor, Ibn 'Arabi.[6]

Miguel Asin Palacios began in 1920 his impressive catalog of convergences that Dante's work presents with various Islamic antecedents.[7] Since the time of the Spanish Jesuit's intuition and research, historians have dwelled on the proof of the Islamic influence Dante experienced, especially through the tales that report the legend of the nighttime journey (*isrâ'*), followed by the ascension (*mi'râj*) in which the Prophet of Islam goes in one night from Mecca to Jerusalem, before rising up into the heavens to meet the prophets who preceded him and to come as close as possible to the divine presence.[8] As soon as Palacios' book appeared, European resistance was strong; that a founding text of European literature had been shaped by Islamic influence seemed intolerable, prejudicial. Some great thinkers even treated the Spanish scholar as an agitator, since he proffered them this piece of truth at the very instant when all of Italy was preparing for the celebrations that would honor the sixth centenary of Dante.[9]

It seems difficult for a European, even an enlightened one, to admit that the one who constitutes the beginning of the creative historical development opening the way to literary modernity could be under Islamic influence. Yet the example of Dante proves that until the beginning of the fourteenth century, the Mediterranean scene was under the domination of Islamic culture. Even in the recent discussions between Benoît Chantre and Philippe Sollers on Dante, this question remains off limits; it is out of the question. The awareness of political urgency does not even cross the minds of the two interlocutors.[10] Through the mere presence of Islam in France and elsewhere in Europe and in the West, such a question deserved at least to be recalled; it could constitute a pledge and an argument for our time, so rich in "interdependencies." Here is how Sollers reduces the space in which the "sacred poem" is deployed:

> Dante is the diamond of Catholic art. He condenses in his "sacred poem" all the possibilities that this art contains at its height. Before him, the Greeks. After him, modern times. Through him, Latinity is refounded in the "dolce stil nuovo," the Bible and especially the Psalms.[11]

I want to add: "With Dante, and all the way down to you, the repression of Islam."

Saïd thinks it would be more pertinent to think of the crisis and the tension our world is experiencing "in terms of powerful and powerless communities, secular politics of reason and ignorance, universal principles of justice and injustice."[12]

As much as I agree with Saïd when he recalls Islam's contribution to universality, I distance myself from him when he evades the specificity necessary for the understanding of its tendencies, if not its sickness. He evokes the terrible events of September 11:

> From this carefully planned huge massacre, from the horror these suicide attacks inspired by pathological motivations and executed by a small group of militants with disturbed minds, a proof has been offered of Huntington's theory. Instead of seeing these events for what they are, that is to say the forced appropriation of great ideas (I use the term in the sense of "large") by a tiny group of fanatics whipped into a frenzy for criminal aims, international experts, from the ex-Prime Minister of Pakistan, Benazir Bhutto, to the Italian Prime Minister, Silvio Berlusconi, have pontificated on the troubles inherent in Islam.
>
> But why not rather see the parallels, certainly less spectacular in their destructive potential, of Osama bin Laden and his partisans, in sects like the Branch Davidians, or the disciples of the preacher Jim Jones in Guyana, or even the members of Om Shinrikiyo in Japan?[13]

I was not aware of the analysis offered by Bhutto, and I can only condemn the racist and imbecilic suggestions of Silvio Berlusconi, but this does not prevent me from reflecting on "the troubles inherent in Islam" which, unarguably, exist. This book has sought to identify them and to analyze them. I will make one more appeal to the use, as nuanced as possible, of the dialectic art to distinguish between the specific and the universal qualities of Islam. It is even a duty of humankind to have recourse to that, at least to preserve human diversity, or what remains of it, in a time when interference and interdependence contribute to establishing uniformity.

I once knew a venerable sheikh, a great scholar of the religious sciences, a master with a prodigious memory who could effortlessly recite traditional pieces, and who was intimately familiar with the Qur'an, of which he was an expert interpreter. He was full of prudence, all nuance and subtlety in his interpretations when he was in an untroubled state, far from the melancholic agonies of depression and not possessed by the raging excitation of the manic. But if his chemical regulation became unbalanced, and if at the approach of his manic period the poorly prescribed lithium salts didn't succeed at leveling the harshness that sends the patient into crisis, the system of Qur'anic reference changed. Now the sheikh no longer cited the gentle, tolerant verses, full of compassion for those of other beliefs; he was excited by the warlike, fearsome sections of the Qur'an, and began to attack the traces of Jahiliyya and idolatry that still encumber the contemporary era. If he had been allowed to act, he would have destroyed archaeological remains, statues or other traces of some pagan cult of images. In his excitation, he was in the same state that led the Taliban to destroy the Buddhas of Bamiyan as well as the archeological pieces preserved in the museum in Kabul. This portrait should be seen as an allegory that reveals the double face that Qur'anic literature has and that confirms that the sickness of Islam can be seen in the face of the maniac.

From this point of view, the Qur'an is a book similar to the Bible as Voltaire rediscovers it in his *Traité sur la tolérance* (Treatise on toleration).[14] There is in monotheist revelations a warlike, fanatical, violent, frightening aspect. It is this face that the sickness favors. And the sickness spotted by Voltaire in his co-religionists also stems from the manic state: "The great method of diminishing the number of madmen, if some remain, is to abandon that sickness of the mind for the system of Reason, which slowly but infallibly enlightens mankind."[15]

In Islam, this sickness has expressed itself many times throughout history. It has manifested itself twice in the Muslim West, through the two dynasties of Berber origin, in the twelfth and thirteenth centuries: that of the Almoravids, followed by that of the Almohads. The former advocated an elementary, exclusive, frustrated *Malekism* (translators' note: the Islamic legal system of North Africa). They were, in the beginning, enemies of the arts. After conquering Seville, they made enormous pyres of musical instruments; entire libraries fed the flames of their auto-da-fé. Not even the works of Ghâzali (1058–1111) escaped, even though, from the depths of his eastern site, he had praised their military actions, which had broken the spirit of the *Reconquista* and reestablished order and unity in the Islamic realms of the Iberian peninsula. The fanatic zeal of the Almohads is probably the source of the extinction of the native Christianity in the Maghreb, which was ancient and rooted as the Coptic Christianity of Egypt or the Arab, Syrian or Chaldean Christianity of the Near East. But it is always the same aspect of the Qur'an that is invoked by those who enthrone fanaticism and intolerance at the heart of their Islam.

32

THAT IS THE SICKNESS OF ISLAM. It has existed throughout history. It exists now. It is identifiable through the actions and words of the fundamentalists. But I do not confuse Islam with its sickness, even if I can see the undeniable component of it that predisposes it to that sickness. He who diagnoses the sickness prescribes the remedy. If this is not a case of "the remedy is in the sickness," what treatment can be prescribed for Islam?[1] I see a double treatment: It concerns in turn external rationale and internal rationale.

The external rationale involves the integration of Islam into the common scene, and that has to begin by abolishing its separation from the rest of the world. To do this, I recommend doing away with the myth of Ishmael, which has even been reactivated, taken up and developed by Islamophiles like Louis Massignon, who borrows the Sufi notion of *badaliyya* to elaborate his theory of compassion-substitution. In this way, the Christian, like Massignon himself, substitutes himself for the Muslim and lives in his place the nonfulfillment of his belief as a banished person.² Massignon's compassion for the faithful of excluded Islam, exiled and orphaned, descendants of Ishmael, even extended to political involvement.³ Thus he brought his active support to the Algerians and the other colonized peoples struggling for the liberation of their country in the distress of nonrecognition.

This idea of banishment loses its pertinence when we reflect on the time of Islamic hegemony. Entering into sovereignty and its brilliant exercise makes the notion of exclusion invalid, even if this situation engendered the chagrin of a Yehuda Halevi, who remained inconsolable before the triumph of the son of an amorous liaison with a servant who had now become the master subjugating Sara's child. Consider these verses taken from various poems in the *Divan* of the Jewish poet formed in the framework of the Arabic culture of Spain:

> *The son of the slave clothes me in terror*
> *and flings his arrow with his hand high . . .*
> *The kingdom of Hagar rises up and mine is lowered.*
> *Seïr works wonders and the son of my maidservant triumphs . . .*
> *Perhaps he has made you see your enemy*
> *Weakened, brought low—and you, your head high,*
> *Saying to Hagar's son: withdraw your proud hand*
> *From the son of your mistress whom you have vexed? . . .*
> *Revenge my injury so I may no longer be forced*
> *to call my slave, "my master" . . .*
> *My Beloved, You have abandoned me,*
> *caught in the trap of my desolation*
> *You have set free that wild son of a slave . . .*
> *My enemies rejoice, and you have let them ride on my mount.*⁴

The sovereignty reserved for the descendants of these servants seems to have engendered a cry of poetic revolt in this man who called for the confirmation of his people's chosen status by material signs like the return to Zion. His desire was that they would end their captivity in the prison of the Ishmaelites, the *agarim* (children of Hagar), the two names by which the Jews designated the Muslims, referring to the banished one whose descendants knew an imperial destiny, transforming their orphan origin.

This myth of banishment seems confirmed by Western nonrecognition, not only of the historic contribution of Islam, but especially of the pertinence of the *topoi* it offers.[5] I even see a sort of therapeutic necessity for Westerners to work on themselves to get rid of the conscious or unconscious Islamophobia inherited since undergoing the influence of the caricatured, polemical, denigrating and malicious image constructed by the Middle Ages and admirably elucidated by Norman Daniel. For Daniel, the medieval survival of these visions has never ceased, not in the Islam seen by the Age of Enlightenment, or even in the Islam perceived through the criteria of the "scientific" age; none of these methodologies have escaped the prejudices they inherited.[6] Norman Daniel concludes with this thought:

> It is essential that Christians perceive Mohammed as a sacred figure, that is to say, that they see him as the Muslims see him. If they do so, they will share through empathy the prayers and devotions of others. They should "agree to suspend their skepticism," according to Coleridge's phrase (*a willing suspension of disbelief*).[7]

This recommendation goes beyond the position of Massignon, and is like the one, for instance, that the Dominican monks adopt when visiting or staying at the Institute for Arab Studies, which they own, in Cairo. Emilio Platti explains, legitimizes and puts into practice such a position. He approaches Islam as an authentic belief in which he has discussions with the religion of the other, without trying either to evade or deform or reduce or neutralize the other's difference. When he recalls the tendencies and dangers that threaten the Islam of today, one almost has the feeling that his critique comes from within, so well has he been able to keep the other company in his truth.[8]

To this gradual progression toward the recognition of Islam among religious people, I will add the importance of such a recognition in the secular fields of art, poetry, philosophy. The poetics of the in-between, of the interstitial, of crossing over, which is natural for me, should be extended to the field of Islamic culture and should be the poetics of everyone.[9] This integration of the Islamic legacy into the sources of thought and creation (just as much as Greek, Latin, Hebrew, Japanese, Chinese and Indian sources) should be an additional warranty of the constitution of a community that would be world culture, whose products would be creative works, situated beyond traditions but without interrupting dialogue with them. Each person should choose the ancients who suit him or her, so that in the adventure of the new, the living can catch hold of the dead.

Goethe was already persuaded in his day that a universal literature (*Weltliteratur*) was being born and that its coming should be hastened.[10] To this end, he thought of the relationship between the specific and the universal. It is within each particularity that the universal will shine and be reflected through the national and individual mirror. Each of us should appropriate the poetic works that realize such an aim, whatever our language or nation might be. We must learn to know the particularities of each language, and of each nation, for it is through them that the exchange works and is realized in all its amplitude. Thus we will reach reciprocal mediation and recognition. Hence the role of translation in this poetics of interval and crossing. Translation is what will serve as an intermediary between the languages. On this question, Goethe was prophetic, for in our day, in the world tribe of poetic creation, often the poet attributes his talent and his mastery to the act of translating.

> Every translator should be seen in the same way: he tries to be the mediator of this spiritually universal activity and undertakes to promote reciprocal exchange. For whatever one may say about the insufficiency of translations, translation is and will remain one of the worthiest and most important activities in universal world exchange.

The Koran says: "God gave each people a prophet speaking in its own language."[11] Thus each translator is a prophet among his people.[12]

Goethe wrote his *West-Östlicher Diwan* (1814–1818) in the perspective of this *Weltliteratur*, which would thereafter have its source outside Europe, in emulation of the pre-Islamic Arabian poets whom he began to know in 1783 through their English translation by W. Jones. The German poet appreciated Persian lyricism, to which he was initiated by Herder in 1792, before coming to study Hafiz (circa 1325–circa 1390), even identifying with him after becoming enthusiastic over reading the full translation of his *Divan* by Hammer (1812–1813). Goethe lived his hegira toward the East, his expatriation toward the poetry of Islam and the ambivalence it maintains by singing of divine love with the techniques of carnal love, by singing the praises of spiritual drunkenness by means of profane, bacchic poetry.

> *I want, in the baths and taverns,*
> *O Saint Hafiz, to think of you;*
> *When the beloved raises her veil*
> *And from her ambered hair*
> *Sweet perfumes emanate.*
> *Yes, may the poet's murmur of love*
> *Arouse desire even among the houris.*[13]

In this migration to the East, the sixty-year-old poet was transformed into a new youth, finding in the company of Islam a confirmation of his sensuality and of the Spinozism of his youth.[14] One can hear surprising Islamic echoes through his deism, and the pulverization of the divine in the world, in that immanence of the transcendent theorized by Ibn 'Arabi, which profoundly impregnates the Persian lyricism that the poet from Weimar adopted.

One single aspect seemed insurmountable to the German poet, however: the despotism of God in the Islamic interpretation of him, and the representation of God as embodying political authority. Goethe speaks of this in the notes and essays that accompany the volume of poems in his *West-Eastern Divan:*

> But what will never enter into the Western spirit is the spiritual and bodily servility toward a lord and master that stems from the most ancient times, when kings first took the place of God. . . .
>
> What Westerner could find it bearable that the Easterner not only strikes the earth nine times with his forehead, but offers his head for the king's pleasure to use as he likes?[15]

Finally with this remark we find Western incompatibility with Eastern despotism, the first expression of which dates back to Aeschylus' *Persians* (472 B.C.), a tragedy based politically on the opposition between the acceptance of the yoke of servitude by the Persian subject and the insubordination in the name of freedom that animates the Athenian citizen. This opposition is eloquently expressed in the form of an allegory in the dream of Queen Atossa, wife of Darius and mother of Xerxes, the two emperors involved in the Persian wars, and who both experienced defeat, one at Marathon (490 B.C.), the other at Salamis (480 B.C.):

> *I had the impression that two women, in beautiful clothes,*
> *one arrayed in Persian robes,*
> *the other in Dorian robes, came into my sight,*
> *surpassing by far the women of today in stature*
> *and of faultless beauty; they were sisters from*
> *the same blood; one lived in Greece, having received it*
> *by lot*
> *as ancestral land, and the other in a barbarous land.*
> *I seemed to see them showing me*
> *strife between them; and my son, learning of*

this,

tried to contain and appease it. He harnessed them
to the yoke of a chariot, passing girths
around their necks. One, with this gear, became
proud as a citadel,
and her mouth in the reins was easy to command;
but the other struggled; with both hands she tears
the harness from the chariot, pulling it towards her roughly,
without a bit, and breaks the yoke in half.[16]

We would have to wait for Louis Aragon's *Le Fou d'Elsa* to find a work that takes its inspiration from Islamic culture as extensively and intensively as Goethe's *Divan*.[17] In this polyphonic book, which is not just a poem, as it is called on the cover, Aragon takes up the theme of the madness of loving. This theme, invented by the Arabs at the end of the seventh century through the legend of the madman from Leyla, in *Laylâ and Majnûn*, was illustrated in Europe by Tristan and Yseult, Romeo and Juliet, Werther, and even Nerval and Breton.[18] With this book, Aragon honored the Arab vocation of culture, and his arch literary gesture has a political reach, since the poet-novelist made this work a gift from the French language to the Arab aspect of Algeria. Aragon had conducted an erudite investigation into Arabic culture before writing his book, at the end of the 1950s and the beginning of the 1960s, at the very instant when Algeria was covered in blood and when Camus knew that the outcome he dreamed of (reconciling all the native constituents of Algerian soil) demanded first "the recognition of the Arabic personality," denied in Algeria by more than a century of colonial servitude.[19] With *Le Fou d'Elsa*, Aragon realized this "recognition" in the work itself.

Such an experience also reveals that the Islamic corpus introduced into French literature, as well as the other great European languages, is dense enough to offer the poet an inexhaustible source of inspiration. It does not necessarily require mastery of the languages of Islam to enter the profundities, the secrets, the particularities of this culture and to exploit the devices and connections that enriched the European poet's own work. Aragon showed in his book an extraordinary capacity for assimilation and an amazing mimetic force that engaged him with the path of identification. It is the poetic and metaphysical Arab and Islamic code that gives structure to the work, and that is confronted with allusions to other places and centuries (from Russia, from the myth of Grenada and from the Spain that was formed inside the French literature, with Chateaubriand and Barrès, etc.). Grenada, just before its downfall, is the place where the poetic fiction unfolds. By opening the controversy about the future (a tense the Arabic language ignores), the question of the Granadan future joins the great queries of the twentieth century, between twilight melancholy (the theme of the fall, of old age) and the exaltation of resistance. With such varied techniques, Aragon achieved a work that honors the poetics of the heterogeneity engendered by crossing borders and circulating among languages, cultures, places and centuries.

Opening up to the subject of Islam attracted that thinker and philosopher who wanted to integrate a part of Islam into his materials. This is what Jacques Derrida tried to do in his teaching in Ehess, during the public lectures devoted to the theme of the foreigner and of hospitality. There, he put forward the need to enroll in an Islamic-Judeo-Christian perspective. When he analyzes the philoxenia of Abraham, he draws inspiration from the studies of Louis Massignon to integrate Islamic issues into his field of thought. The publication of part of these lectures bears witness to this contribution, which integrates the notions of sacred hospitality and of the sworn word elaborated on by Massignon after growing familiar with the texts and people of Islam.[20] Finally, Jean-Luc Nancy is also eager to work with a perspective that integrates Islam into his reflections on monotheism. Alluding to the events of September 11, he contrasts Huntington's "war of civilizations" with the term that irrevocably annuls it, "civil war":

The present state of the world is not a war of civilizations. It is a civil war: it is the internecine war of a city, of a civility, of a community spreading to the ends of the world and, because of this, to the extreme of their own concepts. At its extreme, a concept is broken, a distorted visage swells out, a gaping hole appears.

Nor is it a war of religions, or rather every war called religious war is a war inherent to monotheism, a religious scheme from the West and within it, from a division that spreads, again, past borders to extremes: to the East from the West, until it cracks and gapes wide in the very heart of the divine. Thus the West will turn out to have been only the exhaustion of the divine, in all the forms of monotheism, whether it be exhaustion by atheism or by fanaticism.[21]

And finally I come to political integration. Here, I am speaking to America, which felt the shock of September 11 and which uses power that authorizes it to be the judge of the universe, if it decides to apply the universal principle of justice. I speak to America, even if I know that such an address risks being useless, vain. I see three urgencies here. Two concern the recurring issues that are the state of Iraq and the Palestinian question. Here the politics of the double standard triumphs, by which the arrogance of injustice is expressed, which in turn feeds the rage of resentful men. When I witness current events unfolding as I write this, when I hear the suggestions made by responsible Americans, always partisan in the positions they express about the burning issues that reach us from the Near East, I tell myself that even the tragedy of September 11 was not enough to open the eyes of America and enlighten its discernment about the reasons for the hatred it arouses. Why doesn't this America act to reestablish the sovereignty of Iraq, by putting an end to its leaders who have held the country hostage, by freeing the Iraqi people from the yoke they are under, and by proposing a Marshall Plan that would reconstruct the resources of a nation that could then become an ally of reason and good sense?

Why doesn't America use its clout to find a reasonable resolution between Israel and Palestine, in the logic of two sovereign states, whose territories could be defined by international law recognizing the legitimacy of Israel with the borders drawn up before June 1967, and the sovereignty of Palestine as a viable and continuous geographical entity, with Jerusalem as a shared capital? Why not act to compel the Palestinians to deny the right of Palestinian refugees to return to Israel, while legitimizing their inclusion with the Palestinian state, along with financial compensation for their losses in Israel? Why not make Israel dismantle and abandon the settlements, as numerous in Gaza as they are in the West Bank? Why doesn't America use its influence to make Israel realize the moral wrongs, the damages and the harm done to the Palestinians? Why not convince Israel of the necessity to recognize that its foundation was the origin of Palestinian misery, and to repent in its turn? Do we need to recall that before the creation of the state of Israel, the same land was inhabited by another people, which knew it as their home? About this situation, the inventor of modern Hebrew, Eliezer Ben-Yehuda, wrote in September 1881, upon disembarking at Jaffa:

> I must admit that this first meeting with our Ishmael cousins was far from joyful. A depressing feeling of fear filled my soul, as if I were before a huge, menacing wall. I saw that they felt they were citizens of this country, land of my ancestors, and I their descendant, I was returning to this land as a stranger, son of a foreign land, of a foreign people. . . . I was suddenly crushed, overwhelmed with regrets rising up from the depths of my being. Perhaps my whole enterprise was vain and hollow, perhaps my dream of a rebirth of Israel on the ancestral land was only a dream that had no place in reality.[22]

Clearly, it was the realization of the Zionist dream that created the Palestinian nightmare. This is a truth that will have to make its destined way into Israel's consciousness.

How is it, moreover, that no one brings up the troubled past of Ariel Sharon, implicated in a war crime, since his responsibility was recognized in the Sabra and Chatila massacres by the investigation conducted by the democratic processes of the state of Israel itself? By what divine power is he protected, so that no political or moral authority dare raise this deed of his earlier life, one that so dishonors and disqualifies him?

It is the exercise of injustice in impunity that feeds hatred and horrifying terrorism and that remains the weapon of the impoverished, the weak, those who have exhausted the resources of the law. Add to this disaster a demonization of the Palestinian, the Arab, the Muslim, revealing a racism as devastating as the new Arab anti-Semitism whose practices and pernicious effects I reported earlier. One of the highest religious authorities of Israel, one of its most prestigious rabbis, maintained racist anti-Arab ideas that were just as reprehensible as the anti-Semitic schemings of the sheikh from al-Azhar.

Israelis should realize that their country was created at the time when Islam suffered the most unfavorable balance of power in its history. By coming into existence, Israel abrogated a legitimacy at least thirteen hundred years old (if you take away the century's interruption when political authority in the Holy Land was exercised by the Frankish kingdom of Jerusalem). Israelis should recognize that such a divestiture can only inflict a deep wound. Voltaire had explained that one of the rare "reasonable intolerances" he could imagine would be what would ensue if the people of Israel decided to reconstruct their state on the lands that the Bible attributes to them, for that would lead to an immense disorder. The fulfillment of such a plan would have conflicted with the "more than a thousand-year-old Mohammedan usurpation":

[The Jews] would necessarily be obliged to destroy all the Turks, which goes without saying: for the Turks own the country of the Hittites, the Jebusites, the Amorites, Girgashites, Hevites, Araceans, Cineans, Hamateans, Samarians: all these peoples were put under a curse; their country, which was more than twenty-five leagues long, was given to the Jews by a number of successive covenants; they should come back into their property, which Mohammedans have usurped for more than a thousand years. But if the Jews reasoned thus today, it is clear that we could respond only by condemning them to the galleys. These are just about the only cases when intolerance seems reasonable.[23]

But it is true that Voltaire was writing at a time when the balance of power did not reduce Islam to powerlessness.

The third political problem that deserves to be addressed is one that concerns the alliance between Saudi Arabia and the United States. An urgent debate should be opened on the nature of this alliance. Why are such privileged ties not dependent on the political obligations of freedom and democracy? How can the United States treat as a friend a country whose women are demeaned to the point that they are not even allowed to drive? How long will the United States refuse to consider Wahhabism, which in its fanatical version of the truth is implicated morally in the events of September 11 that struck the heart of America?

How can it be that the main adviser to the American president on Islamic questions, the lawyer David Forte, a professor at Cleveland-Marshall College, breathes not a word against Wahhabism?[24] Perhaps because he himself seems fascinated by extreme religion, and because he secretly admires the state of things in Wahhabite Arabia, out of some fundamentalist affinity, given the closeness of his sensibility with that of the most conservative circles of American Catholicism. Each time he deals with an anti-American Saudi, such as Osama bin Laden or one of the numerous Saudis counted among the terrorists of September 11, each time he criticizes one of them, he denounces the man's "Kharijite" tendencies. Why refer to that vanished sect of earliest Islam, which was in fact a paragon of fanaticism and violence, prescribing *takfir*, excommunication, at the least sign of halfheartedness or deviance? The criticism that unearths Kharijism to attack the fanatical tendencies of present-day fundamentalism was advanced in order to denounce the strictly legalistic tendencies of someone like Mawdûdi, who excludes from the Islamic community whoever does not perfectly apply the law modeled on the life of the Prophet and those of his companions most sanctified by tradition.[25]

The Americans will have to explain themselves to the Saudis; they will have to tell them, eye to eye, that Wahhabism in itself is enough to lead to murderous fanaticism. To the Saudi official who thinks, "We Saudis want to modernize and not necessarily westernize ourselves," a phrase Huntington reports to illustrate his thesis, the Americans should dare to say, "You're free to act as you like, but don't be surprised if you engender monsters with such policies, all the more dangerous since they are sure of their innocence. Osama bin Laden is not an accident; he carries to its ultimate consequences the Wahhabism in which he was educated."[26]

Finally, I will briefly discuss a few internal reasons, although an exhaustive discussion of them lies outside the scope of this book. The first remedy for the sickness of Islam concerns the necessity of returning to a profound awareness of the polemics, controversies and debates that have nourished the tradition. To struggle against forgetting requires a labor of anamnesis. It is important to articulate the reconstitution of meaning (starting with medieval traces and survival) with a modern critical awareness so that the liberty of a plural, conflicting language, enduring disagreement with civility, can be established.

This critical attitude should embrace the legal question. To shape a law adapted to the advances of modern times, the Tunisian lawyer Mohammed Charfi, commenting on the case of the reforming jurist in Tunisia, recommends using *talqîf,* the makeshift form of fixing things invented and used by the fundamentalist reformers of the nineteenth century, Jamâl ad-Dîn Afghâni and Mohammed 'Abduh:

> For each rule inherited from Muslim law and judged today to be inhuman or ill-adapted to our time because it is contrary to the rights of man or to the principles of freedom and equality, one should try to go back to its origins to find a flaw. If it is attached to a *hadîth,* one should verify if it is authentic, and try to reinterpret it. This is

not dishonest research, in the sense that one will not make the verse say the opposite of what it says, or introduce any doubt where the *hadîth* has strong chances of being authentic. But neither is this an entirely objective research without *a priori*. On the contrary, the researcher has already fixed an objective for himself, and tries to find the historical or semantic arguments to achieve it. He does not seek to understand the religion in itself, but rather to establish in it the justification of the new norm, which he thinks is fairer, and which he wants to establish. Without being erroneous or subjective, this is a goal-directed research.[27]

Moreover, it is up to the Islamic states to rethink their teaching policies, in order to rid educational programs of the prevailing fundamentalism. Diffuse Wahhabism contaminates consciousnesses through the teaching transmitted in schools and now supported by television. In this conspicuous area, we have the valuable, practical precedent methodically thought out by its promoter: the elaborate reform conducted by the same Mohammed Charfi, who was minister of national education (from 1989 to 1994) in his country, Tunisia:

Teaching in Arab-Islamic countries is by nature conducive to the rise of fundamentalism. It needs to be purged of all aims contrary to the rights of man and to the foundations of the modern State. With a radical reform of the educational system . . . the school could, in the near future, contribute to curing society of religious extremism.[28]

33

NOW THAT I'VE COME TO THE end of this book, written in urgency, I would like to enrich the "testimonies against intolerance" collected by Voltaire in his *Traité sur la tolérance* with two verses from the Qur'an:

No coercion in religion.[1]

Râzî comments on this: The interpretation (*ta'wil*) of this sentence is that God did not construct the question of faith on force (*ijbâr*) and violence (*qasr*), but based it on the possibility of persuasion (*tamakkun*) and free choice (*ikhtiyâr*). God made clear and obvious the path that leads to faith. When all the ways to convince are exhausted in the Book, only coercion remains to lead the hesitant to the truth. But recourse to constraint is unacceptable: The use of violence annuls the testing (*imtihân*) and effort prompted by assiduous application (*taklîf*) of the rules. To illustrate the line of argument that he borrows from a previous authority (al-Qaffâl), Râzi cites other Qur'anic verses: "May he who wants to, believe, and may he who wants to, remain unbelieving"; "If your Lord had wanted it, all those who people the Earth would believe. Is it up to you to force people to believe?"[2] Râzi recalls that constraint is exercised as soon as the Muslim says to the unbeliever: "Convert or I kill you." This verse sheds light on the right of the people of the Book and of the Manicheans. If they agree to pay the tax on minorities (*jizya*), they earn the protection of the law. Legal advisors (*fuqahâ'*) differ in their opinions as to whether this verse applies to all the unbelievers, or only the people of the Book.[3] In any case, the interpretation of this verse authorizes some metaphysicians or theologians of Islam to suspend the notion of jihad.

And here is the second verse:

Discuss with people of the Book only in the finest manner—except with those among them who are unrighteous. Say: "We believe in what was revealed to us and in what was revealed to you. Our God as well as yours is unique. To him we submit."[4]

Such a verse is explicit enough; it gives Islam an absolute legitimacy to belong to the ethical and metaphysical sphere of monotheism, which should be expressed by the notion of Islamic-Judeo-Christianity. Allah is not the name of the God of Islam; it is the Arab word that designates God, the same God that is at the basis of monotheism in its formal, cultural and symbolic ternary variety. The power of this verse imposed the peaceful way on the fundamentalist Mawdûdi, the way of civility implied by the courtesy of persuasion and recourse to words as opposed to weapons. This peaceful recommendation was of course rejected by his successors.[5] The expression *bi'llatî hiya ahsan,* which I have translated as "in the finest manner," becomes an idiomatic phrase in Arabic, and is amply used in current language to signify respect for courtesy in any dispute or controversy.

It is this aspect of the Qur'an of which the fanatics of Islam, sick with their suicidal fervor full of hatred, should be reminded. Several times we have evoked Voltaire, who calls for good sense. The master from Ferney calls on reason, which he conceives as the radical remedy against the mental sickness of fanaticism. I would like to confirm this recourse to reason to restrain the monotheists' summons to the sickness of intolerance and war in the name of God. Ernest Renan too invokes reason as remedy for evil:

> If religions divide men, reason brings them closer. . . . There is only one single reason. The unity of the human spirit is the great, consoling result that comes from the peaceful clash of ideas, when one puts aside the opposing claims of so-called supernatural revelations. The covenant of the good minds of the whole Earth against fanaticism and superstition is on the surface the act of an imperceptible minority; at bottom, it is the only covenant that lasts.[6]

For the sake of this thought, I pardon his racism, his essentialist vision of languages and symbolic systems, his hierarchy of expression and imagination; I pardon his wanderings of another era, for he also helped me understand the chimera represented by Pan-Arabism as well as by Pan-Islamism. His pamphlet *Qu'est-ce qu'une nation?* (What is a nation?) reminded me that the nation is founded not on linguistic unity, not on the community of faith or on geographical continuity or the sharing of history. It is based on the single wish to be together.[7] It is this wish that made me choose the French community, where my foreign name is pronounced with sounds amputated, where I continue to maintain my Islamic genealogy and to cross it with my other, European genealogy. Thus the inherited and the chosen are combined inside one single being.

And as much as I work to make manifest Islamic allusion in my poetic and literary work as well as in my teaching or my presence in the heart of the city, I am still surprised by those who, invoking their Islam, demand that the French Republic change, as the representative of about thirty Islamic associations suggests:

> Just as Islam is asked to change, so should secularity change, for today secularity cannot be content with a definition according to

which it restricts the religious to the private sphere. The return of the religious is general, and it questions the whole social sphere.[8]

To this unreasonable claim, I will answer with a Talmudic precept that should serve as a teaching for the recognition of the Islamic presence in France: *Dina dé-malkhuta dina:* "The law of the State takes precedence over the law of the Torah."[9]

Finally, I would like to take a definitive stance as coming from the solidarity of the community, as an instinctual reflex, a principle of survival and existing, and would recall the old precept that Eratosthenes taught Alexander. Disapproving of the division of humanity into Greeks and Barbarians, the former as friends and the latter as enemies, he urges changing the criterion so as to distinguish instead between virtue and dishonesty: "Many Greeks are base people, and many Barbarians have a refined civilization."[10] And I am happy to find an Islamic formulation of this precept, the echo of which I grasp from the pen of the divine Ibn 'Arabi:

How many beloved saints there are in the synagogues and churches!
How many enemies full of hatred in the rows of mosques![11]

PARIS-DAMASCUS
OCTOBER 19–DECEMBER 9, 2001

Afterword:
War Chronicles

I

Paris, March 21, 2003

It's war in Iraq. In the universal spirit of perpetual peace proposed by Kant, the first Gulf War could have been legally and morally legitimized, since the dictator of Baghdad had broken one of the basic rules that protect perpetual peace: didn't he decide to abolish the borders of a constituted State? But what reasons are there for the present war, which is spreading flames on the shores of the Tigris? The reasons invoked by American power focus on the liberation of the Iraqi people from the yoke imposed on them by their despot, and on the actualization of a democratic model that would save the entire region and the local culture which seems to be either incompatible with it, or at least refractory toward it.

But when we deepen our investigation, we become aware of a fear that such reasons constitute an alibi to conceal a less avowable intention. Without having to go far back in time to find texts written by any of the neoconservatives whose ideas guide the actions of the American government, without leafing through the writings emanating from that sphere of influence active since the 1970s, we will content ourselves with glancing over the ninety-page document made public in September 2000—before the arrival of George W. Bush in the White House. The twenty-eight tenors of neoconservativism took part in drafting it, including Lewis Libby, director of the team that surrounds Vice-President Dick Cheney, and Paul Wolfowitz, second-in-command in the Pentagon and to the Secretary of Defense, Donald Rumsfeld. This document—written for the neoconservative think-tank Project for a New American Century (PNAC)—is entitled *Rebuilding America's Defenses: Strategy, Forces and Resources for a New Century*.[1]

This report incites political authority to act so that American hegemony will last "as far as possible into the future" (p. i). To accomplish such an aim, the conditions of a "global *Pax Americana*" (p. 1) must be created. Thus it is important to "discourage any attempt on the part of advanced industrial nations to pose a threat to our leadership or even to aspire to play a more ample regional or global role." And to reach such a goal, an invasion of Iraq is recommended so that absolute control of the region can be assured—by more completely controlling the politics of oil and reinforcing the local hegemony of the surest ally, Israel. The realization of such a project is one of the conditions necessary for universal governance. The United States, during the decades to come, will be summoned to play a central role in order to guarantee regional security in the Gulf. Thus it seems obvious to us that the still-unresolved conflict with Iraq provides an ideal justification. The need for a substantial presence of American forces in the Gulf "would endure even should Saddam pass from the scene" (p. 17).

Reading such a document reveals to us at least a part of the rationale that motivates the American war in Iraq. Note first of all that September 11 was not the instigator of this war. It was only its accelerator. You will then note that the American government has gone from being pragmatic to becoming ideological. That is to say, it is acting so that reality conforms to its vision. The American action is far from being improvised: it is ordered by a concept and intends to submit reality to its own a priori vision. The American theoreticians of neoconservatism were formed by the disciples of Leo Strauss—one of the great masters of political philosophy, the foundations of which, still able to be actualized, he derives from Plato, Aristotle, al-Farabi, etc. But today's American politics do not seem consistent with Straussian theory, which aims to establish the norm on the basis of natural law. America's actions recall rather the adversary of Strauss's theory, Carl Schmitt, who thinks that it is the executive decision that establishes the norm. I can readily perceive a possible link to Leo Strauss when the American neoconservatives intend their action to promote the civilization denied by that barbarism to which Saddam's dictatorship, founded on the Ba'ath ideology, is likened: this ideology follows Fascism and Communism (along with Islamism [a term for various Islamic fundamentalisms—Trans.]) in that resistance to democracy decried by Strauss.[2] Perhaps they are trying to equate the horizon of civilization and democracy with that of natural law. Still, when the Americans unilaterally impose on Iraq the norm thus recognized, they cannot avoid decisionism [Schmitt's term for executive decision made without consultation or deliberation—Trans.]. Through the conceptual premises that led to the Iraq war, should we perceive a theoretical confusion where the phantoms of Leo Strauss and Carl Schmitt clash? These two enemies from long ago did, however, treat each other with a certain form of respect, as witnessed by a correspondence that, although intermittent, was unbroken by their antagonistic involvement.

By taking on this confusion, though, we notice that the reference to the norm equating natural law with civilization and democracy becomes blurred when we learn that the other master they value is none other than Reinhold Niebuhr who, in *Moral Man and Immoral Society*, studied European totalitarianism in the 1920s and '30s, and concluded by rejecting naïve pacifism and inciting action in politics in the name of what he calls "Christian absolutism." If that is the case, every norm, every civilization, every natural law can be based only on its own cultural assumptions. No transcendence can be envisaged to construct a universal that could be shared by aspirants from another tradition. Islam, as an absolute that does not wholly correspond to the Judeo-Christian absolute, proves incapable of being assimilated with the norm emanating from natural law or from civilization or democracy. It would then be appropriate to subdue it by a decision of war. It is within this deadly crossroads that the two reductions of universality meet, that of the Judeo-Christian neoconservatives and that of the Islamists. Ignoring the challenging effort necessary for the encounter, this reasoning calls on humanity (to the world's misfortune) to do its utmost to play universality against universality. With the extraordinary difference between the two forces in plain sight, we will then be led to witness, as impotent voyeurs, the obscene spectacle of war between "intelligent" weapons and sacrificial terrorism.

And there is more. Or perhaps less. By invoking the liberation of a people from an abominable dictatorship and the advent of democracy to Iraq, the United States clothes hegemonic reasoning with a moral task. That is precisely the mechanism of colonial discourse illustrated notably by Jules Ferry at the end of the nineteenth century in his answers to the attacks of Clemenceau and the radicals on colonial policies.[3] Jules Ferry will have us believe that "the duty of civilization entrains a right of intervention." He says especially: "Superior races have a right with regard to inferior races [...] because they have a duty. They have the duty to civilize inferior races." Now when even the notion of race no longer belongs to usable language, the idea thus expressed and the mechanism in which it is operative are still current.

Thus it is clear that the American war in Iraq—as incredible as "shock and awe" are—refers back to an earlier form of discourse. It establishes a regression that leads us back to the colonial era. But this reference is neither in the vocation nor in the "essence" of American politics, whose hegemonic accession after 1945 was active in the process of de-colonialization and in the collapse of colonial empires.

Thomas Friedman, the famous editorialist for the *New York Times*, himself a conservative and proponent of the current war, is aware of the risks that such a regression brings. He is anxious that it not undermine the spirit that presides over American politics. In one of his editorials that appeared in the first half of March, he implicitly says this by recalling an anecdote that takes on the aspect of an apologue.[4] When Roosevelt, returning from Yalta, expressed his wish in 1944 to meet Ibn Saud during his stop in the Mideast, Ibn Saud asked two questions of his guest, who had been presented to him as the man who commands the most powerful country in the world: Does he believe in God? Does he possess colonies? Those were the questions posed by the unsophisticated Bedouin leader, king of the Wahhabite State, which he had founded twelve years earlier. This signifies that the archaic being did not lack political intuition. It goes without saying that Roosevelt's answers—first yes, then no—contributed to sealing the American-Saudi alliance, at least until its weakening by the attacks that made the twin towers of New York vanish and that destroyed a wing of the Pentagon.

II

Paris, March 27, 2003

In the way that Hegel thought about Napoleon's effect on Europe, I am convinced that the countries of Islam cannot avoid benefiting from pressure from outside (even if it is violent and even war-producing) towards reforming and adapting profoundly to the demands of the century. Faced with Napoleonic conquest, Hegel could go beyond the national sentiment and patriotic invocation that animated someone like Kleist, who called on Prussia to get back on its feet and fight the foreign emperor who came to invade their country. The German philosopher saw further than his compatriot the writer, reckoning that the cannons of the French conqueror were contributing to the spread of new ideas heralding the modern State that the peoples of the continent were awaiting.

Similarly, many Arabic historians figure that the expedition to Egypt led by Bonaparte at the very end of the eighteenth century constituted the electroshock the drowsy Orient needed to awaken to the truth of the time and to the ideas illuminating the technical and political transformations that were in the process of shattering the old order of things. Beyond its imperialist premises, the Nile sojourn of the future emperor revealed to Egypt and to the region the distance that kept widening and hierarchically separating Europe and Islam, distributing opposing roles to them, granting to some the privilege of power and hegemony, and to others the affront of weakness and submission.

After the two centuries that witnessed in succession colonial domination, decolonialization, and a return to sovereignty, it seems that the drama in which Islam and the West confront each other has not changed its nature. And the events of September 11 have again spectacularly confirmed both the persistence, if not the aggravation, of the problems that Islam is confronting, and the necessity to find a remedy for them. Faced with the immensity of the harm done in its name, Islam is transformed into a question that every human being has the duty to focus on. This is the urgent task that must concern the humanity of Islam as well as European or American humanity. Thus I have the innermost conviction that Islam cannot resolve its problems or extricate itself from its shackles unless it is *also* changed into a Western question. For such a course to take place, isn't it time finally to take Islam seriously?

Such an urgency was already called for in 1919, when, emerging from the Great War, the most firmly established Islamic power, the Ottoman Empire, had just been defeated, when the Caliphate was heading toward its abolition, when the quasi-integrality of the peoples of Islam was undergoing foreign domination. During the sessions when the Treaty of Versailles was being developed, a meeting was devoted to Islam through the initiative of M.E.S. Montagu, Secretary of State for India; among the Muslim invitees asked to speak with President Wilson, Clemenceau, Lloyd George and Baron Sonnino, Yussof Ali ends by concluding: "*It seems that sometimes Europe forgets Islam and all that it represents. It is our duty to say that it still exists, and that if its interests and its feelings are neglected, it will be a source of great dangers for the future."*[5]

Aren't the events of September 11 the distant effect of this negligence, which continues to persist, and yet which was expressed at a time when Islam was anemic? What other catastrophe should we wait for so that Islam may finally be internalized by everyone as a fateful question? One cannot form an alliance with Islam, one cannot contribute to its appeasement, except through such a concern, not just to separate Islam from Islamism and despotism, but also to mobilize Islam to act against the demons of fundamentalism and dictatorship. It is in this common war against Islamists and dictators that Western-Islamic solidarity can be contemplated. And it is in this perspective that I would have imagined the exercise of external pressure, of Western war, on Islam. But for such a war to gain its efficacy, there would first have had to be a policy that established confidence between Islam and the West. Such a confidence cannot be shared without the application of justice, a pledge that connects its moral horizon to political and military action. And it is in the resolution of the Israeli-Palestinian conflict that such a moral earnest could have been manifest. Only the intervention of a third party could have cleanly decided the tragedy that the two competing legitimacies are establishing. And the third party expressly designated to impose the division of territory through the solution of creating two viable states protected by "sure and recognized borders" is none other than the United States.

But September 11, instead of imposing such an obvious fact, had the opposite effect. It inverted priorities. It led to the consecration of the Sharon point of view in the heart of the White House through the influence of neoconservative ideologists. Do you know that the adviser to the American president who is in charge of Middle-Eastern affairs is none other than Elliot Abrams, who was one of the people who directed and guided Benyamin Netanyahu, the Israeli prime minister determined to undermine, if not paralyze, the Oslo agreement, inspired and supervised by the Democrat administration? The most radical partisans of the Likud dictate politics in Washington. They are the ones who sold the idea of war against Iraq as a first priority to resolve the problems of

Islam, inviting Islam to the feast of democracy and ridding it of the unbearable alternative between secular military dictatorship and Islamist totalitarianism. But good sense would have been satisfied if the Americans had begun to resolve with authority the Israeli-Palestinian conflict, thereby making credible the utopian aim of its war against Iraq.

I personally discovered that it could not be that way after meeting Christopher Caldwell, in the beginning of June 2002. (In the article where he recounts our meeting, he attributes "brio and courage" to me for *The Malady of Islam*—but he also thinks me ingenuous for defending a "dreamed Islam" contradicting "actual Islam": as if a conceivably united Islam were in his eyes a utopia that could not be rescued from its fundamentalist fate. The blurring of such a nuance forces Islam to be equated with Islamism, to be reduced, with no other possibility, to that inassimilable part that, as a last resort, understands only the discourse of war.)[6] After an hour of conversation, I told my interlocutor that I was surprised by the American misinterpretation of September 11, as it becomes manifest in the partisan and unjust conduct of the Israeli-Palestinian conflict (we had just experienced the nightmare of Jenin). At that point he became angry and answered that the absolute support of the United States for the present Israeli policy is not negotiable. Faced with such a refusal of dialogue, our conversation ended abruptly. When we realize that Christopher Caldwell is one of the associates of William Kristol, founder of the *Weekly Standard*, the quasi-official megaphone for neoconservativism, we grasp the fanaticism blinding this ideological tendency that has established itself in the Pentagon and the White House. Moreover, it is Christopher Caldwell, as one responsible for French affairs in the neoconservative milieu, who led the polemics awakened by the French opposition to the war against Iraq, a campaign of dubious taste that led him to suggest an inept rewriting of the *Marseillaise*.

How can we detect some positive future created by the war that the English and Americans are now waging in Iraq? I repeat: We have been given no believable pledge that this war has the aim either of liberating the Iraqi people from the dictatorship it has undergone for ages or of bringing democracy to Mesopotamia. I demonstrated in the preceding chronicle how such a stated intention constitutes a mask that hides the true aim revealed in the documents written by the neo-conservatives. What we are witnessing actually shows the action of a partisan, hegemonic force blinded by an ideological belief aggravated by the fanaticism established by the revival of religious motivation by the very person who embodies supreme authority in America. Instead of experiencing a violence intended to bring the new idea (democracy) that the states and peoples of the Near East need, we are experiencing the effect of a violence that will revive the worst of Islam. It is as if the arrogance and conceit of neoconservative fundamentalism were destined to strengthen the fateful terror of Islamist fundamentalism through the intolerable violence of their weapons. Violence of weapons fanned by the "pornographic" way the images diffused by Arabic satellite televisions are portrayed, new arrivals in the semiography that does not shrink from the effects of the close-up and of wide-angle shots, lingering indecently over the bleeding, mutilated bodies of the innocent dead or wounded, disfigured forever, a way of filming that urgently calls for the development of an ethical charter that would oversee the iconography of information during armed conflict.

The present war cannot be equated with Napoleon's, admired by Hegel. It does not divide Islam to incite it to banish its demons and fight its fantasies. I fear it will lead Islam to regroup around an anti-Western hatred in a hysterical reflex destined to maintain misunderstanding of the least intelligent kind.

III

Damascus, April 3, 2003

In Proust's *Le Temps retrouvé* (Time regained), the war of 1914–18 is constantly introduced into the fiction, both as a sequence of events that touch the characters (Robert de Saint-Loup, Gilberte's husband, lost his life in it) and as a subject of discussion between the narrator and his friends on the science or art of battles, on the relationship between strategy and politics, culture and war, destruction and art, on patriotism or philoxenia in a time of hostilities, on the way in which critics and journalists report feats of arms without bothering about analyses that lead to predictions that the outcome belies, none of which induces repentance in their authors, to whom Proust grants the circumstance of "sincere forgetfulness" (this phrase seems to be a constant that animates all chroniclers, since it is certainly borne out in the present conflict). During one of the sequences evoked in the last section of the *Remembrance*, I recall that Proust makes a foray into Mesopotamia as a theater of war.[7] And he locates this place among those where time is fixed in a "stagnation of the past that [. . .], through a sort of specific heaviness, is paused indefinitely, so much so that one can recover it again just as it is." Doesn't he see in the maneuvers of the English on the shores of the Tigris and the Euphrates, in their ebb and flow, a likeness to the retreat of Xenophon?

And, following a digression, Susan Sontag, in her last book on photography,[8] teaches me a fact (well-known among historians) in which I recognize the persistence and repetition of experiences in the theater of operations that is Mesopotamia. I see in this space a stubborn history that keeps returning. It is as if certain places contained a memory that predisposes them to undergo the same kind of experience until their destruction. As it did in 1924, as it did in 1991, Iraq in the war of 2003 will constitute a field of experimentation for the technology that transforms weaponry and, consequently, the manner of combat. The American writer recalls the English pilot, squadron leader in the Royal Air Force, amazed in 1924 at seeing from ten thousand feet the transformation of seditious market towns into piles of dust: after the detonation of four or five bombs that he had just dropped, "a third of their population is killed." It was especially in Iraq that aerial bombardments were tested on populated areas. And, twenty or so years later, the same English pilot will have directed, according to the same procedure, in February 1945, the annihilation of more than a hundred thousand civilians in Dresden whose calcination was not necessary for victory.

Strangely, Sontag's digression intersects Proust's remark which opens the passage leading to the mention of the Mesopotamian episode. Planes are mentioned in it as an invention that transforms the war; Gilberte recalls this when recounting the felicitous expression of her late husband: "Each army must have an Argus with a hundred eyes,"[9] to which the narrator replies: ". . . in the battle of the Somme, [. . .] they began by blinding the enemy by puncturing his eyes, by destroying his planes and his barrage balloons." Since then, the field of the military gaze was amply enlarged when satellites and missiles were added to planes. This multiplication of eyes was made in the refinement of computation and the high precision of observation. (How could Saddam have had the madness to accept a confrontation with America, knowing not just that he did not possess an army that was "an Argus with a hundred eyes" but also that he had no chance of "blinding the enemy by puncturing his eyes"?)

And who remembers the name of the two English generals whom Proust cites a paragraph later, about the siege of Kut-al-Amara, an event that impressed the narrator when he saw the name of Basra rise up next to Baghdad, two cities that will remain in memories as long as they circulate through the imaginations of readers traveling with *The Thousand and One Nights*: Doesn't Sinbad the Sailor return to the Baghdad of Harun al-Rashid, after coming back exhausted from his adventures? And once he has tired of the indolence and relaxation the city of the Caliphs offers, isn't he carried away by the wish to be buffeted about on the waves leading him again to Basra to load his ships before embarking toward destinations the winds will thwart, to our delight as readers excited by the expanse our cartography of the marvelous will take on? To precipitate them into the same oblivion that buries the English generals who led the Iraq operations of 1914, I will not speak the names of the American generals who are as I write carrying out experimentation with their new weapons, transforming their infantrymen into Martians disembarking on a land of a people whose actions remain subject to ancient ways of life. I am trying to erase from my memory the names of these directors of a fight so unequal that it is wrong to call it a war.

In the echoes of the American expedition, I will join to the names of Baghdad and Basra those of Karkh and Russafa, of A'zhamiya and

Rashidiya, of Najaf and Kerbala, of Mosul, Wasît, Samarra. . . . Each of these names revives in my memory the familiar history of Arabic arts and letters, so many episodes and deeds of language through which files a gallery of princes, viziers, saintly personages, revolutionaries, leaders of men, rebels, and other patrons of the arts, poets, polygraphs, Sufis, heresiarchs, painters, miniaturists, calligraphers, female singers, musicians, translators, astronomers, doctors, geometricians, algebraists, botanists, agronomists, grammarians, linguists, theorists of poetics, lexicographers, folklorists, creators of scientific or poetic works, inspired, sometimes libertine, products of minds often skeptical and free, peopling the literary salons, scholarly meetings, prestigious voices feeding doctrinal discussions, dogmatic controversies, theological disputes, trials preceded by inquisitorial examinations (where metaphysical arguments clash with political considerations), sparring matches, Socratic midwiferies, bacchic scenes, passion plays (which, with the Shiites, commemorate the founding sacrifice sacralized by analogy to the Passion of Christ). This Arabic era of Mesopotamia belongs to "that stagnation of the past" signaling the eternity of the place fed by other previous traces receding much further in the count of millennia (from the epic of *Gilgamesh* to the myth of Abraham, via the Code of Hammurabi).

And it is the ones who are supposed to be the guardians of this memory who find themselves confronted with the technological innovations capable of the most effective destruction. How have we come to this deadly conflict between the most immemorial antiquity and the modern which, through the mediation of technology, sets a convenient distance between the instrument that aims to annihilate and the human being who was formed to make use of it? It is as if cutting edge technology had freed itself from any necessary discourse with the ancestors and could choose for its theater of experimentation the very scene of its origins (anticipating the *mise-en-abîme* of the invention of writing and of state archives by the Sumerians).

And, in this theater of origins that Proust celebrates through the imperishable rejuvenation of *A Thousand and One Nights*, oblivion watches in its turn, oblivion and palinode, for many energetic beings belonging to this region refuse, in the name of conformity to the divine letter, to identify themselves with the Arabic tales that fanatics among them consign to the pyre of purgation. Not to speak of the misinterpretation of the notion of *jahiliyya*, that charge of ignorance that properly concerns only pagans who lived before Islam, castigated as "willfully ignorant" with respect to unitarianist, monotheist dogma, a class that the fundamentalists enlarge, in their poor but virulent polemics, to include all of human creation not illumined by the grace of divine Revelation, preferably in its rectifying and ultimate version. By this reductive reading of the notion of *jahiliyya*, the subjects of Islam change their condition: in the beginning, up until their willful ignorance, they were aware of belonging to a great enterprise that drew its greatness from assimilating all the pertinent things created by the communities that preceded them (and for them assimilation was not the same as abolition); now they limit their useful field to the narrow space authorized by obedience to the Qur'anic letter. All the rest is abrogated; whether they are the beautiful anteriorities that pierce all origins, watching in the patient labor of research over another origin to origin; or the works that, in the heart of Islam, like *The Thousand and One Nights*, somehow found a way to preserve the vital dynamics faced with a divine law that escapes with difficulty the crude context in which it first appeared. By struggling against the products of *jahiliyya* and of what they think are its recurrent and regressive effects, realizable at any moment and particularly in our century, the fundamentalists end up establishing in the ranks of their reactionaries and conspirators a veritable state of ignorance that no cure can mend.

Such is the strange world in which we live. Anxiety gnaws me when I see the American, the new man, busy playing with his inventions on exposed and helpless bodies; he leads the final avatar of Technology to its destructive destination despite the awareness that is supposed to enlighten him and that reminds him that this war is a new kind of war, one of extreme discernment that compels him to distinguish between a people for whose liberation he strives, and a regime whose collapse he desires. Thus it is more urgent than usual to deplore the innocent victims.

But, while appreciating the spectacular distance between the two warring parties, I end up finding fallacious the distinction between the regrettable death of civilians and the legitimate death of soldiers and Ba'athist militants in conformity with the political intention of this war. And my anxiety increases when I note that the very ancient peoples who came to Islam are stricken with an amnesia that keeps them from being the living depositories of the antiquities their land conceals. And yet they have not reached that level of contemporary invention that might have reconciled them with this century by enabling them to master the science and know-how that would have rendered them capable of defending themselves against the danger to which Technology and its perpetual mutations expose them.

IV

Beirut, April 10, 2003
We can only rejoice at the fall of a dictator. But the surprising thing is the ease with which the system of the dictator is coming undone, whereas, while he was in power (and until the eve of his overthrow), he wielded terror and seemed irremovable, so perfectly organized he was, recruiting zealous agents to contribute to his triumph. The latest images that reached us of effigies toppled, collapsed, burned, broken, lacerated, smeared, trashed, spit upon and beaten with the soles of shoes integrate the figure of Saddam into the repertory of deposed and desecrated dictators, the foremost of which are Mussolini and Ceausescu. In such scenes we are witnessing a ritual that must have the virtue of being propitiatory. It is an act that resembles the deposition and destruction of idols. A symbolic act that transforms the image to which a cult had been devoted, once an object of adoration, into a heap of scrap iron (or a pile of ashes).

I cannot help but be fascinated by the *a posteriori* acknowledgement of the fragility of the tyranny of the One, from which dictatorship emanates. It becomes obvious at the time of his deposition: there he is in his wretchedness, the very one who had embodied the One and who, an hour before his end, remained enveloped by the mystery of an aura that, in the eyes of his subjects, made his image and body sacred. Beyond the minority who never deviated from their belief, a minority divided into partisans and irredentist opponents of the dictator, beyond this minority, most of those who today are scorning the images of the dictator were themselves the ones who communed in his cult.

One of the mysteries of the human being dwells in this strange adhesion of the multitude to the glory of one single person, to submission to his authority. The efficacy of a dictatorship is evident as much in the terror it establishes as in the consent that La Boétie calls *servitude volontaire* (voluntary servitude).[10] And it is this disposition of the human being that led Montaigne's friend to write his treatise, a work whose thesis appears on every page of what is otherwise a rather confused composition. The tyranny of one single person, he says, cannot succeed without its active acceptance by the many. By revealing such a promptness to link with the One for one's own enslavement, La Boétie's analysis intends to arouse the feeling that rejects the hegemony of the One whether over oneself or over others. Such a conclusion led to an alternative title for *Treatise on Voluntary Servitude*: it was nicknamed *Le Contr'Un* (The Anti-One) (Montaigne contemplated including it in his *Essais*, but instead set poems in its place in order to focus attention on the friend's presence in his work). We also know that La Boétie's treatise was read and commented on in the psychoanalytic milieu, so much does voluntary servitude determine interpersonal relationships. And it is as a psychoanalyst and as an Egyptian that Mostafa Safouan translated it into Arabic, hoping thus to bring a remedy to the soul of his people, psychically and politically stricken by the Boétian syndrome. It remains for us to wonder at the paltry echo this translation encountered among native Arabic speakers, not yet, as a majority, awakened to that internalization of critical thinking, preliminary to psychic and political transformation, which unbinds you from consenting to that servitude, in which the roots of both dictatorship and fundamentalism are plunged.

Political awareness protects us from such a disposition and solicits our vigilance to keep ourselves from succumbing to it. Of course political authority needs to be embodied. And even in the best-established democracies, this need for embodiment is felt. In republics and democracies of a presidential kind, the ones that dispense with delegating to a chancellor or prime minister part of the power that divides and redirects the executive, a remainder of embodiment of authority by one person still exists. That is the case of the [French] Fifth Republic when not tempered by coalition. That is also the case with the American system where the presidential image transforms a mediocre or even moronic man by the aura his function grants him. In such structures, not only are traces of the theological-political foundations (as analyzed by Carl Schmitt)[11] revealed, but even some persistence of the sacredness of the political body is implicit.[12] Curiously, the return of the monarchic imprint is most perceptible through the figures that embody the executive power in the two systems that founded their political modernity on the most radical ruptures: Didn't America declare its independence and build its republic through one of the most virulent anti-royal polemics? Didn't France open the way to its political metamorphosis with a Revolution, followed by a regicide? Perhaps, paradoxically, the mark of persistence is inversely proportional to the virulence of the rupture. Within such a phenomenon can be identified one of the ruses of the unconscious in history and politics. Thus, beyond ruptures that decide modern political foundation, a network of traces emanating from past structures continue to act on the body politic and on the iconography that stages it.[13]

When the embodiment of the political is kept in reserve, deferred, suspended, when the place where it is actualized is found to be vacant, an orphan condition is established. Such a state might be lived as a strangeness that the dissatisfied cannot bear. Then their implicit desire to surmount the horror of the void is relayed by the resounding voice of the multitude demanding the re-establishment of the missing image. Obviously, Iraq will live through this time of vacancy, and its multitude will be led to call on the re-founding of the One in its sacralization. Yet do the subjects that populate Mesopotamia have the means to fulfill their hope of substituting democracy for tyranny in such a sacralizing reconstitution of the One?

The distinction between the two structures is obvious. It can be traced back to antiquity. We are in its presence in one of the first tragedies that came to us, in Aeschylus' *The Persians*. What characterizes the tyrant is that he is not liable for his deeds; no account is asked of him when he leads the community whose leader he is to disaster. Xerxes will continue to be King of kings despite the catastrophe of Salamis; after the calamitous defeat, he will return to his throne in Susa. By contrast, the Athenian victory is not personalized, and the name of the savior of Athens, Themistocles, is not mentioned. If, on the contrary, he had been the source of some wrong, he would no doubt have been deposed. For in democracy, the politician is judged more according to his failures. We can make out in this highly political tragedy another distinction between tyranny and democracy. Tyranny is made easy because of the consenting submission of the multitude to the One (in this, the shade of La Boétie meets the ghost of Aeschylus). Democracy is founded on the vigilance of a people that will not accept the fetters shackling its limbs and shows this by an act of rebellion.

But the people of Iraq did not achieve such an act of revolt by its own initiative. Can violent foreign intervention, the action of the third party, awaken this people to democratic vigilance? Or will we see it waver from dictatorship to the anarchy of civil war, only to return to dictatorship? The case of Iraq is extreme. It belongs to a space, Islam, the Arab world, where almost all the regimes illustrate the ultimate expression of despotism. The conjuncture we are experiencing invites us to meditate on the case of the ordinary dictatorships that are the most widely-shared lot in such latitudes. Aren't we in a propitious situation to set in motion the process that will lead us to abandon the despotic state to arrive at the democratic state? Isn't it right to seize the opportunity offered by the present Iraqi situation to search within us in order to get on with the introduction of the necessary reforms that will rescue us from this intolerable alternative paralyzing political wills, trapped between secular military dictatorships and the totalitarian impulses of Islamist fundamentalism?

These days, even the least deleterious dictatorships tremble when considering the audacity of foreign intervention; their virulence remains suspicious in our eyes, since they could have rid themselves of Saddam at a much slighter cost, so drained was the country, stricken with an entropy engendered by the destructions of 1991, by the embargo that has lasted for twelve years, by the absence of forbidden weapons (whose supposed concealed existence contributed to preparing the *casus belli*). The future will tell us if what we revealed above (in *Chronicles I* and *II*) is the strict truth or if, despite our vigilance, we were not able to abandon the *doxa*, the common opinion, the stereotypes that obscure and trouble the gaze that Arabs direct at themselves and the world. For now, and despite the political and ethical problems that this American intervention raises in the lands that stretch between the two rivers, we rejoice at the end of a dictatorship that we would have preferred to see succumb to the blows of the subjects who had been enduring its crimes. But this wish will remain a pious aspiration as long as such subjects have not acted on themselves through a more persevering metaphysical quest, through a more scrupulous introspection, to extirpate the state of voluntary servitude from within them; without that extirpation, it will be impossible for them to become the political beings who enjoy the democratic process.

V

Bosra du Hauran (Syrian-Jordanian border)
April 14, 2003
Now that all the cities of Iraq are subdued and the war is coming to a close, what can we conclude? Indeed, with the disappearance of the dictatorship, the prime declared objective of this war is reached, practically on schedule. But now the problems begin for the conquerors. In the cities taken over from the authority of a dissolved State, bearing in

mind the long-accumulated deprivations, it is perhaps in the order of things to see the multitude let off steam by theft, pillage, plunderings. Of all the images broadcast, I will mention only two to express my indignation at the disorder and vandalism that have added scars to cities already wounded. First of all the image of chaos is scandalously illustrated by the gazelles set loose from their palatial imprisonment, at each step almost breaking their fragile hooves on the asphalt, followed by the thoroughbred stallion with lustrous black coat, escaped from his stable, adapting to his new condition without deviating from his elegance, yielding to the hands of ragged scoundrels who tied his bridle to the slats of a rusty van, imposing a machine's speed on it, at the risk of ruining its integrity, imagining it being demeaned to a draft animal or even to some butcher's block. Then the damage wrought by barbarous invasion is seen in the burning of the Library and the devastation of the Museum: The loss of more than ten thousand manuscripts (including a rare manuscript of *The Thousand and One Nights*), the damage done to so many archeological remains, bring to the surface of my memory the treasures forever lost during the sacking of Baghdad by the Mongols (in 1258).

Even if the vandals are none other than natives of the place, even if the foreign forces are allied with other forces originating within the country, even if their presence is demanded and legitimized by local voices, it still remains true that with the burned books and the smashed or stolen art objects the responsibility of the invaders is involved. Following the example of the Israeli soldiers in Sabra and Chatila, they let it happen. (Thus these friends and allies—Sharon and Bush—have to their debit the responsibility for a crime carried out by third parties on a site subject to the authority of troops under their command; such a crime is equal in intensity even when it changes its nature: didn't one crime express itself by the massacre of human beings whose corpses were marked by the pleasures of disfiguration and amputation? Didn't the other crime lead to the jubilant vandalizing of symbolic goods by a vengeful crowd, about whom we do not know whether their misdeeds were spontaneous or planned?) Such invaders have revealed their priorities by their promptness in protecting the oil wells in the south and the north and in Baghdad the ministry in charge of their functioning and management, abandoning to the populace or to local custodians the institutions where works of art were preserved. By this last remark I am suggesting that a clue is given that casts doubt on the spontaneity of such vandalisms, provoked to legitimize the calling in of troops: that is why the diplomatic or international representatives targeted by the pillagers are the German embassy, the French cultural center, and the seat of the UN inspectors, three places belonging to three entities that constituted an obstacle to the American war.

This invader likens himself to a liberator; in our judgment, he doesn't really care much about that, such is the arrogance with which he acts, and the certainty of one who possesses a comfortable and triumphant power. His obstinacy doesn't prevent me from asserting that through the priority given to maintaining order, I am forced to recognize an additional sign by which the unavowed aim of the Iraq expedition is revealed, as it was thought out and planned by the neoconservative ideologues who found in Bush the dream executor of their project. If they were acting, as they claim, against barbarism and for civilization, they would never have left unheeded the protection demanded by the caretakers of the places where the works of a heritage that belong not just to Iraq but to all of humanity were preserved.

Given the evolution of events, we see that politics is a scene where the worst is to be feared. Not just that any progress in the resolution of conflicts can be called into question, but that no acquisition is definitive, even the one that seems best established. The ebbtide can carry away what the incoming current brought. Regression lies in wait. Vigilance must be constant, and it is not enough to seize favorable circumstances to transform the virtuality that gleams on the horizon into reality. Who would have thought that what was being offered during Rabin's and Clinton's era would one day be buried, and would correspond to a lost paradise?

Yet the American chroniclers who are proponents of the war call for moderation, some demanding humility in victory in order to arrive more quickly at the construction of democratic utopia,[14] others hoping to win the confidence of the Iraqi people by sparing it the scenes of humiliation observed in the beginning of April at Umm Qasr during the distribution of food to a population whose dignity had been dissolved by want.[15] One has the feeling that these men who shape people's opinions want their political representatives and their military to measure up to the famous phrase the Athenian addressed to his Spartan protagonist: "Strike, then listen." But the proposals that come to us from Washington are not ready to honor such a minimal request. By their extremism, they fill with despair the opinions of those who are most on their side. I am inclined to believe that for them dialogue is desirable only on condition that the interlocutor disappear to himself, a situation that removes civility from conversation and the goal from negotiation, that is to say the search for compromise and the advance, even infinitesimal, toward the contradictor's position. "Submit to me or I dismiss you"—that seems to be the new American motto in its method of dealing with others.

But I will not unveil my crystal ball in order to predict the future. I don't have to wait to see Syria invaded in its turn to know that the Arab disaster is already accomplished. The destruction of Iraq is not the result of this but the reason for it, not the consequence but the cause. Such a disaster is not just characterized by the defeat of the ideological variants of Arabism (which have been in their death throes ever since the defeat of June 1967). It is perceptible through the catastrophic situation of the Arab present, reflected in the UNDP (United Nations Development Program) report published in 2002, the irrefutable nature of which stems from the fact that its researchers and authors are specialists native to the countries concerned. I recall only two statistics from this document which illuminate with symbolic brilliance the economic and cultural state of this expanse of the globe, and spare us the prolixity of experts. The gross national product of all Arab countries (including the countries that produce petrodollars) is less than that of Spain. And the number of translations published each year into Arabic, a language used by three hundred million speakers, is less than into Lithuanian, language of a country which counts scarcely one and a half million inhabitants.[16] It is to such truths that we should turn to explain the confusion and impotence of the Arab crowds who have lived through one more illusion, scandalously maintained by a mediatized discourse equating desire with reality, and creating the fiction of an efficient Iraqi resistance that summoned up the energy to call for combat and mobilize volunteers who came to Baghdad for their destruction from Tunisia, Morocco, Egypt, Syria and other places.

Beyond the chaos, we will not see an Iraq betrothed to a democratic wedding anytime soon. Already political assassination is in the process of making the country slide into civil war. Soon, we will see the Americans lose interest in the fate of an Iraq much more complicated in its daily management than foreseen, a rebarbative, discouraging country that doesn't revive any hope in the mirage of utopias. But an effort will be made to save appearances. There will be an allied government that will facilitate the task of the American protectorate. As in Kuwait, as in the Emirates, as in Saudi Arabia. The zones of oil production will be protected militarily and secured, as they say. And the regional balance of power largely favorable to Israel will be comforted for decades. This situation confirms only one single certainty: we are entering the sphere of limited sovereignty and the establishment of new forms of protectorates adapted to a globalization that it is incumbent on us not to abandon to American decision alone. Faced with such a frustrating context, I do not see toward what cause the feeling of revolt will be directed, if not toward the targets of Islamist terrorism, which will find its most decisive argument in this American interventionism that scorns justice.

VI

Damascus, April 15, 2003

After the events of this war, now more than ever the world—particularly Islam and the Arab countries—would do well to benefit from what I have called, in recent talks, the European nuance. This can be explained by the history of the last sixty years and goes beyond the conjuncture of the French and German opposition to the American machinations in Iraq, an opposition that could be perceived as being one of its manifestations. This nuance goes beyond the two main arguments that were advanced to flesh out the rationale that accompanied this opposition. On one hand, the defenders of the French-German position cite the Treaty of Westphalia (1648) to recall the recourse to dialogue and to the principle that advocates the balance of powers and thus the rejection of unilateralism in the treatment of supra-national crises. On the other hand, they have depended on the obligation not to obscure the appeal to international law when a situation forces them to intervene in the affairs of another country, while rejecting the notion of a rogue state as well as the concept of a preventive war; some go so far as to demonstrate philosophically that perhaps the inventor of the expression "rogue state" is itself the rogue state par excellence;[17] others remind us of the argument for the legitimacy of preventive warfare propounded in the Roman senate by Scipio, who advocated the destruction of Carthage.[18]

The European nuance whose genesis I want to elucidate goes beyond these arguments, which, though circumstantial, scarcely lose their pertinence. In order to determine the two stages that were involved in the appearance of this nuance, I will make use of two texts striking in their brevity, premonitory works of two prophets of reason, whose predictions, later verified by facts, turn out to be much more clairvoyant than the pronouncements of soothsaying visionaries that mysticism has made us familiar with, by the gift of an authentic poetic proximity necessary to existence, far from politics.

At the end of his lecture *Qu'est-ce qu'une nation?* (What is a nation?),[19] Ernest Renan gathers the future of Europe in the coming century into one short paragraph; he says that in the twentieth century the old continent will experience the bloodiest war, and end up by forming a confederacy. And in an article published in October 1943, two months before her death, Simone Weil[20] urges Europeans to temper

American hegemony (whose advent she had predicted after the Nazi collapse, which she also deemed inevitable) by channeling the tension of the two polarities that rule the world's fate and that they are alone in mastering. It is a question of two opposing pairs that constitute the old and the new on one hand, the East and the West on the other. While still feeling deeply rooted in ancient Greece, and much before it, in Sumer or ancient Egypt, the European is nonetheless not conservative or backward-looking; he is still the adventurer capable of new discoveries, inventor in the realms of the mind and of form; and, even beyond the erudition he has accumulated about the East, he knows, without losing his liberty, that in this space his spiritual origins reside.

After the two terrible world wars, we had to wait until the 1950s for the Europeans to decide to constitute themselves as an economic community, the first milestone of a process whose unfolding continues before our eyes, to confirm, in fullness and on both counts, the meaning of the prediction formulated by Renan seventy years earlier. After 1945, Europe, by abolishing war from its theater of operations, has seen a new man develop, marked by peace and the critical gaze he directs at his own history. In the beginning of the century we have just begun, this man seems finally able to realize the program that he had been assigned sixty years ago by Simone Weil. He is also in a position to reconcile the principles he invented (in the "Age of Enlightenment") with the deeds he carries out as an actor on the world's stage. I see him in a state where he can reduce, if not annihilate, the distance between his belief and his actions. Going beyond the historical failing with which he was so reproached (especially during the colonial era) would restore the universality of his invention, from which the various non-European entities, among which I place Islam foremost, could draw greater advantage. (On such premises I build my own life as a European Arab.) And, in this perspective, I can easily see the Western promise split up, divided between American dominance (finally regressive, since it leads us back to the sin from which Europe is absolved) and the European nuance (bearer of a truth not yet experienced by history).

Starting from these distinctions, it is possible to interpret the op-positions that have become manifest during the Iraq crisis, and then the Iraq war. There is a prior example that current events revive, one through which the European nuance can be recognized according to at least one of the two prerogatives I have just mentioned: In Ancient Mesopotamia, the European identifies a part of himself with which he continues to converse: he cannot help but be shocked by the damage wrought to what he has a right to deem a heritage he shares.

But there is another example that comes to us from the heart of the tenth century, and that eloquently illustrates the double weft (ancient/new, East/West) that weaves European nuance. I want to evoke it now so as to lead violence back to the symbolic plane where, through tragic sentiment, it regenerates the human being and distances him from that other form of violence brought by war and the massacres it creates. The European individual, especially the French one, has access in his own language to books that reconstruct the exceptional experiences for which the land of Iraq has been the theater. I am thinking particu-larly of the monumental work that Louis Massignon devoted to al-Hallaj, that mystic of the East with whom the Westerner identified and whose life and work he reconstructed, both men devoted to the Ab-solute to the point of sacrifice, to the point where, through the ardent passion of the Muslim Sufi who was martyred in 924, the Christian, friend of Claudel, discovered the paths of his own conversion.[21]

Surely if he has internalized such an ancient Eastern reference, a contemporary Westerner can only deplore the hubris that has been un-leashed on the soil that preserves the memory of the scattered ashes of the martyr from Baghdad, commemorated by a humble cenotaph. The rare pilgrims to this tomb hear amidst the cooing of turtledoves haunt-ing the neighborhood the inspired paradox (the *shat'ha*) that led their revered teacher to the stake: *Anâ al-Haqq,* "I am the Creating Truth." In this experience of excess that comes to us from Eastern antiquity, the man from the West experiences his own limits by realizing on his own account the extremes of ecstasy, at the risk of confirming the modern craftsman of the poem in his commitment to the unspoken and to social anarchy. During one of the pauses that accentuates this experience of excess, even the question of evil was confronted head-on through a conversation with the devil in which the Sufi records the confidences of the Evil One, giving the reasons for his insubordination towards the divine order that granted privilege to Man in the fiction of the Creation. How can we not think of the *Kitâb at-Tawâsin*,[22] of its blaspheming ardor, of its other form of hubris that consumes the body for the glory of visionary apocalypse, and not for the destruction of patient beings, the multitudes stricken in this present war.

This is the toll of the battles that have lasted for three weeks: hundreds of dead, thousands of wounded. Faced with this American balance sheet, the European nuance is confronted with the question of power. Stripped of its capacity to have any effect on events, it risks losing even the privilege of symbolic violence, which would affect only the people of 'withdrawal' [Heidegger's term for the mystics who preserve a distance from events—Trans.] (in which case the poetic energy would be eroded). This nuance would end up becoming a dead letter if it were expressed only in words, persuasive as they may be. The chronicle of the Near East (from the Israeli-Palestinian conflict to the present invasion of Iraq) shows us the inefficacy of the European nuance on political reality. As long as Europe thinks it is impotent, it will not be otherwise. Isn't it time to awaken a political will that determines to bring to the old and still young continent the means of dissuasion that will color the reality of its nuance? Obviously, in rediscovering armed power, Europe could form new ties with its old demons and excite an itch for hegemony that no morality could restrain. This risk deserves to be run: it will put to the test the tragic paradox from which every human draws his survival, his renewal, his regeneration, even to the point of death.

By deciding to regain power, European nuance would become effective; it would ruin the edifice built by Robert Kagan, who has long attributed weakness to Europe, power to America.[23] To emerge from the angelic pacifism with which the neoconservative polemicist floods us, to correct the proposals of Joschka Fischer from which he draws,[24]

I would say that the return to power would grant European nuance the possibility of re-balancing the powers, not to serve hegemonic desire, but to apply law and justice, and to bring freedom along with its principles, not to disguise an aim supposed to serve its interests with a moral alibi. Then European nuance could become the appropriate answer to American policy as exercised in the Near-East, in Iraq, in Palestine, in these recent months, weeks and days.

Then Sharon could no longer dismiss the European peace initiatives with a wave of his hand, followed by a shrug of his shoulder. Then all ambiguity about the condemnation of dictators and the necessity of acting, even with military force, to bring an end to their misdeeds, would be removed. In such a way, Europe might have intervened with a more controlled force to proceed to the eradication of the system installed by Saddam, while sparing the people a large part of its dead, and avoiding travail and destruction to the country. Through such means, Europe could demand Arafat's departure and denounce him as a despot even more illegitimate than the other despots of the region, since in his case, his despotism precedes the foundation of the State.[25] And such a European nuance will have the duty to be rigorous in its alliances, to the point that in its name one nation cannot cooperate or act in common with other nations if one of the contracting parties overtly contravenes its principles, as is the case with Russia, disqualified by its colonial war in Chechnya.

By returning to power, the European nuance can preserve the diversity that peoples the world when it constitutes an anthropological richness and act against it as soon as it becomes problematic. It could advocate the respect for difference on the ground of symbolism and imagination, in the realm of signs, and be categorical when it comes to the uniqueness and universality of political authority that is the State of law illumined by the Age of Enlightenment.

Having reached this point on our journey, we see that, in the case of Islam, the strategy of relationship couldn't be clearer. Within as well as outside the continent, the European individual, provided with his nuance, can speak to the Muslim in these terms: "I make Islam as a civilization my own, I internalize it: Doesn't it sustain a part of my soul? As a religion, it deserves respect: By the symbolic and imaginal formation it grants to those who believe in it, doesn't it produce subjects who can be loyal citizens? But on the political and legal level, we believe in the universality of our own system, we will defend our values and we will battle any rival so-called axiology, particularly the one that your fundamentalists construct, for human experience teaches us that as soon as the religious absolute is confused with the law and with politics, freedoms are stripped away."

That would be the utopia of European nuance. As you will note, it should not, in principle, reject the right to intervene in other countries, even at the risk of seeing the notion of sovereignty reduced—whose diminishing is, perhaps, inevitable because of progressive globalization and the objective experiences that direct humanity toward a new truth of space/time, founded on transcending the notion of frontiers, and on the real world as it acts on politics as well as on poetics through the travel and intermingling that the intense global circulation of men and women produces, crossing the barriers of countries and continents. Thus, confronting American strategy, European nuance must be exercised under the same horizon. The very clarity of its intention frees it from the ambivalence revealing the moral alibi behind the hidden agenda. What also distinguishes it from the Trans-Atlantic empire (which still remains its ally) is that by continuing to care about a greatness it must maintain and an influence it must make prevail, it no longer aspires to a political hegemony to defend or to make endure as long as possible. It will then have to its advantage the privilege of preserving, by taming, the two forces that drive the world, activated by the tensions between ancient and modern, East and West, polarities that the American consciousness cannot discern, because of its lack of historical profundity, and its geographical distance.

Notes

CHAPTER 1

1. Voltaire, *A Treatise on toleration*, translated extract available at http://www.
   wsu.edu:8080/~wldciv/world_civ_reader/world_civ_reader_2/voltaire.html.
2. Thomas Mann, *The Story of a Novel: The Genesis of Doctor Faustus,* trans.
   Richard Winston and Clara Winston (New York: Alfred Knopf, 1961), 28.
3. Robert Malley, "Surprises et paradoxes," *Le Monde,* October 31, 2001 (trans. PJ
   and AR).
4. This concept will be made clear during certain stops along the itinerary of this text.
   One can measure the universal spread of the American way by reading Italo
   Calvino, *Six Memos for the Next Millennium: The Charles Eliot Norton Lectures,
   1985–1986,* trans. Patrick Creagh (New York: Vintage International, 1993). The
   Oulipo-affiliated writer was amazed in 1959 by many phenomena of daily American life that surprised many other European visitors who crossed the Atlantic, although, forty years later, these same phenomena no longer surprised anybody,
   neither in Europe nor elsewhere, as they have been adopted by everybody.

CHAPTER 2

1. Friedrich Nietzsche, *On the Genealogy of Morals,* trans. Walter Kaufmann (New
   York: Vintage, 1989), 36–40, 121–129.
2. Ibid., 41.

3. Akhbarian: Ibn 'Arabi was known as *el sheikh el-akhbar* (the great sheikh or master) [translators' note].
4. Mikhayil Mishaqa, *Murder, Mayhem, Pillage and Plunder: The History of Lebanon in the Eighteenth and Nineteenth Centuries,* trans. W. M. Thackston, Jr., (Albany: State University of New York Press, 1988).
5. Al-Mawâqif, station 364, vol. 3, 97v and 99r, reproduction *hors commerce* of the partially autographed manuscript, published on the occasion of the emir's centenary (Algiers, 1983). A choice of these stations was translated from Arabic into French by Michel Chodkievicz in Emir Abd el-Kader, *Ecrits Spirituels* (Paris: Le Seuil, 1982).
6. Qur'an, 3:160.

CHAPTER 3

1. For information concerning al-Ma'mun, I draw in part on the article concerning him by M. Rekaya, in *Encyclopédie de l'Islam* (Leiden-Paris: E. J. Brill and G. P. Maisonneuve & Larose, 1991), 6:315–323.
2. Qur'an, 2:62.
3. Abu Tammam, *Divan,* edited and commented by Ilya al-Hawi (Beyrouth, 1981), section 212, p. 718. (The translations with no translator's name appended were done from Arabic into French by the author, and from French into English by PJ and AR).
4. Abu Nuwas, "Wine and the Qur'an" and "The Pleasures of Baghdad," in *Divan,* ed. A. A. M. al-Ghazali (Beirut, 1982), 120, 167. To know this poet better, see Jamal Bencheikh, "Poésies bachiques d'Abû Nuwâs, thèmes et personages," *Bulletin d'études orientales* 18 (1963–1964), 7–83.

CHAPTER 4

1. Ahmed Djebbar, *Une histoire de la science arabe, entretiens avec Jean Rosmorduc* (Paris: Points-Sciences, Seuil, 2001), 101–106, 366–370.
2. Hegel, *Phenomenology of Mind,* trans. J. B. Baillie (Harper Torchbooks, 1967), particularly "Enlightenment," 559–598.
3. Antoine Galland, *Les paroles remarquables, les bons mots et les maxims des Orientaux,* especially the introduction by Abdelwahab Meddeb, "La Sagesse des Orientaux" (Paris: Maisonneuve & Larose, 1999), 5–14.
4. Mary Wortley Montagu, *Selected Letters,* ed. Isobel Grundy (New York: Penguin, 1997).
5. Averroës, *Decisive Treatise and Epistle Dedicatory: Determining the Connection Between the Law and Wisdom,* trans. Charles E. Butterworth (Chicago: University of Chicago Press, 2002).
6. Alain de Libera, *Penser au Moyen Âge* (Paris: Seuil, 1991). Also see Maurice-Ruben Hayoun and Alain de Libera, *Averroès et l'averroïsme* (Paris: Presses Universitaires de France, 1991).
7. See, for example, Henry Corbin, *Histoire de la philosophie islamique* (Paris: Gallimard, 1974).
8. Christian Jambet, *Se rendre immortel* (Montpellier: Fata Morgana, 2000).
9. Régis Morelon, "Panorama général de l'astronomie arabe," in *Histoire des sciences arabes,* comp. Roshdi Rashed (Paris: Seuil, 1997), 1:29–30.

CHAPTER 5

1. Galland, *Les Paroles remarkables,* 101–107.
2. This tendency is represented by the Moroccan scholar Mohamed Abed al-Jabri. See his introduction to Averroës's Arabic paraphrase of Plato's *Republic,* in which he writes: "With the return of this book to Arabic we proudly ascertain that the answers for our present-day political problems are found in our own heritage." Averroës, *Commentary on Plato's* Republic, introduction by Mohamed Abed al-Jabri (Beirut, 1998), 9–10.
3. Hamdane Khodja, *Le Miroir* (Paris: Sindbad, 1983), 38.
4. Carl Schmitt, "Der Gegensatz von Parlamentarismus und moderner Massendemokratie," in *Positionen und Begriffe* (Berlin: Duncker & Humblot, 1994).
5. Ibid., 69.
6. Ibid.

CHAPTER 6

1. Averroës, *Decisive Treatise.* The following development draws on pages 106–113.
2. Ibid., 110.
3. Ibid., 112.
4. We shall see that the movement he gave rise to was called the *salafyia,* in reference to those same *salafs.*
5. E. I. J. Rosenthal, *Averroës' Commentary on Plato's* Republic (Cambridge, 1956). Critics pointed out the errors of translation in this book, which led Ralph Lerner to propose another one, *Averroës on Plato's* Republic (Ithaca, N.Y.: Cornell University Press, 1974). This text returned to Arabic with the help of Ahmed Sha'lân, professor of Hebrew at the University of Rabat (Averroës, *Plato's* Republic).
6. *Hafadha,* the term used by Averroës, is Qur'anic (6:61). It concerns the guardian angels (protectors and recorders); Farabi also uses the term *hurrâs* (guardians) in a more secular way.

CHAPTER 7

1. Qasim Amin information page, available at http://www.nmhschool.org/tthornton/mehistorydatabase/qasim_amin.htm.
2. For information on Sheikh Mohammed 'Abduh, see Donald Malcolm Reid, "Muhammad Abduh," available at http://www.cqpress.com/context/articles/epr_muhammadabduh.html.
3. Hoda Sha'rawi was born in Minya in 1879 and grew up in Cairo. The daughter of a wealthy and respected provincial administrator from Upper Egypt, she was, like all aristocratic young girls, educated at home. Her memoirs tell of her life as one of the last upper-class Egyptian women in the segregated world of the harem. At age thirteen, she was married against her wishes to a cousin many years older. A year later, she separated from her husband for a period of seven years. During these years, Hoda Sha'rawi gradually came to an awareness of the constraints imposed upon women in Egypt and devoted the rest of her life to fight for women's

independence and the feminist cause. With her newfound freedom, she took an increasingly militant stand against the harem and became engaged in Egypt's nationalist struggle, which culminated in independence in 1922. Her daring act of defiance in unveiling herself at a Cairo railway station in 1923 signaled the end of the harem years for herself and the beginning of the end for others. Hoda Sha'rawi was the head of the Egyptian Feminist Union until her death on August 12, 1947. She is remembered in history as the liberator of Egyptian women.

4. Germaine Tillion, *The Republic of Cousins; Women's Oppression in Mediterranean Society,* trans. Quintin Hoare (New York: Prometheus Books, 2000), 18 (in French edition).

5. A concept already adapted by Averroës, as we saw in Chapter 6.

6. Western and Christian connotations are part of the invention of these two neologisms. *Fundamentalism* refers to a conservative element current in American Protestantism between 1900 and 1920; *integrism* was originally applied to the position of those Catholics who refused to accept the reforms instituted by the Vatican or elaborated within the Church, from the 1950s to the 1980s. Despite these connotations, the term *fundamentalism* adapts itself well to the spirit of *Salafism,* whose emulators wanted to modernize Islam while being wary of keeping its "foundation" intact (via a return to the utopia of its origins). Moreover, the term *integrism* is accurately applied to those movements initiated since the 1930s by the Muslim Brotherhood and including all contemporary Islamicist and terrorist deviations. In integrism, we also have in mind the polysemy of the word *integrity:* that state of something that has remained intact, and the old sense of *virtue,* or complete purity. If integrity is qualitative, then integrality is quantitative: the state of a complete thing. To apply a prescription *dans son intégralité* means to do it totally. The Islamist is an integrist when he preaches the integrity of the law, and imposes its application in its integrality. This abolishes all alterity and installs a form of being that adds a new name to the catalog of totalitarian practices that have wrecked the century. Between the two names (fundamentalism and integrism), there is a difference of intensity: Coercion transforms itself into terror, and struggle into war. On the other hand, I hesitate to identify integrism with Islamicism, because that is what Islam was called until the time of Ernest Renan and others after him (by using the same morphological schemata that gives *christianisme* [translators' note: the French word for "Christianity"]). But it is acceptable to designate the integrists as *Islamists,* as that name distinguishes them from the Muslims (*muslimun*) and rhymes well with how they are designated in Arabic today (*islamiyun*). It is further useful to recall that the word had a more general sense: In medieval Arabic, *Islamists* meant "followers of Islam." The term is used in the famous book by al-'Ash'ari (873–935), *Maqalat al-Islamiyyin,* which his German editor Hellmut Ritter translates as *Die dogmatischen Lehren der Anhänger des Islam* ("The dogmatic teachings of the followers of Islam," 3rd ed. (Wiesbaden, 1980).

7. Miskawayh, *Tahdhib al-akhlaq* (Treatise on ethics), 2nd ed., translated from Arabic into French by Mohammed Arkoun (Damascus: Institut Français, 1988). An English version of the book was published as a summary of Miskawayh's ethical system: Ibn Miskawayh, *The Refinement of Character,* trans. C. Zurayk (Beirut: American University of Beirut Centennial Publications, 1966). This work is also known as *Taharat al-a'raq* (Purity of dispositions). Also see http://www.muslimphilosophy.com/rep/H042.htm.

8. Ernest Renan, *L'Islamisme et la science* (Paris, 1883), reprinted in *Discours et Conférences,* 6th ed. (Paris: Calman-Lévy, 1919), 375–409.
9. Albert Hourani, *Islam in European Thought* (Cambridge: Cambridge University Press, 1991). This work remains the best synthesis of the westernization of Arab thought between 1850 and 1950.
10. Taha Husayn, *Fi ash-Shi'r al-Jahili* (Cairo, 1926; reprint, 1991).
11. Taha Husayn, *Mustaqbal al-thaqafah fi Misr* (Cairo, 1938); and English version, Taha Husayn, *The Future of Culture in Egypt,* trans. Sidney Glazer (New York: Octagon Books, 1975).
12. Ali 'Abd ar-Raziq, *Al-Islam wa uçul al-Hukm* (Cairo, 1926). French translation by Abdou Filali Ansari, *L'Islam et les fondements du pouvoir* (Paris: La Découverte, 1994).
13. Filali Ansari, *L'Islam,* 62. The French translator neglects to say that the author cites these philosophers only by reference to the textbook by Arthur Kenyon Roger, *A Student's History of Philosophy* (New York: Macmillan, 1960), 242–250. This is specified by the author in a footnote (see the Arab text [Tunis, 1999], 19). This oblique reference to these philosophers is worth noting because it signals the limit of the Westernization of the minds, which often occurs via textbooks and not through the meditation on, and internalization of, the founding texts. Notably, however, Sheikh 'Abd ar-Raziq points the reader (on page 66 of the French translation) to the monograph by Thomas Arnold, *The Caliphate* (Oxford, 1924). By calling his colleague a "great scholar," the sheikh does not participate in the suspicion that Westernism will later experience.

CHAPTER 8

1. Some portraits of these freethinkers can be found in Dominique Urvoy, *Les penseurs libres de l'islam classique* (Paris: Albin Michel, 1996).
2. Ibn Hazm, *al-Facl fi-l-Milal wa'l-Ah'wa' wa'n-Nihall,* vol. 5 (Cairo, n.d.). Although volume 5 is not dated, the first four are dated between 1317 and 1321 AH (1899–1902 CE).
3. Non-Arab-speaking readers can be introduced to the work of this author by one of the available French translations, for example, al-Ma'arri, *Rets d'éternité,* poetic extracts translated by Adonis and Anne W. Minkowsky (Paris: Fayard, 1988).

CHAPTER 9

1. These polemics can be found in his *Fatwas,* all of which have been published under the auspices of the Saudi state in an edition of more than twenty volumes, the whole of which the Saudi embassies offer as presents! See also his epistles and controversies, Ibn Taymiyya, *Majmu'at al-Rasa'il wa'l-Masa'il,* edited by Rashid Ridha, 5 parts distributed over 2 vols. (Cairo, n.d.). Rashid Ridha (1865–1935) is Mohammed 'Abduh's Syrian student who deviated from his master's horizon by giving a more restrictive meaning to the *salaf,* which 'Abduh had extended from the first Muslims in Medina to include the great traditional thinkers up to Ghazali (1058–1111). Add to this Ridha's suspicions against Sufism, and you will understand the belated interest he developed in Ibn Taymiyya. As a consequence of this

adherence to the Hanbalite doctor from Damascus, he repudiated an early text in which he assimilated Wahhabism to a *bid'a*, a "reprehensible innovation." Toward the end of his life, he showered praise on this same Wahhabism, just before the definitive triumph of Abd al-Aziz Ibn Saud, the founder of Saudi Arabia (in 1932).

2. Ibn Taymiyya, *as-Siyasa ash-Shar'iyya fi Islah ar-Ra'i wa'r-Ra'iyna* (Cairo, n.d.).
3. Immanuel Kant, *La Métaphysique des moeurs*, trans. A. Philonenlo (Paris: Vrin, 1993), 214.
4. Ibid., 215.
5. Ibid., 217. Hegel also showed how such a purity resulted in revolutionary terror; see the section entitled "Absolute Freedom and Terror" in Hegel, *Phenomenology of Mind*, 599–610.
6. Hans Kelsen, *La Théorie pure du droit*, trans. Charles Eisenmann (Paris-Brussels: LGDI Bruylant, 1999).
7. Carra de Vaux and Schact, *Encyclopédie de l'Islam*, s.v. "hadd."

CHAPTER 10

1. "Submission" is the primary meaning of the word *islam*, in conformity with the instinct of natural religion; it is the return to this primary principle of adoration that characterizes Islam as a religion.
2. Two expressions taken from the last verse of the Qur'an's opening Sura, called al-Fatiha. The interpretation proposed here by Ibn Taymiyya, which identifies the Jews with "those who (reap) divine anger" and the Christians with those who have "lost the way," is traditional, though not shared by all.
3. Yehuda Halevi, *Le Diwân*, trans. Y. Arroche and J. G. Valensi (Montpellier: Editions de l'Eclat, 1988), 91–93.
4. The Arab text says, *"illa anna fi 'aqlihi shay'un,"* literally, "but something was perturbing his mind." [Translators' note: Meddeb suggests that this Arabic expression, translated into "good French," means precisely *"mais il avait un grain,"* which could be translated as "but there was a grain of folly in him."]
5. According to tradition, men are not supposed to wear silk.
6. Ibn Battuta, "Voyages et périples," in *Voyages Arabes,* (Paris: Bibliothèque de la Pléiade, Gallimard, 1995), 454–455.

CHAPTER 11

1. This Boheman is sort of a European equivalent of today's Osama bin Laden.
2. D. A. F. Sade, *Cahiers personnels* (Paris: Oeuvres Complètes, J. J. Pauvert, 1966), 13:9–10.
3. My friend, the poet Salah Stétié, has told me that when visiting Arabia, he learned that whenever the smallest archaeological item relating to the history of early Islam and even to later Islamic periods is discovered, it is immediately covered in concrete.
4. Concerning the Hanbalism that the master from Herat followed, see Ansari, *Chemin de Dieu*, trans. Serge de Laugier de Beaurecueil (Paris: Sindbad, 1985), 24–30. [Translators' note: Also see A. G. Ravan Farhadi, *Abdullah Ansari of Herat: An Early Sufi Master* (London, New York: RoutledgeCurzon Sufi Series, 1996).]

5. He was a redoubtable polemicist against intellectualist theologians.

6. Qur'an, 2:165.

7. Ansari, *Cris du coeur,* trans. Serge de Laugier de Beaurecueil (Paris: Sindbad, 1988), 82.

8. Ibn Taymiyya, *Ar-Radd 'alâ al-Mantiqiyyîn* (Bombay, 1949).

9. Dawud al-Baghdadi, *al-Mihna al-Wahbiyya fi Radd al-Wahhabiyya,* followed by *Ashaddal-Jihad fi Ibt'al Da'wa al-Ijtihad* [1305 A.H./1887 C.E.] (reprint, Istanbul: Ikhlas Vkfi Yayinidir, 1986).

10. The Arab expression *Haddara dammahu* means exactly "to suffer, to permit the blood of a man to be spilled, without the executioner's being susceptible to being pursued" (used for a prince or judge). Fundamentalists use this expression a lot, which constitutes a call for murder exonerating in advance the one who executes it.

11. Al-Baghdadi, *al-Mihna al-Wahbiyya fi Radd al-Wahhabiyya,* 40–41.

12. Such as the Cordovan Zhahirite Ibn Hazm (994–1063) and Ibn Qudama (1147–1223), the Hanbalite from Jerusalem.

13. Al-Baghdadi, *al-Mihna al-Wahbiyya fi Radd al-Wahhabiyya,* 41–44.

CHAPTER 12

1. Jacques Berque, *Langages arabes du présent* (Paris: Gallimard, 1974), 124.

2. E. R. Dodds, *The Greeks and the Irrational* (Boston: Beacon Press, 1957), 270–278. For the scenes of *sparagmos* (the absorption of live animal or human flesh) as they are shown in Euripides' play, see C. K. Williams, trans., *The Bacchae of Euripides* (New York: Noonday Press, 1990), especially verse 139, p. 14, concerning the consumption of Theban cattle, and verses 1239ff, concerning the dismemberment of Pentheus.

3. Abdelwahab Meddeb, "Art et transe," *Esprit* 220 (1996): 72–79.

4. "On the Point of Departure and Its Importance for the Future of the Anglo-Americans," in: Alexis de Tocqueville, *Democracy in America,* trans., ed. and with an introduction by Harvey C. Mansfield and Delba Winthrop (Chicago and London: The University of Chicago Press, 2000).

5. The reader will notice that it is exactly that genealogical approach that the book underhand tries to honor.

6. Tocqueville, *Democracy in America,* http://xroads.virginia.edu/~HYPER/DETOC/1_ch02.htm

7. Ibid.

8. Ibid.

9. Qur'an, 6:19; and Al-Qushayri, *Lat'aif al-Isharat,* ed. I. Al-Basyuni (Cairo, 1981), 1:524.

CHAPTER 13

1. But we must remember that the Crusades were preceded by the loss of Sicily (1063) and the fall of Toledo (1085).

2. Djebbar, *Une histoire de la science arabe,* 56.

3. In Japanese, the character *mei* means "clear," and *ji* means "reign." Together, the two characters signify a "clear reign," or in French, *gouvernement éclairé,* an enlightened government. The victory of Japan over Russia in 1905 was perceived in Egypt as the sign that an Asian country could succeed in the double perspective corresponding to the program of the nationalists: to fight against the domination of Europe while at the same time adopting its civilization. For an Egyptian nationalist's view on renovated Japan, see Mustafa Kamil, *ash-Shams al-Mushriqa* ("The sun that illuminates") (Cairo, 1906).
4. [Translators' note: See http://www.arabworldbooks.com/authors/refaa_eltahtawi .html; and http://www.ahram.org.eg/weekly/2002/568/cu1.htm.]
5. Rifa'a Rafe' Tahtawi gave the eclectic list of his readings during his Parisian sojourn in his book translated as *L'or de Paris,* trans. Anouar Louca (Paris: Sindbad, 1988), 224; also available in English: Rifa'a Rafe' Tahtawi, *An Imam in Paris: Al-Tahtawi's Visit to France (1826–1831),* trans. Daniel L. Newman (London: Saqi, 2002). In his introduction, the French translator, Anouar Louca, recalled that Tahtawi assiduously read the *Aperçu historique sur les moeurs et coutumes des nations,* whose author was a certain Depping. It is in fact an installment of the *Encyclopédie portative ou Résumé universel des sciences, des lettres et des arts.* One can see toward what illusory knowledge such reading can lead; how can such minor, concise, schematic publications lead him "by the shortest roads to the discovery of unsuspected societies," as his translator claims?
6. Ali 'Abd ar-Raziq, *Al-Islam wa uçul al-Hukm.*

CHAPTER 14

1. Simone Weil, "A propos de la question coloniale dans ses rapports avec le destin du peuple français" ("On the colonial question in its relation to the fate of the French people"), *Écrits historiques et politiques* (Historical and political writings) (Paris: Gallimard, 1960).
2. Ibid., 377.
3. Harold Bloom, *The American Religion: The Emergence of the Post-Christian Nation* (New York: Simon & Schuster, 1992).

CHAPTER 15

1. Thomas Hobbes, *De Cive* (Oxford: Oxford University Press, 1983), 196, 248, 249.
2. Denis Diderot, *Encyclopédie,* vol. 8 (Neuchâtel, 1765).
3. Carl Schmitt, *Political theology: four chapters on the concept of sovereignty,* trans. George Schwab (Cambridge, MA: MIT Press, 1985). See before all, Chapter 1, "Definition of Sovereignty," 5-15. See also "A legend: the liquidation of all political theology" (1969) where, on page 128, Schmitt deplores the absence of Islam in [Erik] Peterson's treatment of the question: "Islam, whose political pertinence is considerable, and whose theological respectability is incontestable, is purely and simply absent, despite the fact that its God merits that name more than the *One* of Aristotelian or Hellenistic metaphysics."

4. I include in this observation the states whose legislators were conscious of the rupture introduced by their borrowing from the spirit of European constitutionality. I am thinking, among others, of the states refounded by Atatürk and Bourguiba.
5. Abu al-Hasan al-Mawardi, *Al-Ahkam as-Sult'aniyya* (The Principles of power) (Beirut, n.d.), 39–41. [Translators' note: For a partial translation with an introduction and annotations by Darlene R. May, also see http://members.tripod.com/~wzzz/MAWARDI.html.]
6. The creators of the constitution of the Fifth Republic counted among them attentive readers of Carl Schmitt, including René Capitant, "The National-Socialist State" (1938; reprint Brussels: Eclectica, 1990).

CHAPTER 16

1. Qur'an, 2:30. In this passage, God, just before creating Adam, announces to the assembled angels, "I will place a caliph on this earth" (through this verse, man is invested with the divine vice regency).
2. 'Abd ar-Raziq, *Al-Islam wa uçul al-Hukm*, 67.
3. Qur'an, 38:26.
4. Had the spiritual function been assigned to the imam, the title of caliph would have had to be granted him.
5. The cube at the center of the temple is called the Ka'ba. The angle that looks east is called Iraqi, the angle that is oriented toward the north is called Syrian, the one that throws its shadow toward the south, Yemeni; finally it is along the Western angle that the Black Stone is sealed. Esoteric tradition identifies this angle with God's right side; the pilgrim who touches the Black Stone and kisses it is supposed to state his allegiance to God through that gesture.
6. Zayn al-'Abidin belonged to the descendants of the Prophet via the latter's daughter Fatima and cousin Ali; he is recognized by the Shiites as the third imam.
7. Farazdak, *Diwan* (Beirut: Dar Sader, n.d.), 2:178–181.

CHAPTER 17

1. Baybars was of the first Mameluke dynasty, whose sultans were of Turkish origin; this first dynasty produced twenty-five sultans between 1250 and 1382.
2. The reader who has not visited Cairo can get a sense of this splendor by consulting two works, valued for their illustrations as well as for the texts that accompany and explain them: Jean-Claude Garcin, *Le Caire* (Paris: Mazenod & Citadelle, 2000), especially the text on 147–275 and the illustrations on 166–312; and Henri and Anne Stierlin, *L'Egypte des mille et une nuits* (Paris: Imprimerie Nationale, 1996), for its photographs depicting the sublime details of Mameluke architecture.
3. At that time, Cairo was under the reign of al-Zahir Barquq, the first Mameluke sultan of Circassian origin. This second Mameluke dynasty produced twenty-four sultans.
4. Ibn Khaldun, *Le Voyage d'Occident et d'Orient*, trans. Abdessalam Cheddadi (Paris: Sindbad, 1980), 148. The admiration generated by Cairo signals that this

city was far more important than any of the Western cities Ibn Khaldun had fre-
quented (Tunis, Bejaïa, Tlemcen, Fez, Grenada, Seville).
5. Philip Mansel, *Constantinople: City of the World's Desire, 1453–1924* (New York:
St. Martin's Press, 1996), 6–7.
6. Ibid., 42.

CHAPTER 18

1. Throughout this development, I am drawing on the excellent monograph by Ernst
Kantorowicz, *Frederick the Second, 1194–1250,* trans. E. O. Lorimer (New
York: Unger, 1957).
2. The dynasty of the Ayyubids, founded by Saladin, reigned over Egypt (to which it
added Syria) from 1171 to 1249.
3. Kantorowicz, *Frederick the Second,* 192.
4. Ibid., 191.
5. Ibid., 192–193.
6. Ibid., 237.
7. Ibid., 247.

CHAPTER 19

1. Rashid Ridha, *al-Wahhâbiyyûn wa'l-Hijâz* (Cairo, 1926). See also Chapter 9, note 1.
2. Two prime ministers are counted among the Muslim Brotherhood's victims: Ahmad Maher (1945) and Nuqrashy Pasha (1948). Hassan al-Banna' was assassinated in his turn in 1949. Among the brotherhood's violent actions was the
failed attempt against Nasser (October 1954), an act that, after the dissolution of
the movement (January 1954), led officers of its junta to chase them down, exe-
cute some of them, and imprison or expel the rest.
3. Hassan al-Banna', *Nahwa an-Nûr* (Toward the light), discourse sent by the author
in 1946 to various Islamic heads of State, including King Farouk. See *Majmû'at
ar-Rasâ'il* (Alexandria, 1990), 72.
4. Translators' note: By *magmatic,* the author refers to a single flow of lava, that is, a
relentlessly advancing, homogeneous entity.

CHAPTER 20

1. Qur'an, 12:40.
2. Jacques Berque translates: "Power belongs only to God" *(Le pouvoir n'appartient
qu'à Dieu)* (Le Coran [Paris: Sindbad, 1990], 249). Si Hamza Boubakeur translates: "In truth, to judge belongs to God alone" *(En vérité, il appartient à Dieu
seul de juger)* (Le Coran [Paris: Maisonneuve & Larose, 1995], 767).
3. Qur'an, 12:40.
4. *Amr* and *taklîf* are two synonyms that Fakhr ad-Dîn Râzi (1149–1209) proposed
in his great commentary *Mafâtîh al-Ghayb* (The keys to the mystery), ed. Muhyi
ad-Dîn (Cairo, 1933), 18:114.
5. Abû al-A'lâ Mawdûdi, *The Meaning of the Qurân* (Lahore, 1967–1988).

6. It is possible that Mawdûdi's interpretation was influenced by the presence of the word *sult'ân* just before the word *hukm*. *Sult'ân* derives from the root *s.l.t'.*, which means "to be absolute in commandment, to exercise absolute power." *Sult'ân* signifies "power, empire, strength, violence"; it also signifies "prince," which gives us "sultan" in French and English. In the context of the verse that concerns us, I translated it as "authority." Again, no traditional commentary retains the political meaning that the words *hukm* and *sult'ân* contain.

7. I cannot avoid such a judgment, even if I know that the solution offered *in fine* by Mawdûdi is the paradoxical (and unrealizable) form of a democracy.

8. From a paraphrase of Mawdûdi's doctrine in Emilio Platti, *Islam . . . étrange? Au-delà des apparences, au coeur de l'acte d'islam, acte de foi* (Islam . . . strange? Beyond appearances, in the heart of the act of Islam, act of faith) (Paris: Le Cerf, 2000), 277–279. For my discussion of Mawdûdi's doctrine, I owe much to the part of Platti's book devoted to this topic. See especially "L'islamisme: Une réforme à la dérive" (Islamism: A drifting reform), 270–292.

9. These critiques make up the body of an article that Mariam Jameelah published in 1987 in the *Islamic Quarterly*, published by the Islamic Cultural Center of London.

10. Sayyid Qutb, *Khasâ'is at-Tasawwur al-Islâmî wa Muqawwimâtihi* (Specifics and foundations of Islamic conception) (Cairo-Beirut, 1978), 236.

CHAPTER 21

1. Gilles Kepel, *Le Prophète et Pharaon* (The prophet and pharaoh) (Paris: La Découverte, 1986).

2. Note that the fundamentalists, as children of Americanization, already cared about the televisual appearance of their horrendous crimes; they were already marked by the narcissism of the media, beyond the impact on the public that the image procures for them to propagate their ideology and intimidate the world through terror.

3. St. François de Sales, *Introduction à la vie dévote* (Introduction to the devout life) (Paris: Seuil, 1961), 22–23.

4. Sayyid Qutb, *Khasâ'is at-Tasawwur al-Islâmî wa Muqawwimâtihi*, 29–44, shows how this passage from myth to a reality based on reason remained insufficient with the Jews as well as with the Christians, whose Scriptures are still full of legends (*asât'îr*) and are scarcely free of the prevailing paganism (*wathaniyya*). Though he cites Biblical legends, he remains blind to the Qur'anic recollections of these same legends, as well as to those that are unique to the Book of the Muslims, or that this book reaps from post-Biblical literature.

CHAPTER 22

1. Yehuda Halevi, *Le Kuzari, Apologie de la religion méprisée* (The Kuzari: In defense of the despised faith), trans. Charles Touati (Louvain-Paris: Peeters, 1994).

2. See Henry Laurens, *La question de Palestine*, vol. 1, *L'Invention de la Terre Sainte* (The question of Palestine, vol. 1, The invention of the Holy Land) (Paris: Fayard, 1999), 18. In his demonstration Laurens draws from Mayir Vreté, "The Restoration of the Jews in English Protestant Thought, 1790–1840," *Middle Eastern Studies* 8 (1972): 3–50. Also see George Robinson, "Jérusalem, 21 Août

1830," in *Dédale/Multiple Jérusalem* 3 and 4 (Paris: Maisonneuve & Larose, spring 1996), 196–200.

3. The state of Israel was founded three years after the revelation of the disaster caused by the "final solution."

4. Sheikh Ahmad Tantâwi, *Beni Isrâ'îl fi-l'Qur'ân wa's-Sunna* (Cairo, 1987), 9.

5. Abdelwahab Meddeb, "Comme un ange déchu au Caire" (Like an angel fallen in Cairo), in *Dédale/La Venue de l'étranger* 9 and 10 (Paris: Maisonneuve & Larose, fall 1999), 402–426.

CHAPTER 23

1. Abdelwahab Meddeb, *La Sexualité en Islam,* 6th ed. (Paris: PUF, 2001).

2. Norman Daniel, *Islam and the West* (Oxford: Oneworld Publications, 1993), 131–156.

3. Gustave Flaubert, *Correspondance,* vol. 1, letter to Louis Bouilhet, March 13, 1850 (Paris: La Pléaide, Gallimard, 1973), 605–607.

4. Sheikh Nafzawi, *Le Jardin parfumé* (The perfumed garden), trans. Baron R. (Paris: Philippe Picquier, 1999).

5. Nietzsche, *L'Antéchrist* (Paris: Pauvert,1967), 103.

6. I use the word *epiphanic* in the sense that the Irish novelist James Joyce gives it, a meaning that revives in me the echo of the Sufi notion of *tajalli,* which describes the process of revealing the invisible in concrete things; it is a question of visions and revelations that transform the urban hours of the walker and establish poetry in the city.

CHAPTER 24

1. Mohammed Mukadam, "Rihlat al-Afghân al-Jazâ'iriyyîn mina 'l-Qâ'ida ilâ 'l-Jamâ'a" (Journey of Algerian Afghans from al Qa'ida to the GIA), *Al-Hayat* (London-based Arab daily), November 23–30, 2001. This investigation should be read with caution, for it seems inspired by the Algerian Secret Services, which opened their archives to the journalist.

CHAPTER 25

1. See Abû Faraj al-Isfahâni (897–967), *Kitâb al-Aghâni,* 25 vols., commented on and annotated by A. A. Mhanna and S. Y. Jâbir (1986). This famous book is a magnificent summa (peppered with savory anecdotes) telling the history of song and poetry throughout the first three centuries of Hegira. In the beginning of his book, Isfahâni devotes numerous pages to the Medina, where poets, musicians, singers, and lovers jostled to woo, sing, dance and improvise in the harmony between the melody of sound and language.

2. Immanuel Kant, *Perpetual Peace,* trans. M. Cambell Smith (Bristol: Thoemmes Press, 1992).

CHAPTER 26

1. The word *hyle* ("matter") is the same Greek word that Ibn 'Arabi used in Arabic (*hayûli*) to designate the matter that will accept form (Ibn 'Arabi, *Fusus al-Hikam* [Cairo: Abû al-'Alâ' al-'Afîfî, 1946], 113).

2. Ibn 'Arabi, *Tarjumân al-Ashwâq* (Bezels of wisdom), poem 12, translated in Abdelwahab Meddeb, *Dédale/L'Image et l'Invisible,* 1 and 2 (Paris: Maisonneuve & Larose, fall 1995), 69. See also the translation of the poem and the original commentary in Maurice Gloton, *L'Interprète des désirs* (The interpreter of desire) (Paris: Albin Michel, 1996), 128–133.

3. Muslim ibn al-Hajjâj, *Sahîh,* with the *sharh* by Nawawi, 18 vols. (Cairo, 1349 A.H./1930 C.E.).

4. Abdelwahab Meddeb, "L'Icône mentale," in *Dédale/L'Image et l'Invisible,* 1 and 2 (Paris: Maisonneuve & Larose, fall 1995), 45–66.

5. Qur'an, 39:3.

6. Qur'an, 38:4.

7. 'Arabi, *Fusus al-Hikam,* 194–196.

8. Bîrûni, *Tahqîq mâ li'l-Hind* (Hyderabad, 1958), 84–85. See the partial translation into French by Vincent Monteil, *Le Livre de l'Inde* (Paris: Sindbad/Unesco, 1996), 125.

9. Ibn Hazm, *al-Facl fi-l-Milal wa'l-Ah'wa' wa'n-Nihall,* 5:35.

10. Shahrastani, *Le Livre des sectes et des religions,* trans. J. Jolivet and G. Monnot (Paris-Louvain: Peeters/Unesco, 1993), 2:530.

11. Guy Monnot, *Islam et religions* (Paris: Maisonneuve & Larose, 1986), 115.

12. Ibn Nadîm, *Al-Fihrist,* ed. R. Tajaddud (Tehran, 1971), 409–412. In this passage, the author is probably describing the two Buddhas in Bamiyan: "They have two statues whose forms were cut from the walls of the cliff, in a high valley; each of these statues is over eighty cubits high, and they can be seen from far away" (410). Mas'ûdi, *Murûj adh-Dhahab,* revised and corrected by Charles Pellat (Beirut: Barbier de Meynard and Pavet de Courteille, 1966), 1:84–98, 1:245–281.

13. Monnot, *Islam et religions,* 117. The treatise *Majma' al-Bahrayn* was introduced, translated, and commented on in Daryush Shayegan, *Hindouisme et soufisme, une lecture du "Confluent des deux océans"* (Hinduism and Sufism, a reading of "The confluence of two oceans") (Paris: Albin Michel, 1997).

14. Friedrich Hölderlin, *Hyperion,* in *Oeuvres,* trans. Philippe Jaccotet (Paris: La Pléiade, Gallimard, 1967), 190.

CHAPTER 27

1. Averroës, *Decisive Treatise,* 155ff.; for "the elite," Averroës uses *khawâs* (pl. of *khâs*), and for "mass," *jumhûr,* of the quadriliteral verbal form *j.m.h.r.,* which means "to unite," "to gather the people," "the public," and so forth. *Jumhûr* in ancient Arabic can have a pejorative connotation; in its plural form (*jamâhîr*), it signifies "populace, multitude." In modern Arabic, the neologism that designates the republic derives from the same root (*jumhûriya*).

2. Bistâmi, *Les Dits de Bistâmi* (The sayings of Bistâmi), trans. Abdelwahab Meddeb (Paris: Fayard, 1989), especially sayings 91, 99, 456.
3. Christian Jambet, introduction to Jalâluddin Rûmî, *Soleil du réel* (Sun of reality), trans. Christian Jambet (Paris: Imprimerie Nationale, 1999), 45–46.
4. Antonin Artaud, *Oeuvres complètes* (Paris: Gallimard, 1971), 8:256–286, noted precisely this distinction between instruction and culture during his travels to Mexico (May–August 1936), and the harm the generalization of the one causes, to the detriment of the other.
5. 'Abd ar-Rahmân Sulami, *Dhikr an-Nisâ al-Muta'abbidât as-Sûfiyât* (On Sufi women and female devotees) (Cairo, 1993), 77. For Umm 'Alî's relationship with Bistâmi, see Bistâmi, *Les Dits de Bistâmi,* passage 372.
6. Ibn Manz'ûr, *Lisân al-'Arab* (Cairo, 1882), 3:361.
7. Qur'an, 2:127.
8. Qur'an, 16:26.
9. It can seem presumptuous "naturally" to equate the September 11 terrorists with al Qa'ida while no proof of their belonging to such an organization has been confirmed. Doesn't the act itself reveal its signature? It is perfectly consistent with bin Laden's discourse and program. The echo it revives resounds in the very interior of his ideological sphere. If bin Laden did not organize it, there is no doubt he inspired it. It is possible that those who acted in New York and Washington belonged only to the diffused mass that extends the base maintained by bin Laden in person, but it is legitimate to guess that both the clearly established structure and the nebula that surround him constitute one single, unique organization whose name is *al Qa'ida.* (This note was written before the broadcast of the two videotapes of December 13 and 31, 2001, whose contents implicate bin Laden even more.)

CHAPTER 28

1. Bernard Lewis, *The Assassins: A Radical Sect in Islam* (Oxford: Oxford University Press, 1987). Translated into French as *Les Assassins, terrorisme et politique dans l'Islam médiéval* by Annick Pélissier (Brussels: Editions Complexe, 2001).
2. Joseph von Hammer, *History of Assassins Derived from Oriental Sources* (1818; reprint from the German edition, Burt Franklin, 1935).
3. Ibid., 182.
4. Lewis, *Assassins,* 77.
5. William Burroughs, *Cities of the Red Night* (New York: Holt, Rinehart, and Winston, 1981). [Translators' note: Meddeb used William Burroughs, *Les Cités de la nuit écarlate,* trans. Philippe Mikriammos (Paris: Christian Bourgois, 1981), 14.]
6. Nasiri Khusraw, *Sefer Nameh, Relation de voyage* (Sefer Nameh: Travelogue), trans. Charles Schefer (Paris, 1881).
7. Nasiri Khusraw, *Le Livre réunissant les deux sagesses* (The book joining the two wisdoms), trans. Isabelle de Gastines (Paris: Fayard, 1990), 321–322.

CHAPTER 29

1. Lewis, *Assassins,* 175.
2. Ibid., 186.

3. Ibid., 172.
4. Alain Rey, *Dictionnaire historique de la langue française* (Paris: Dictionnaire Le Robert), 1992, 2:1198.
5. Qur'an, 3:169.
6. Fakhr ad-Dîn Râzi, *Mafâtîh al-Ghayb*, 9:72–77.
7. Sayyid Qutb, *Khasâ'is at-Tasawwur al-Islâmî wa Muqawwimâtihi*, 20.
8. See the article that recounts this event by Michaël Prazan in *Libération*, September 14, 2001.
9. Abdelwahab Meddeb, "Le partage," *Dédale, Multiple Jérusalem*.
10. Qur'an, 37:102–107.
11. Averroës, *Talkhis Kitâb Arist'ût'alîs fî-Shi'r*, in an appendix of translations in ancient and modern Arabic of *The Poetics* by Aberrahman Badawi (Beirut, 1973), 220.
12. Aristotle, *The Poetics*, trans. Roselyne Dupont-Roc and Jean Lalo (Paris: Seuil, 1981), 53b 19, chapter 14, p. 81.
13. Goethe, "Supplementary Remarks on Aristotle's *Poetics* (1827)," in *Ecrits sur l'art*, comp. and trans. Jean-Marie Schaeffer (Paris: Klincksieck, 1983), 257.
14. Abdelwahab Meddeb, "Cous coupés" (Cut necks), in *Algérie, textes et dessins inédits* (Algeria: Unpublished texts and drawings) (Casablanca: Le Fennec, 1995), 65–67.

CHAPTER 30

1. Lewis, *Assassins*. For these various anecdotes, see, respectively, pp. 160, 159–160, 104, 85, 114–115.
2. For this idea of *takiyya*, see ibid., 61, 122, 134, 176.
3. The "deserters" (or dissidents) that constitute the oldest sect of Islam, whose followers first manifested themselves on the occasion of the battle of Siffin (July 657), by leaving the ranks of the two armies to express their refusal to participate in the arbitration between the two claimants for the caliphate, Mu'âwiya and 'Ali. This extremist sect with exalted fanaticism had the special feature of declaring an infidel anyone who did not share its points of view. It also practiced political assassination and terrorism, and does not even spare women. For that reason it is often invoked in relation to contemporary fundamentalists. See G. Levi Della Vida, in the *Encyclopédie de l'Islam*, 4:1106–9. Also see H. Laoust, *Les Schismes dans l'Islam* (Paris: Payot, 1965), 36 and following.
4. Qur'an, 3:28.
5. Qur'an, 2:195.
6. Rodrigo de Zayas, *Les Morisques et le racisme d'Etat* (Paris: La Différence, 1992), 218–219.
7. Leila Sabbagh, "La Religion des Moriscos entre deux fatwas," in *Les Morisques et leur temps* (Paris: CNRS, 1983), 50. I owe much to this analysis, especially concerning *taqiyya*.
8. See Muslim, *Sahîh*, 2:175–176.
9. Sabbagh, "La Religion des Moriscos," 53.
10. Qur'an, 16:106.
11. T. E. Lawrence, *The Seven Pillars of Wisdom* (Garden City, N.Y.: Doubleday, 1938), 46–47. [Translated into French as *Les Sept piliers de la sagesse*, trans. Julien Deleuze (Paris: Folio-Gallimard, 1992), 55–56.]

12. Usama Ibn al-Munqîdh, *Des enseignements de la vie, Souvenirs d'un gentil-homme syrien du temps des croisades* (On the lessons of life: Memoirs of a Syrian gentleman at the time of the Crusades), trans. André Miquel (Paris: Imprimerie Nationale, 1983).

13. Bistâmi, *Les Dits de Bistâmi,* passages 47, 48, 49, 50.

14. Ibn Khaldun, *Le Voyage d'Occident et d'Orient.*

15. Ibid., 230–239.

16. Babur, *Le Livre de Babour: Mémoires du premier Grand Mogol des Indes* (Babur's book: Memoirs of the first Great Mogul of the Indies), trans. Jean-Louis Bacqué-Grammont (Paris: Imprimerie Nationale, 1985).

CHAPTER 31

1. Samuel P. Huntington, "The Clash of Civilizations," *Foreign Affairs* (summer 1993). The article was subsequently developed into a book: Samuel P. Huntington, *The Clash of Civilizations and the Remaking of World Order* (New York: Simon & Schuster, 1996).

2. Daryush Shayegan, *La Lumière vient de l'Occident* (The light comes from the West) (l'Aube: La Tour d'Aigues, 2001), especially chapter 3 of book 1, "Le Choc des civilisations" (The clash of civilizations), 31–41.

3. Edward Saïd, "The Shock of Ignorance," trans. Françoise Cartano, *Le Monde,* October 27, 2001.

4. Dante, *The Divine Comedy: Hell,* 23:22–36.

5. Ibid.; they are mentioned, respectively, in lines 129, 143 and 144 of canto 3.

6. Abdelwahab Meddeb, "Le Palimpseste du bilingue: Ibn 'Arabi et Dante," in *Du bilinguisme* (Paris: Denoël, 1985), 125–140.

7. Miguel Asin Palacios, *L'Eschatologie musulmane dans "La Divine Comédie,"* trans. Bernard Dubant (Milan: Arché, 1992). The first Spanish edition came out in Madrid in 1920.

8. Enrico Cerulli, *"Il Libro della Scala" e la questione delle fonti arabo-spagnole della "Divina Commedia"* (Vatican City: Biblioteca Apostolica Vaticana, 1949). Also see Enrico Cerulli, *Nuove Ricerche sul "Libro della Scala" e la conoscenta dell'Islam in Occidente* (Vatican City: Biblioteca Apostolica Vaticana, 1972). This *Libro della Scala* is now available in contemporary French; see *Le Livre de l'Échelle de Mahomet* (Paris: Livre de Poche, Lettres gothiques).

9. Asin Palacios added to the second edition of his book (1944) a copious dossier entitled "History and critique of a polemics," integrated into the French translation, pp. 501–632.

10. Philippe Sollers, *La Divine Comédie,* discussions with Benoît Chantre (Paris: DDB, 2000).

11. Ibid., 9.

12. Saïd, "Shock of Ignorance."

13. Ibid.

14. Voltaire, *Traité sur la tolérance.* See chapter 12, described in the title: "Whether intolerance was by divine law among the Jews, and if it was always put into practice," 89–96.

15. Ibid., 56.

CHAPTER 32

1. The "remedy is in the sickness" quote comes from Rousseau, *Confessions* (Paris: Gallimard, La Pléiade, 1959), 19.

2. Louis Massignon, *Explication de la badaliyya* and *La badaliyya et ses statuts* (Cairo: Cahier Vert, 1947).

3. Louis Massignon, "L'Hégire d'Ismael," in *Les Trois Prières d'Abraham* (Paris: Le Cerf, 1997), 68–73.

4. Halevi, *Divan,* 91, 107, 117, 127, 137, 138.

5. Abdelwahab Meddeb, "L'Autre Exil occidental" (The other Western exile), in *Le Récit de l'exil occidental par Sohrawardi* (The tale of Western exile by Sohrawardi), trans. Abdelwahab Meddeb (Paris: Fata Morgana, 1993), 27–43.

6. Norman Daniel, "The Survival of Medieval Concepts," in *Islam and the West,* 302–326.

7. Ibid., 394–395.

8. Platti, *Islam . . . étrange?*

9. The reader has seen this poetics at work all throughout this book.

10. Goethe, *Goethe's Conversations with Eckermann,* Wednesday, January 31, 1827, trans. Jean Chuzeville (Paris: Gallimard, 1949, 1988).

11. Qur'an, 14:4.

12. Article devoted to "German Romance," *Über Kunst und Altertum* 6, no. 2 (1828). See Goethe, *Writings on Art,* 263.

13. Goethe, *West-Eastern Divan,* bilingual (French and German) ed., trans. Henri Lichtenberger (Aubier, 1940), 57.

14. Goethe, *Goethe's Conversations with Eckermann,* 393.

15. Goethe, *West-Eastern Divan,* 362.

16. Aeschylus, *The Persians,* trans. Myrto Gondicas and Pierre Judet de La Combe (Chambéry: Comp'act, 2000), lines 181–196.

17. Louis Aragon, *Le Fou d'Elsa* (Paris: Gallimard, 1963).

18. André Miquel, Percy Kemp, *Majnûn et Laylâ: L'Amour fou* (Majnûn and Laylâ: Mad love) (Paris: Sindbad, 1984).

19. Albert Camus, *Actuelles III, Chroniques algériennes, 1939–1958* (Paris: Gallimard, 1958), 151.

20. Anne Dufourmantelle invites Jacques Derrida to respond, in Jacques Derrida, *De l'hospitalité* (Paris: Calmann-Lévy, 1997), 135. In this book two sessions of Derrida's courses are transcribed. The fourth (January 10, 1996) was entitled "Question d'étranger: Venue de l'étranger," and the fifth (January 17, 1996) was entitled "Pas d'hospitalité."

21. Jean-Luc Nancy, *La Communauté affrontée* (Paris: Galilée, 2001), 11–12.

22. Eliezer Ben-Yehuda, *Rêve traversée* (A dream come true), translated into French from Hebrew by Gérard Haddad and Yvan Haddad (Paris: Editions du Scribe, 1988), chapter 6; English edition translated by T. Muraoka and edited by George Mandel (Boulder, Colo.: Westview Press, 1993).

23. Voltaire, *Traité sur la tolérance,* 123.

24. For information about David Forte, see Franklin Foer, "Blind Faith," *The New Republic,* October 22, 2001.

25. Mariam Jameelah, in the article already cited in which she criticizes her master Mawdûdi.

26. The phrase "We Saudis want to modernize and not necessarily Westernize ourselves" comes from Huntington, "Clash of Civilizations," 110.
27. Mohammed Charfi, *Islam et liberté, le malentendu historique* (Islam and freedom, historic misunderstanding) (Paris: Albin Michel, 1999), 137–138.
28. Ibid., 228.

CHAPTER 33

1. Qur'an, 2:256, quoted in Voltaire, *Traité sur la tolérance,* 109–111.
2. Qur'an, 18:29 and 9:99.
3. Fakhr ad-Dîn Râzi, *Mafâtîh al-Ghayb,* 7:13–14.
4. Qur'an, 29:46.
5. Emilio Platti, *Islam . . . étrange?,* 282–283.
6. Ernest Renan, "L'Islamisme et la science," in *Discours et conférences,* 6th ed. (Paris: Calmann-Lévy, 1919), 402–403; Appendix (Response to Afghâni), *Journal des débats,* May 18, 1883.
7. Ernest Renan, *Qu'est-ce qu'une nation?* (What is a nation?) (Paris: Imprimerie Nationale, 1996).
8. Fouad Alaoui, *Libération,* October 16, 2001. Alaoui is a neuropsychologist of Moroccan origin.
9. Literally: "The law of the country is the law."
10. Strabo, *Geography,* translated into French by Germaine Aujac (Paris: Belles Lettres, 1969), 1:4, 9.
11. Ibn 'Arabi, *At-Tajalliyât al-Ilâhiya* (Tehran: Osman Yahia, 1988), 458.

AFTERWORD

1. This document can be viewed online at http://www.newamericancentury.org.
2. Leo Strauss, "The Crisis of Modernity" (published in its original version in 1962). See its French translation in *Nihilisme et politique* (Paris: Bibliothèques Rivages, 2001), p. 87.
3. See the speeches analyzed by Tzvetan Todorov in *Nous et les autres* (Paris: Le Seuil, 1989), pp. 290–292.
4. The authenticity of this anecdote was questioned by one of the Saudi princes in the letters to the editor that appeared in the Arab-language daily published in London, *Asharq al-Awsat.* Whether such an anecdote was invented or not matters little, so significant is it in the chronicler's argument.
5. Paul Mantoux, *Les Délibérations du Conseil des Quatre, 24 mars–28 juin 1919* (Paris: CNRS, 1955). I thank Gérard D. Khoury for drawing my attention to this document.
6. Christopher Caldwell, "Allah Mode," Part 2, *The Daily Standard,* June 7, 2002.
7. Marcel Proust, *A la recherche du temps perdu* (Remembrance of things past) (Paris: Gallimard, 1999), p. 2351.
8. Susan Sontag, *Regarding the Pain of Others* (New York: Farrar, Strauss and Giroux, 2002), p. 67.

9. Proust, *op. cit.*, p. 2350.

10. Etienne de la Boétie, *Traité de la servitude volontaire* (Paris: Garnier-Flammarion).

11. Carl Schmitt, *Political Theology*, trans. George Schwab (Cambridge, MA: MIT Press, 1985).

12. This refers back to the survival in the modern democratic state of the medieval structure as it was analyzed by Ernst Kantorowicz in his study on Western monarchy in *The King's Two Bodies* (Princeton: Princeton University Press, 1997).

13. See the analyses, connections and intuitions of Giorgio Agamben, in *Homo Sacer*, trans. Daniel Heller-Roazen (Stanford: Stanford University Press, 1998).

14. Robert Kagan in the *Washington Post*, April 12, 2003.

15. Thomas L. Friedman in *The New York Times*, April 10, 2003.

16. See my article in the journal *Histoire*, Paris, December 2002.

17. Jacques Derrida, *Voyous* (Paris: Galilée, 2003). See p. 138 (where the author refers to Noam Chomsky's book, *Rogue States: The Rule of Force in World Affairs* [Cambridge: South End Press, 2000]); and p. 139 (where he quotes *Rogue States and U.S. Foreign Policy*, by Robert S. Litwak [Baltimore: Johns Hopkins University Press, 2000]); see also pp. 145–6 where, in his "deconstruction" of the expression, Derrida ends by saying, "as soon as there is sovereignty, there is abuse of power and rogue state"; in short, there are nothing but rogue states in actuality or in potentiality.

18. Example reported by the German law historian Michael Stolleis, professor of international law at the University of Frankfurt, during a conversation we had in Damascus.

19. Ernest Renan, *Qu'est-ce qu'une nation?* (Paris: Imprimerie nationale, 1996).

20. Simone Weil, "A propos de la question coloniale dans ses rapports avec le destin du peuple français" (On the colonial question in its connections with the fate of the French people), republished in *Ecrits historiques et politiques* (Paris: Gallimard, 1960), p. 375.

21. Louis Massignon, *La Passion de Mansûr Hallâj*, 4 vol. (Paris: Gallimard, 1974). Translated as *The Passion of al-Hallaj: Mystic and Martyr of Islam* by Herbert Mason, 4 vol. (Princeton: Princeton University Press, 1982).

22. *Idem*, III, pp. 300–344.

23. Robert Kagan, *Of Paradise and Power: America vs. Europe in the New World Order* (New York: Knopf, 2003).

24. "The concept of Europe after 1945 has been and continues to be the rejection of the European principle of balance of power and of the hegemonic ambitions of the individual States that appeared in 1648, after signing the Treaty of Westphalia." Quoted by Robert Kagan, *Of Paradise and Power*, p. 90.

25. Arafat corresponds to the definition of the despot I gave earlier, in *Chronicle IV*. Doesn't he continue to exercise authority even though he has led his people to disaster?